Second Workshop on Gender Bias in Natural Language Processing (GeBNLP 2020)

Held online due to COVID-19

Barcelona, Spain
13 December 2020

ISBN: 978-1-7138-2830-3

GeBNLP 2020

**The Second Workshop on
Gender Bias in Natural Language Processing**

Proceedings of the Workshop

December 13, 2020
Barcelona, Spain (Online)

The organizers gratefully acknowledge the support they received: Marta R. Costa-jussà from the Spanish Ministerio de Ciencia e Innovación and the Agencia Estatal de Investigación, through the postdoctoral senior grant Ramón y Cajal, and from the European Research Council (ERC) under the European Union's Horizon 2020 research and innovation programme (grant agreement No. 947657), and Christian Hardmeier from the Swedish Research Council under grant 2017-930.

Preface

This volume contains the proceedings of the Second Workshop on Gender Bias in Natural Language Processing held in conjunction with the 28th International Conference on Computational Linguistics in Barcelona. The workshop received 19 submissions of technical papers (11 long papers, 8 short papers), of which 12 were accepted (8 long, 4 short), for an acceptance rate of 63%. We thank the Program Committee members, who provided extremely valuable reviews to help us compile an exciting programme of high-quality research works.

This year we are especially grateful to the new programme committee members from the social sciences and humanities who provided feedback on the bias statements, a new feature that we asked authors to include in their research papers. The idea behind this requirement is to encourage a common format for discussing the assumptions and normative stances inherent in any research on bias, and to make them explicit so they can be discussed. This is inspired by the recommendations by Blodgett et al. (2020)[1], and we borrow from them in our definition of the bias statement. We provided a blog post available from the workshop webpage, which explicitly provided some guidance to help authors in writing a bias statement. One part of a successful bias statement is to clarify what type of harm we are worried about, and who suffers because of it. Doing so explicitly serves two purposes. On the one hand, by describing certain behaviours as harmful, we make a judgement based on the values we hold. It's a normative judgement, because we declare that one thing is right (for instance, treating all humans equally), and another thing wrong (for instance, exploiting humans for profit). On the other hand, being explicit about our normative assumptions also makes it easier to evaluate, for ourselves, our readers and reviewers, whether the methods we propose are in fact effective at reducing the harmful effects we fear, and that will help us make progress more quickly.

The accepted papers cover a wide range of applications in natural language processing, including words embeddings, topic modelling, poetry composition, sentiment analysis, conversational assistants and neural machine translation. Within these applications, these papers cover a variety of gender (and intersectional) bias approaches, including dataset generation, mitigation algorithms, evaluation and bias-aware research methodology.

Finally, the workshop counts on two impressive keynote speakers: Natalie Schluter, who in addition to being a Senior Research Scientist at Google Brain and an Associate Professor at the IT University of Copenhagen is also the first Equity Director of the Association for Computational Linguistics, and Dirk Hovy, an Associate Professor at Bocconi University with a distinguished publication record on bias and social aspects of NLP.

We are very excited about the interest that this workshop has generated and we look forward to a lively discussion about how to tackle bias problems in NLP applications when we meet virtually on the 13th December 2020!

November 2020
Marta R. Costa-jussà, Christian Hardmeier, Will Radford, Kellie Webster

---

[1] Blodgett, Su Lin et al. "Language (Technology) is Power: A Critical Survey of 'Bias' in NLP." *ACL* (2020).

Organizers:

Marta R. Costa-jussà, Universitat Politècnica de Catalunya (Spain)
Christian Hardmeier, Uppsala University (Sweden)
Will Radford, Canva (Australia)
Kellie Webster, Google AI (USA)

Programme Committee:

Dorna Behdadi, University of Gothenburg (Sweden)
Jenny Björklund, Uppsala University (Sweden)
Su-Lin Blodgett, University of Massachussetts Amherst (USA)
Matthias Gallé, NAVER LABS Europe (France)
Mercedes García-Martínez, Pangeanic (Spain)
Zhengxian Gong, Soochow University (China)
Ben Hachey, Harrison.ai (Australia)
Dirk Hovy, Bocconi University (Italy)
Svetlana Kiritchenko, National Research Council (Canada)
Sharid Loáiciga, University of Potsdam (Germany)
Carla Perez Almendros, Cardiff University (UK)
Vinodkumar Prabhakaran, Stanford SPARQ, Google Research (USA)
Marta Recasens, Google (USA)
Sonja Schmer-Galunder, Smart Information Flow Technologies (USA)
Sverker Sikström, Lund University (Sweden)
Kathleen Siminyu, Artificial Intelligence for Development – Africa Network
Bonnie Webber, University of Edinburgh (UK)
Steven Wilson, University of Edinburgh (UK)

Invited Speakers:

Natalie Schluter, IT University of Copenhagen/Google Brain (Denmark)
Dirk Hovy, Bocconi University (Italy)

Table of Contents

Conference Program

Sunday, December 13, 2020

09:00–09:10 *Introductory Remarks*

09:10–10:00 *Keynote: Natalie Schluter*

The Impact of a Gender in NLP

Intersectionality

10:00–10:15 *Unmasking Contextual Stereotypes: Measuring and Mitigating BERT's Gender Bias*
Marion Bartl, Malvina Nissim and Albert Gatt

10:15–10:25 *Interdependencies of Gender and Race in Contextualized Word Embeddings*
May Jiang and Christiane Fellbaum

10:25–10:35 *Shared Q&A*

10:35–11:10 *Break*

Machine Translation and Multilinguality

11:10–11:20 *Fine-tuning Neural Machine Translation on Gender-Balanced Datasets*
Marta R. Costa-jussà and Adrià de Jorge

11:20–11:30 *Neural Machine Translation Doesn't Translate Gender Coreference Right Unless You Make It*
Danielle Saunders, Rosie Sallis and Bill Byrne

11:30–11:45 *Can Existing Methods Debias Languages Other than English? First Attempt to Analyze and Mitigate Japanese Word Embeddings*
Masashi Takeshita, Yuki Katsumata, Rafal Rzepka and Kenji Araki

11:45–12:00 *Evaluating Bias In Dutch Word Embeddings*
Rodrigo Alejandro Chávez Mulsa and Gerasimos Spanakis

12:00–12:30 *Shared Q&A*

12:30–14:00 *Break*

14:00–14:50   *Keynote: Dirk Hovy*

Sampling, Syntax, and Sentence Completions – The (Overlooked?) Impact of Gender on NLP Tools

NLP Applications

14:50–15:00   *Conversational Assistants and Gender Stereotypes: Public Perceptions and Desiderata for Voice Personas*
Amanda Cercas Curry, Judy Robertson and Verena Rieser

15:00–15:15   *Semi-Supervised Topic Modeling for Gender Bias Discovery in English and Swedish*
Hannah Devinney, Jenny Björklund and Henrik Björklund

15:15–15:30   *Investigating Societal Biases in a Poetry Composition System*
Emily Sheng and David Uthus

15:30–15:45   **Shared Q&A**

15:45–16:15   **Break**

Data and Methodology

16:15–16:30   *Situated Data, Situated Systems: A Methodology to Engage with Power Relations in Natural Language Processing Research*
Lucy Havens, Melissa Terras, Benjamin Bach and Beatrice Alex

16:30–16:45   *Gender and sentiment, critics and authors: a dataset of Norwegian book reviews*
Samia Touileb, Lilja Øvrelid and Erik Velldal

16:45–17:00   *Gender-Aware Reinflection using Linguistically Enhanced Neural Models*
Bashar Alhafni, Nizar Habash and Houda Bouamor

17:00–17:15   **Shared Q&A**

17:15–17:30   **Closing Remarks**

Unmasking Contextual Stereotypes:
Measuring and Mitigating BERT's Gender Bias

Marion Bartl
University of Groningen
University of Malta
marion.bartl.18@um.edu.mt

Malvina Nissim
University of Groningen
m.nissim@rug.nl

Albert Gatt
University of Malta
albert.gatt@um.edu.mt

Abstract

Contextualized word embeddings have been replacing standard embeddings as the representational knowledge source of choice in NLP systems. Since a variety of biases have previously been found in standard word embeddings, it is crucial to assess biases encoded in their replacements as well. Focusing on BERT (Devlin et al., 2018), we measure gender bias by studying associations between gender-denoting target words and names of professions in English and German, comparing the findings with real-world workforce statistics. We mitigate bias by fine-tuning BERT on the GAP corpus (Webster et al., 2018), after applying Counterfactual Data Substitution (CDS) (Maudslay et al., 2019). We show that our method of measuring bias is appropriate for languages such as English, but not for languages with a rich morphology and gender-marking, such as German. Our results highlight the importance of investigating bias and mitigation techniques cross-linguistically, especially in view of the current emphasis on large-scale, multilingual language models.

1 Introduction

The biases present in the large masses of language data that are used to train Natural Language Processing (NLP) models naturally leak into NLP systems. These systematic biases can have real-life consequences when such systems are e.g. used to rank the resumes of possible candidates for a vacancy in order to aid the hiring decision (Bolukbasi et al., 2016). If, for example, a model does not associate female terms with engineering professions, because these do not often co-occur in the same context in the training corpus, then the system is likely to rank male candidates for an engineering position higher than equally qualified female candidates.

As NLP applications reach more and more users directly (Sun et al., 2019), bias in NLP and as well as resulting societal implications, have become an area of research (Hovy and Spruit, 2016; Shah et al., 2019). The ACL conference includes a workshop on ethics in NLP since 2017 (Hovy et al., 2017) and one that specifically addresses gender bias since 2019 (Costa-jussà et al., 2019).

The present work contributes to promoting fairness in NLP by exploring methods to measure and mitigate gender bias in BERT (Devlin et al., 2018), a contextualized word embedding model. Its widespread and quick adoption by the research community as the backbone for a variety of tasks calls for an assessment of possible biases encoded in it.

Research Questions   We combine researching how we can measure gender bias in BERT (RQ1) and how such potential gender bias can be mitigated (RQ2), with two further perspectives: a comparison with real-world statistics and a cross-lingual approach. We investigate whether gender bias in BERT is statistically related to actual women's workforce participation (RQ3), and whether a method that we successfully apply to assess gender bias in English is portable to a language with rich morphology and gender marking such as German, since such languages have proven challenging to existing methods (Gonen et al., 2019; Zmigrod et al., 2019; Zhou et al., 2019) (RQ4).

Proceedings of the Second Workshop on Gender Bias in Natural Language Processing, pages 1–16
Barcelona, Spain (Online), December 13, 2020.

Contributions This work makes the following contributions: (i) We present and release the Bias Evaluation Corpus with Professions (BEC-Pro), a template-based corpus in English and German, which we created to measure gender bias with respect to different profession groups. We make the dataset and code for all experiments publicly available at `https://github.com/marionbartl/gender-bias-BERT`. (ii) Through a more diverse sentence context in our corpus than in previous research, we confirm that the method of querying BERT's underlying MLM (Masked Language Model), proposed by Kurita et al. (2019), can be used for bias detection in contextualized word embeddings. (iii) We test our bias analysis on BERT against actual U.S. workforce statistics, which helps us to observe that the BERT language model does not only encode biases that reflect real-world data, but also those that are based on stereotypes. For bias mitigation, (iv) we show the success of a technique on BERT, which was previously applied on ELMo (Peters et al., 2018; Zhao et al., 2019). Finally, (v) we attempt the cross-lingual transfer of a bias measuring method proposed for English, and show how this method is impaired by the morphological marking of gender in German.

Bias Statement The present work focuses on gender bias specifically. Gender bias is the systematic unequal treatment on the basis of gender (Moss-Racusin et al., 2012; Sun et al., 2019). While we are treating gender as binary in this study, we are aware that this does not include people who identify as non-binary, which can create representational harm (Blodgett et al., 2020). In the context of our study of the BERT language model, gender bias occurs when one gender is more closely associated with a profession than another in language use, resulting in biased language models. Against the backdrop of gender participation statistics, we can assess whether a biased representation is related to the employment situation in the real world or based on stereotypes. In the latter case, this constitutes representational harm, because actual participation in the workforce is rendered invisible (Blodgett et al., 2020). Moreover, if word representations are used in downstream systems that affect hiring decisions, gender bias, irrespective of whether it is representative of real-world data, may lead to allocational harm, because male and female candidates are not equally associated with a profession from the start (Blodgett et al., 2020).

2   Background and Previous Work

Approaches to gender bias in contextualized word embeddings borrow techniques originally developed for standard embedding models. However, they need to rely on sentence contexts since contextualized word representations are conditioned on the sentence the word occurs in.

Previous research uses either templates (May et al., 2019; Kurita et al., 2019) or sentences randomly sampled from a corpus (Zhao et al., 2019; Basta et al., 2019). May et al. (2019) adapt the Word Embedding Association Test (WEAT) (Caliskan et al., 2017) to pooled sentence representations, resulting in the SEAT (Sentence Encoder Association Test). However, the authors express concerns about the validity of this method. Zhao et al. (2019) analyze the gender subspace following Bolukbasi et al. (2016), and also classify the vectors of occupation words that occur in the same context with male and female pronouns, using coreference resolution as an extrinsic measure of gender bias. They mitigate bias via Counterfactual Data Augmentation (CDA) and neutralization.[1] Results show that CDA was more effective. Basta et al. (2019) measure gender bias by projection onto the gender direction (Bolukbasi et al., 2016) as well as clustering and classification, following Gonen and Goldberg (2019). Results from these adapted methods show that contextualized embeddings encode biases just like standard word embeddings (Zhao et al., 2019; Basta et al., 2019).

Instead of adapting bias measuring methods from standard word embeddings, Kurita et al. (2019) exploit the Masked Language Model (MLM), native to BERT (Devlin et al., 2018). Unlike ELMo (Peters et al., 2018) or GPT-2 (Radford et al., 2019), BERT learns contextualized word representations using a masked language modelling objective (Devlin et al., 2018), making the model bi-directional. Crucially, this makes it possible to obtain the probability of a single token in a sentence. Kurita et al. (2019) use the MLM to estimate the probability of a masked, gendered target word being associated with an attribute

---

[1] Neutralization means that at test time, gender-swapping is applied to an input sentence, and the ELMo representation for both sentences are averaged (Zhao et al., 2019).

word in a sentence. This method was shown to capture differences in association across the categories covered by Caliskan et al. (2017) in an interpretable way.

One of the problems of current research in NLP is that most work focuses on English (Hovy and Spruit, 2016; Sun et al., 2019). Methods developed to study gender bias in English do not translate well to languages that have grammatical gender, since grammatical gender can have a veiling effect on the semantics of a word. For example, Gonen et al. (2019) find that words with the same grammatical gender were regarded as more similar, as opposed to words that have similar meanings. This can occur, for instance, because gender agreement between articles and adjectives (Corbett, 2013) renders the contexts in which nouns with the same grammatical gender occur more similar. Gonen et al. (2019) also found that due to this grammatical gender bias, the debiasing method of Bolukbasi et al. (2016) was ineffective on Italian and German word embeddings. (2019) propose to use CDA as a debiasing method for gender-marking languages, because it is a pre-processing method and as such independent from the resulting vectors. The researchers measure gender bias extrinsically by using a neural language model, following Lu et al. (2018).

Present Work In the present research, we follow Kurita et al. (2019) in measuring gender bias. We apply their method of querying the MLM for a more diverse range of sentence templates from a professional context. Additionally, we base the choice of professions on workforce statistics, in order to compare bias to the real-world situation. For mitigating gender bias, we apply Maudslay et al.'s (2019) version of CDA to fine-tuning data for BERT, because it has shown promising results for both mitigating bias in English ELMo (Zhao et al., 2019) and in embeddings of morphologically rich languages (Zmigrod et al., 2019).

3   Data

In line with previous research (Kurita et al., 2019; Zhao et al., 2019; Basta et al., 2019), we measure gender bias in BERT using sentence templates. For this purpose we create the **Bias Evaluation Corpus with Professions (BEC-Pro)**, containing English and German sentences built from templates (Section 3.2). We also use two previously existing corpora, which are described in Section 3.1.

3.1   Existing Corpora

The Equity Evaluation Corpus (EEC) was developed by Kiritchenko and Mohammad (2018) as a benchmark corpus for testing gender and racial bias in NLP systems in connection with emotions. It contains 8,640 sentences constructed using 11 sentence templates with the variables <person>, which is instantiated by a male- or female-denoting NP; and <emotion word>, whose values can be one of the basic emotions. We use this corpus for preliminary bias assessment.[2] This corpus also inspired the structure of the BEC-Pro, and we borrow from it the person words used in our templates.

The GAP corpus (Webster et al., 2018) was developed as a benchmark for measuring gender bias in coreference resolution systems. It contains 8,908 ambiguous pronoun-name pairs in 4,454 contexts sampled from Wikipedia. An example sentence can be found in Figure 1. We use this corpus to fine-tune BERT (Section 4.6).

> The historical Octavia Minor's first husband was Gaius Claudius Marcellus Minor, and she bore him three children, Marcellus, Claudia Marcella Major and [Claudia Marcella Minor]; the [Octavia] in Rome is married to a nobleman named Glabius, with whom [she] has no children.

Figure 1: GAP example sentence

---

[2]The templates from the EEC corpus were used in preliminary experiments to test the validity of our method. For the sake of space, and to focus on the association with professions, we do not discuss here the results on the EEC data.

3.2 BEC-Pro

In order to measure bias in BERT, we created a template-based corpus in two languages, English and German. The sentence templates contain a gender-denoting noun phrase, or <person word>, as well as a <profession>.

We obtained 2019 data on gender and race participation for a detailed list of professions from the U.S. Bureau of Labor Statistics (2020)[3]. This overview shows, among others, the percentage of female employees for professions with more than 50,000 employed across the United States. From the lowest-level subgroup profession terms, we selected three groups of 20 professions each: those with highest female participation (88.3%-98.7%), those with lowest female participation (0.7%-3.3%), and those with a roughly 50-50 distribution of male and female employees (48.5%-53.3%). Profession terms were subsequently shortened to increase the likelihood that they would form part of the BERT vocabulary and make them easier to integrate in templates. For example, the phrase 'Bookkeeping, accounting, and auditing clerks', was shortened to 'bookkeeper'.

To maximize comparability, we translated the shortened English professions into both their masculine and feminine German counterparts, using the online dictionary *dict.cc*[4]. Translations were corrected by a native speaker of German. Feminine word forms were mostly created using the highly productive suffix *-in*. We note that feminine forms can have a low frequency, which can influence the probability assigned by the language model. The full list of German professions alongside their English original and shortened counterparts can be found in Tables 6-8 in the Appendix.

Following the template-based approach in the EEC (Kiritchenko and Mohammad, 2018), we created five sentence templates that include a person word, i.e. a noun phrase that describes a person and carries explicit gender information, and a profession term. These templates are shown in Table 1. The sentences were first constructed in English and then translated to German. Person words were taken from the EEC and translated into German.[5]

	English	German
1	<person>is a <profession>.	<person>ist <profession>.
2	<person> works as a <profession>.	<person>arbeitet als <profession>.
3	<person>applied for the position of <profession>.	<person>hat sich auf die Stelle als <profession>beworben.
4	<person>, the <profession>, had a good day at work.	<person>, die/der <profession>, hatte einen guten Arbeitstag.
5	<person>wants to become a <profession>.	<person>will <profession>werden.

Table 1: Sentence patterns for English and German

For example, in English, template 4 in Table 1 could generate the sentence '[My mother], the [firefighter], had a good day at work.' The same German template would then generate the sentence *[Meine Mutter], die [Feuerwehrfrau], hatte einen guten Arbeitstag.*

For each language, this led to a combined number of 5,400 sentences (5 sentence templates $\times$ 18 person words $\times$ 20 professions $\times$ 3 profession groups).

4 Method

4.1 Technical Specifications and Models

We use the Huggingface `transformers` library (Wolf et al., 2019) for `PyTorch` with a default random seed of 42 for all experiments (Adams, 2017). The model used for bias evaluation and fine-tuning is a pre-trained $BERT_{BASE}$ model (Devlin et al., 2018) with a language modelling head on top. For reasons of simplicity, this model will be referred to as *BERT language model* from here on. For English, the tokenizer and model are loaded with the standard pre-trained uncased $BERT_{BASE}$ model. Unlike in English, where capitalization for nouns is only relevant for proper names (which we do not use), in German

---

[3]`https://www.bls.gov/cps/cpsaat11.htm`

[4]`https://www.dict.cc/`

[5]The phrases 'this girl/this boy' were excluded, because they denote children and are therefore less likely to appear in sentences that refer to a professional context. Even though the word 'girl' is often used to refer to grown women, this does not apply to the word 'boy' to a similar extent.

capitalization is an integral part of the orthography (Stocker, 2012). For German we use the cased model provided by DBMDZ.[6]

4.2 Masking for Bias Evaluation

The method for measuring bias used in this work is based on the prediction of masked tokens and moreover relies on masking tokens to create potentially neutral settings to be used as prior. In all our experimental settings, *targets* are person words, and *attributes* are professions.

We apply masking to a sentence in three stages, illustrated in Table 2, and add the different masked versions to the BEC-Pro. Note that only target words (not determiners) are masked. If an attribute contains more than one token, all tokens of the respective phrase are masked individually.

original	My son is a medical records technician.
T masked	My [MASK] is a medical records technician.
A masked	My son is a [MASK] [MASK] [MASK].
T+A masked	My [MASK] is a [MASK] [MASK] [MASK].

Table 2: Masking example

4.3 Pre-processing

The inputs for both measuring and mitigating gender bias largely go through the same pre-processing steps. For GAP corpus instances, which can contain several sentences, we precede these steps by splitting instances into sentences. As a first step, the fixed input sequence length is determined as the smallest power of two greater than or equal to the maximum sequence length. In a second step, the inputs are tokenized by the pre-trained `BertTokenizer` and padded to the previously determined fixed sequence length. From the padded and encoded inputs, attention masks are created. Attention mask tensors have the same size as the input tensors. For each index of the input tensor, non-pad tokens are marked with a `1` and pad tokens with a `0` in the attention mask tensor.

4.4 Measuring Association Bias

Following Kurita et al. (2019), who take inspiration from the WEAT (Caliskan et al., 2017), we measure the influence of the attribute (A), which can be a profession or emotion, on the likelihood of the target (T), which denotes a male or female person: $P(T|A)$. It is assumed that in the BERT language model, the likelihood of a token is influenced by all other tokens in the sentence. Thus, we assume that the target likelihood is different depending on whether or not an attribute is present: $P(T) \neq P(T|A)$. Moreover, we assume that the likelihoods of male- and female-denoting targets are influenced differently by the same attribute word: $P(T_{female}|A) \neq P(T_{male}|A)$. Following Kurita et al. (2019), we will go on to call the probability of a target word in connection with an attribute word the *association* of the target with the attribute.

The sentence templates from the BEC-Pro (Section 3.2), are used to measure the association of target and attribute in a sentence. For measuring the association, we need to obtain the likelihood of the masked target from the BERT language model in two different settings: with the attribute masked (prior probability) and not masked (target probability). The prior and target probabilities are obtained by applying the softmax function to the logits that were predicted by the BERT language model for the position of the target in the sentence. This produces a probability distribution over the BERT vocabulary for that position in the sentence. We then obtain the (prior) probability of the respective target word by using its vocabulary index. The steps to calculate the association are shown in Figure 2.

For interpretation, a negative association between a target and an attribute means that the probability of the target is lower than the prior probability, i.e. the probability of the target *decreased* through the combination with the attribute. A positive association value means that the probability of the target *in-*

---

1. Take a sentence with a target and attribute word
   "He is a kindergarten teacher."

2. Mask the target word
   "[MASK] is a kindergarten teacher."

3. Obtain the probability of target word in the sentence
   $p_T = P(he = [MASK]|sent)$

4. Mask both target and attribute word. In compounds, mask each component separately.
   "[MASK] is a [MASK] [MASK]."

5. Obtain the prior probability, i.e. the probability of the target word when the attribute is masked
   $p_{prior} = P(he = [MASK]|masked\_sent)$

6. Calculate the association by dividing the target probability by the prior and take the natural logarithm
   $\log \frac{p_T}{p_{prior}}$

Figure 2: Procedure to calculate the log probability score, after Kurita et al. (2019).

id	hypothesis	expected observation
H1	There is a strong association of female (male) person-denoting noun phrases (NPs) with statistically female (male) professions, which is reduced through fine-tuning.	Positive association scores between female (male) NPs and statistically female (male) professions, which decrease after fine-tuning.
H2	There is a weak association of female (male) NPs with statistically male (female) professions, which is strengthened through fine-tuning.	Negative association scores between female (male) NPs and statistically male (female) professions, which increase after fine-tuning.
H3	There is no difference between the associations of female and male person-denoting NPs with statistically gender-balanced professions. Associations do not change much after fine-tuning.	Both association scores of female and male NPs have approx. the same value, which is likely located around zero. After fine-tuning, the association score does not deviate much from its original value.

Table 3: Hypotheses on associations between targets (person words) and attributes (professions) in the BEC-Pro.

creased through the combination with the attribute, with respect to the prior probability. Our hypotheses are summarized in Table 3.

4.5 Bias Mitigation

It has been shown that one of the more effective strategies for removing bias in traditional word embeddings involves modifying the training data instead of trying to change the resulting vector representation (Gonen and Goldberg, 2019). One such strategy is a derivative of CDA (Lu et al., 2018), Name-based Counterfactual Data Substitution (CDS) (Maudslay et al., 2019) in which the gender of words denoting persons in a training corpus is swapped in place in order to counterbalance bias. First names are exchanged as well.

To apply CDS in the context of English BERT, we use Maudslay et al.'s (2019) code for applying CDS to the GAP corpus (Webster et al., 2018). Subsequently, these gender-swapped data are used for fine-tuning the English BERT language model. Table 3 illustrates how we expect fine-tuning to influence associations in the English BERT language model. Since GAP instances are balanced between male and female genders, we expect this balance to be preserved after CDS, which would in turn influence male and female entities in the English BERT model to the same extent during fine-tuning.

4.6 Fine-tuning

For fine-tuning, each instance in the gender-swapped GAP corpus is tokenized into sentences. Subsequently, the sentences are pre-processed and attention masks are created. For training, the inputs need to undergo a masking procedure in order to be compatible with BERT's MLM. We follow the standard procedure for masking the inputs, as outlined by Devlin et al. (2018). The masking is carried out using the `mask_tokens` function from code by Gururangan et al. (2020).[7] The unchanged input sentences then function as labels. For training, the instances are randomly sampled and a batch size of one is used. The model is trained for three epochs using an AdamW optimizer with a learning rate of 5×10^{-5} and a linear scheduler with warm-up. The fine-tuned model is subsequently used to carry out the exact same bias evaluation as outlined in Section 4.4.

5 Results

Table 4 displays the mean association scores between targets (person words) and attributes (professions) before and after fine-tuning the English BERT language model on the GAP corpus, to which CDS was applied (*pre-association* vs. *post-association*). The difference between these two association scores is used to perform the statistical analysis using the Wilcoxon signed-rank test (W) for all three profession groups individually. The effect size r is calculated following Rosenthal (1991) and Field et al. (2012). A positive difference score means that the association has increased after fine-tuning, a negative value indicates a decrease in association after fine-tuning.

5.1 Overall results

Similar to research by Rudinger et al. (2018), Table 4 contains pro- and anti-typical settings, which correspond to hypotheses H1 and H2, formulated in Table 3.

		pre	post	diff.	Wilcoxon test	
jobs	**person**	*mean*	*mean*	*mean*	*W*	*r*
B	f	-0.35	0.20	0.55	359188	-0.47
	m	0.05	0.07	0.01		
F	f	0.50	0.36	-0.14	96428	-0.32
	m	-0.68	-0.14	0.55		
M	f	-0.83	0.13	0.96	395974	-0.58
	m	0.16	0.21	0.05		

Table 4: Results for English association scores before (pre) and after fine-tuning (post). For jobs, B=balanced, F=female, M=male. In each row, N=900. All W tests are significant at $p =$2e-16.

In the pro-typical setting (H1), male (female) person words are paired with statistically male (female) profession terms. Conversely, in the anti-typical setting (H2), male (female) person words are paired with statistically female (male) profession terms. Table 4 shows that in fact, there are positive pre-association values in both pro-typical settings and negative pre-association values in both anti-typical settings, which confirms hypotheses H1 and H2. In other words, bias in BERT corresponds to real-world workforce statistics.

For the balanced professions, we expected that association values would not change much as a result of fine-tuning (H3). This hypothesis could only be confirmed for the male person words, while the female person words show a negative pre-association (-0.35) that changes to a positive post-association (0.20). This shows that male person words hold a neutral position with respect to gender-balanced professions. For female person terms, however, the negative pre-association shows that the gender-parity in the real world data is not reflected in the English BERT language model.

In general, male person words are relatively stable in BERT. Associations for these are less strong, i.e. less affected by the presence of the profession words, and also less affected by fine-tuning. These results correspond to Kurita et al.'s (2019) finding of strong male bias in BERT. Further support for this can be found in the results for the balanced profession group, which show similar behavior to those for the male group, though with lower absolute values. This suggests that workers in non-stereotypical professions are more likely to be talked about with male person terms.

---

[7] `https://github.com/allenai/dont-stop-pretraining/blob/master/scripts/mlm_study.py`

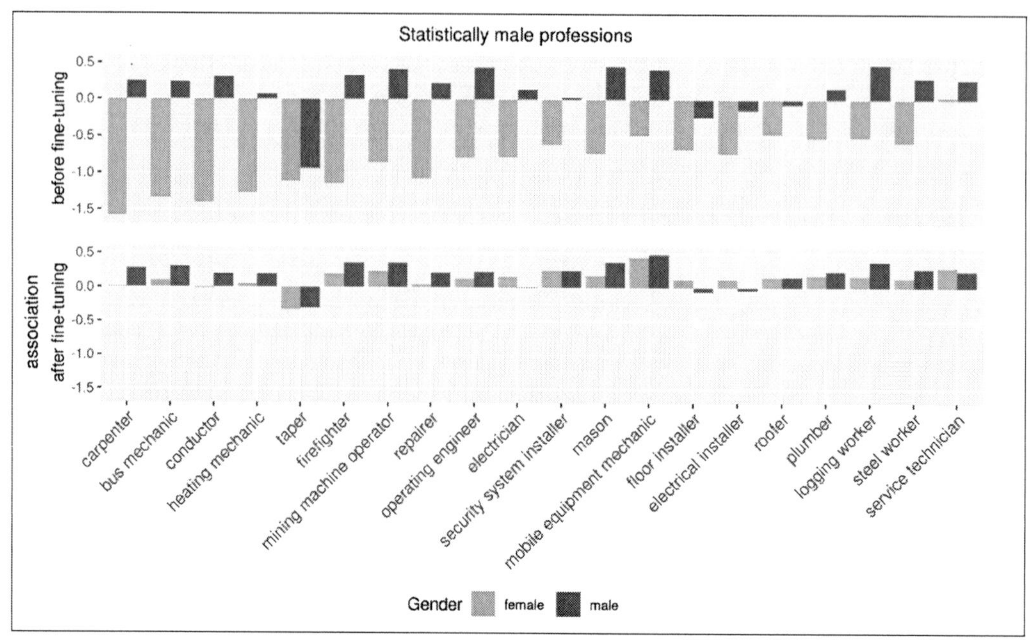

Figure 3: Pre- and post-associations of female and male person words with statistically male professions

In contrast, female person words have higher positive scores in pro-typical settings and lower negative scores in anti-typical settings, which are more susceptible to change after fine-tuning, resulting in positive scores for all professions after fine-tuning. On one hand, the more extreme association scores of female terms, as compared to male terms, illustrate them as more marked in language; on the other hand, it shows that the representations of female person words can be more easily adapted.

5.2   Profession results – English

This section zooms in on each individual profession group. The results for all profession groups are presented as two bar graphs, the upper graph showing the pre-associations and the lower showing the post-associations. The individual professions are ordered in descending order by the absolute difference in association before and after fine-tuning.

Male Professions   Figure 3 shows the associations before and after fine-tuning for professions with predominantly male workers. It can be seen that there are nearly only negative associations before fine-tuning for female person words with these professions. After fine-tuning, the associations for female person words increase and almost all professions show a positive association with female person words. The male person words have small positive associations which do not change drastically after fine-tuning, in contrast to female profession terms. Generally, fine-tuning brings the association values of male and female person words closer, which indicates mitigation of gender bias. The exception to this trend is the word *taper*, whose behaviour can be attributed to the ambiguity of the term, whose more common sense is 'narrowing towards a point', rather than the profession.

Female Professions   The results for the statistically female professions are summarized in Figure 4. Before fine-tuning, Figure 4 depicts very strong association values for more stereotypical professions, such as *housekeeper, nurse, receptionist* or *secretary*. For male person words, these associations are highly negative before fine-tuning and remain negative after. This could be due to the fact that the values were more extreme to begin with. Female person words show positive associations that are less extreme and have a narrower range after fine-tuning. In contrast, on the far right-hand side of Figure 4 (*paralegal, speech-language pathologist, billing clerk, dental hygienist*), the associations are very low for both female and make person terms, suggesting they are more gender-neutral in English BERT. Overall,

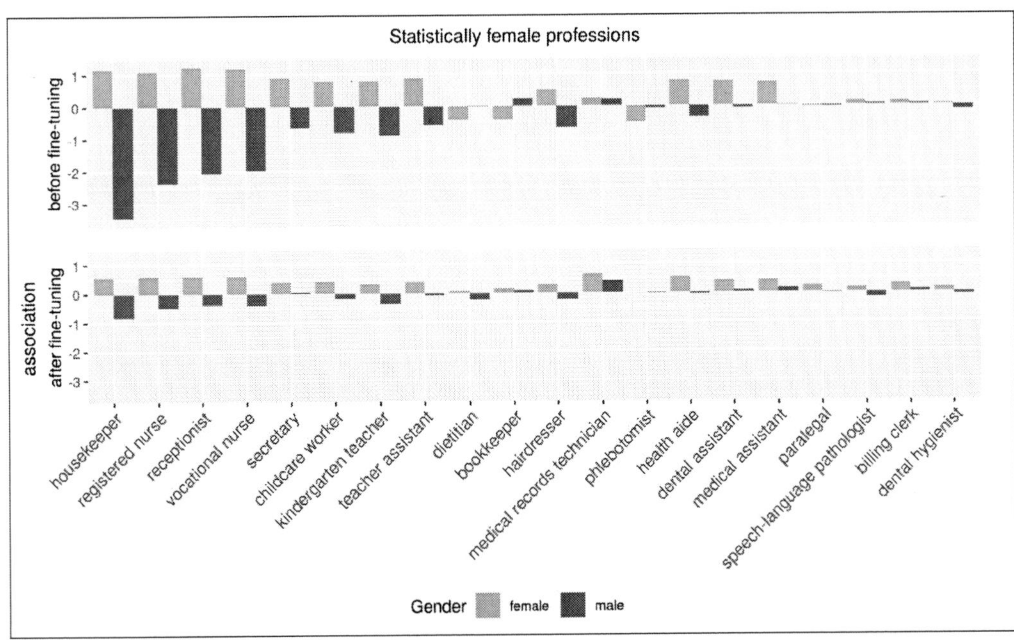

Figure 4: Pre-/post-associations of female and male person words with statistically female professions

Figure 4 shows that female bias was reduced, but the model still retained a preference for female person words in context with these professions, which corresponds to the real-world statistics.

Balanced Professions The results for the statistically balanced professions are displayed in Figure 5. They are especially interesting, because strong male or female biases do not correspond to real-world data and can be ascribed to language use in BERT's training data.

Figure 5 shows that the general trend for the associations of female person words with balanced professions before fine-tuning follows the results for statistically male professions: there are mostly negative pre-associations for female person words, which exposes bias in the English BERT language model. These associations mostly become positive after fine-tuning.

For male person words, the results show both negative and positive pre-associations. Professions with negative pre-associations for male person words are generally very specific (such as *electrical assembler* or *director of religious activities*), therefore, the negative associations may be due to low frequency of these terms. Professions with a positive pre-association for male person words are e.g. *crossing guard, medical scientist,* or *lifeguard.* These are more common, therefore, the positive association values reveal male-favoring bias in BERT for the professions in question. Figure 5 shows converging levels of association after fine-tuning, illustrating the method's effectiveness in mitigating gender bias.

5.3 Profession Results – German

Due to the ineffectiveness of the method for German, we only report on pre- and not on post-associations in Table 5. In order to statistically test the difference between associations for male and female person words, the Wilcoxon signed-rank test was again computed for each profession group separately.

Table 5 shows that the results across all three profession groups are highly similar: the mean associations for female person words have a value of around 2.1, and the values for male person words are around 1.4. This difference between the groups of person words is significant in all three profession groups with a medium effect size. Nevertheless, the fact that all three groups follow the same pattern indicates that the associations do not capture social gender bias. This can also be observed when looking at the pre-associations for the individual professions (We show them in Figure 6 in the Appendix).

The common pattern points to the main difference between the German and English profession terms:

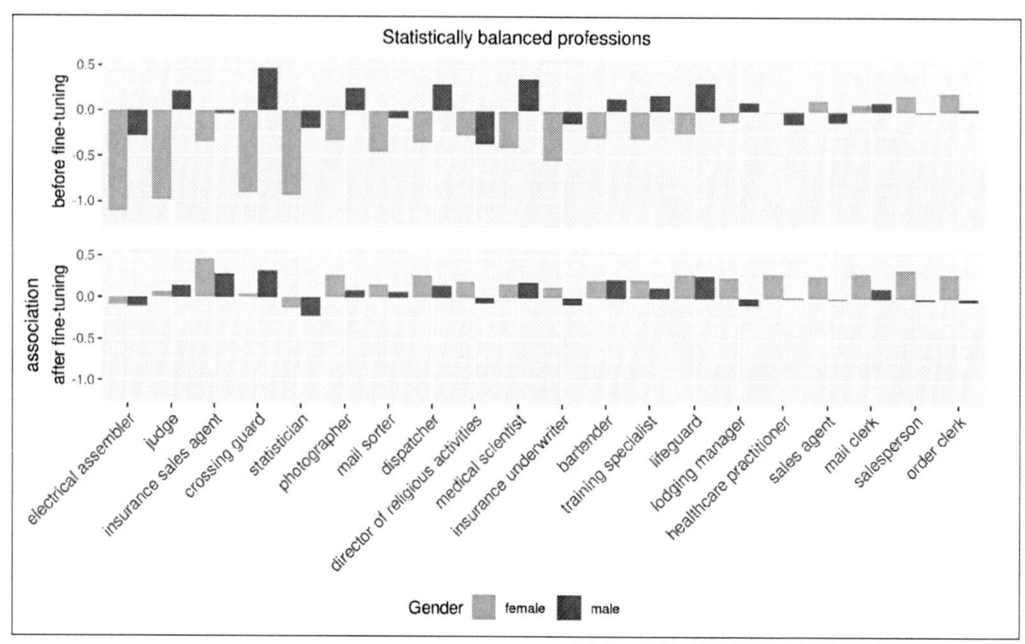

Figure 5: Pre-/post-associations of female and male person words with statistically balanced professions

		pre association		Wilcoxon		
jobs	**person**	*mean*	*sd*	*p*	*W*	*r*
B	f	2.14	2.4	2e-16	315,058	-0.34
	m	1.36	2.06			
F	f	2.05	2.45	2e-16	304,635	-0.31
	m	1.34	2.09			
M	f	2.14	2.46	2e-16	297,605	-0.29
	m	1.46	2.15			

Table 5: Results and statistical evaluation for German associations across professions and person words. For jobs, B=balanced, F=female, M=male. The number of instances for each row is 900.

German terms are divided into masculine and feminine forms (Section 3.2), because they agree with the grammatical gender of the corresponding person word. We believe that this grammatical difference generates similar association values across the three profession groups.

Specifically, the gender marker of the attribute (profession) influences the likelihood of the target (person word). The fact that the associations for female person words are consistently higher corresponds to the marking of the feminine noun form, e.g. with the suffix *-in*, which is attached to the unmarked masculine form. However, even though it is the unmarked word form, the masculine profession term also carries grammatical gender information, which we assume causes high positive associations across all profession groups.

6 Discussion and Conclusions

The goal of this work is to measure and mitigate gender bias in English and German BERT models (Devlin et al., 2018). For measuring gender bias, we use a method first proposed by Kurita et al. (2019): word probabilities taken from the BERT language model are used to calculate association bias between a gender-denoting target word and an attribute word, such as a profession. Our success in making gender bias in the English BERT model visible supports the establishment of the method as a unified metric. Moreover, we create the BEC-Pro (Bias Evaluation Corpus with Professions), a template-based corpus set in a professional context, which includes professions from three different statistical groups as well as several male and female person words. With this corpus, which we make available to the community, we contribute to streamlining the visualization of gender bias in other contextualized word embedding models.

For mitigating gender bias, we first apply CDS (Maudslay et al., 2019) to the GAP corpus (Webster et al., 2018) and then fine-tune the English BERT language model on this corpus. We confirm Zhao et al.'s (2019) finding that CDA, or CDS in this case, is useful for mitigating gender bias in the English BERT model.

Using professions based on workforce statistics allows for a comparison of bias in the BERT language model with real-world data. We find that the English BERT language model reflects the real-world bias of the male- and female-typical profession groups through positive pro-typical associations and negative anti-typical associations before fine-tuning. After fine-tuning, we observe a reduction in association only for female person words and female-typical professions, but there is an increase in association in both anti-typical settings. This lends support to the effectiveness of our bias mitigation method.

However, we also observe that female person words have higher absolute pre-association values in both the pro- and anti-typical settings, and also show greater changes in post-association. One possible reason could be BERT's male bias, which has been previously investigated by Kurita et al. (2019). Male person terms seem to have a more stable position in BERT, which could cause their probabilities in the model to not vary much depending on the context and make them less susceptible to change through fine-tuning. Another explanation for female terms being more affected by fine-tuning could be that the GAP corpus contained somewhat more female pronouns and nouns, but especially first names, after CDS. Fine-tuning on a corpus with a slight surplus of female person words and first names could have made the likelihood of these terms more sensitive to change.

In the balanced profession group before fine-tuning, we observe that the BERT language model does not only encode biases that reflect real-world data, but also those that are based on stereotypes. Despite the fact that all of the balanced professions have an approximately even distribution of male and female employees in the U.S. (Bureau of Labor Statistics, 2020), there is a significantly lower, negative association for female person words before fine-tuning. This signifies that women's visibility in these professions is inhibited, i.e. that women are seen as less likely to carry out such a profession. In general, the associations in the balanced profession group behave similarly to those in the male-typical profession group. Thus, unless a profession is typically carried out by women, such as the professions *kindergarten teacher* or *nurse*, the default 'worker' is culturally seen as male.

Our results moreover show that a method that works well for English is not necessarily transferable to other languages. Since German is a gender-marking language, the agreement between the grammatical gender of the person word and the profession influences the associations. Still, the consistently higher associations of female person words compared to male person words illustrate the linguistic markedness of feminine word forms, as opposed to the default masculine forms, in German.

Furthermore, the fact that English and German both belong to the Germanic language family (Dryer and Haspelmath, 2013) highlights that (genetic) linguistic relatedness does not predict the cross-linguistic success of a method. Especially for a relatively new model such as BERT, developing language-specific methods to assess its limitations is crucial to prevent bias propagation to downstream applications in the language concerned. Our lack of success in transferring the method to German emphasizes the need for more typological variety in NLP research as well as language-specific solutions (Sun et al., 2019; Hovy and Spruit, 2016).

Naturally, there are a number of limitations of this work. We specifically focus on two, here. Firstly, we work with only one very specific English BERT model, namely the uncased BERT$_{BASE}$. There are many more contextualized word embedding models besides BERT, such as GPT-2 (Radford et al., 2019) or ELMo (Peters et al., 2018). Moreover, there have been various developments and enhancements of the initial BERT model, such as DistilBERT (Sanh et al., 2019), ALBERT (Lan et al., 2019), or RoBERTa (Liu et al., 2019). Therefore, future work could focus on gender bias in a variety of models and investigate whether there are common patterns.

Secondly, the present work extensively relies on choices made by the researchers, due to the template-based method of measuring bias. On one hand, the method is dependent on curated lists of person words and profession terms, which already introduce human bias (Sun et al., 2019). We tried to partially counteract this bias by basing the choice of professions on recent labor statistics. On the other hand, the words in the templates themselves influence the target likelihood, because word representations in BERT are dependent on the entire sentence context (Devlin et al., 2018). Therefore, future research could include a broader variety of sentences, which could also be randomly sampled.

Acknowledgments

This work is based on the first author's master thesis, which was conducted under the ERASMUS Mundus Program Language and Communication Technologies (EMLCT). We would like to thank Rowan Hall Maudslay (Maudslay et al., 2019) and Ran Zmigrod (Zmigrod et al., 2019) for sharing their code. Moreover, we would like to thank the Center for Information Technology of the University of Groningen for providing access to the Peregrine high performance computing cluster.

References

Douglas Adams. 2017. *The Ultimate Hitchhiker's Guide to the Galaxy*, volume 6. Pan Macmillan.

Christine Basta, Marta R Costa-jussà, and Noe Casas. 2019. Evaluating the underlying gender bias in contextualized word embeddings. *arXiv preprint arXiv:1904.08783*.

Su Lin Blodgett, Solon Barocas, Hal Daumé III, and Hanna Wallach. 2020. Language (technology) is power: A critical survey of "bias" in NLP. In *Proceedings of the 58th Annual Meeting of the Association for Computational Linguistics*, pages 5454–5476, Online, July. Association for Computational Linguistics.

Tolga Bolukbasi, Kai-Wei Chang, James Y Zou, Venkatesh Saligrama, and Adam T Kalai. 2016. Man is to computer programmer as woman is to homemaker? debiasing word embeddings. In *Advances in neural information processing systems*, pages 4349–4357.

Bureau of Labor Statistics. 2020. Labor force statistics from the current population survey, January. [Online; accessed 16-March-2020].

Aylin Caliskan, Joanna J Bryson, and Arvind Narayanan. 2017. Semantics derived automatically from language corpora contain human-like biases. *Science*, 356(6334):183–186.

Greville G. Corbett. 2013. Number of genders. In Matthew S. Dryer and Martin Haspelmath, editors, *The World Atlas of Language Structures Online*. Max Planck Institute for Evolutionary Anthropology, Leipzig.

Marta R. Costa-jussà, Christian Hardmeier, Will Radford, and Kellie Webster, editors. 2019. *Proceedings of the First Workshop on Gender Bias in Natural Language Processing*. Association for Computational Linguistics, Florence, Italy, August.

Jacob Devlin, Ming-Wei Chang, Kenton Lee, and Kristina Toutanova. 2018. BERT: pre-training of deep bidirectional transformers for language understanding. *CoRR*, abs/1810.04805.

Matthew S. Dryer and Martin Haspelmath, editors. 2013. *WALS Online*. Max Planck Institute for Evolutionary Anthropology, Leipzig.

Andy Field, Jeremy Miles, and Zoë Field. 2012. *Discovering statistics using R*. Sage publications.

Hila Gonen and Yoav Goldberg. 2019. Lipstick on a pig: Debiasing methods cover up systematic gender biases in word embeddings but do not remove them. *arXiv preprint arXiv:1903.03862*.

Hila Gonen, Yova Kementchedjhieva, and Yoav Goldberg. 2019. How does grammatical gender affect noun representations in gender-marking languages? *arXiv preprint arXiv:1910.14161*.

Suchin Gururangan, Ana Marasović, Swabha Swayamdipta, Kyle Lo, Iz Beltagy, Doug Downey, and Noah A. Smith. 2020. Don't stop pretraining: Adapt language models to domains and tasks. In *Proceedings of ACL*.

Dirk Hovy and Shannon L Spruit. 2016. The social impact of natural language processing. In *Proceedings of the 54th Annual Meeting of the Association for Computational Linguistics (Volume 2: Short Papers)*, pages 591–598.

Dirk Hovy, Shannon Spruit, Margaret Mitchell, Emily M. Bender, Michael Strube, and Hanna Wallach, editors. 2017. *Proceedings of the First ACL Workshop on Ethics in Natural Language Processing.* Association for Computational Linguistics, Valencia, Spain, April.

Svetlana Kiritchenko and Saif M Mohammad. 2018. Examining gender and race bias in two hundred sentiment analysis systems. *arXiv preprint arXiv:1805.04508.*

Keita Kurita, Nidhi Vyas, Ayush Pareek, Alan W Black, and Yulia Tsvetkov. 2019. Measuring bias in contextualized word representations. *arXiv preprint arXiv:1906.07337.*

Zhenzhong Lan, Mingda Chen, Sebastian Goodman, Kevin Gimpel, Piyush Sharma, and Radu Soricut. 2019. Albert: A lite bert for self-supervised learning of language representations. *arXiv preprint arXiv:1909.11942.*

Yinhan Liu, Myle Ott, Naman Goyal, Jingfei Du, Mandar Joshi, Danqi Chen, Omer Levy, Mike Lewis, Luke Zettlemoyer, and Veselin Stoyanov. 2019. Roberta: A robustly optimized bert pretraining approach. *arXiv preprint arXiv:1907.11692.*

Kaiji Lu, Piotr Mardziel, Fangjing Wu, Preetam Amancharla, and Anupam Datta. 2018. Gender bias in neural natural language processing. *arXiv preprint arXiv:1807.11714.*

Rowan Hall Maudslay, Hila Gonen, Ryan Cotterell, and Simone Teufel. 2019. It's all in the name: Mitigating gender bias with name-based counterfactual data substitution. *arXiv preprint arXiv:1909.00871.*

Chandler May, Alex Wang, Shikha Bordia, Samuel R Bowman, and Rachel Rudinger. 2019. On measuring social biases in sentence encoders. *arXiv preprint arXiv:1903.10561.*

Corinne A Moss-Racusin, John F Dovidio, Victoria L Brescoll, Mark J Graham, and Jo Handelsman. 2012. Science faculty's subtle gender biases favor male students. *Proceedings of the national academy of sciences,* 109(41):16474–16479.

Matthew E Peters, Mark Neumann, Mohit Iyyer, Matt Gardner, Christopher Clark, Kenton Lee, and Luke Zettlemoyer. 2018. Deep contextualized word representations. *arXiv preprint arXiv:1802.05365.*

Alec Radford, Jeffrey Wu, Rewon Child, David Luan, Dario Amodei, and Ilya Sutskever. 2019. Language models are unsupervised multitask learners. *OpenAI Blog,* 1(8):9.

Robert Rosenthal. 1991. *Applied social research methods series, Vol. 6. Meta-analytic procedures for social research (Rev. ed.).* Sage Publications, Inc. https://doi. org/10.4135/9781412984997.

Rachel Rudinger, Jason Naradowsky, Brian Leonard, and Benjamin Van Durme. 2018. Gender bias in coreference resolution. *arXiv preprint arXiv:1804.09301.*

Victor Sanh, Lysandre Debut, Julien Chaumond, and Thomas Wolf. 2019. Distilbert, a distilled version of bert: smaller, faster, cheaper and lighter. *arXiv preprint arXiv:1910.01108.*

Deven Shah, H Andrew Schwartz, and Dirk Hovy. 2019. Predictive biases in natural language processing models: A conceptual framework and overview. *arXiv preprint arXiv:1912.11078.*

Paul Stocker. 2012. Nouns. In *A Student Grammar of German,* page 11–29. Cambridge University Press.

Tony Sun, Andrew Gaut, Shirlyn Tang, Yuxin Huang, Mai ElSherief, Jieyu Zhao, Diba Mirza, Elizabeth Belding, Kai-Wei Chang, and William Yang Wang. 2019. Mitigating gender bias in natural language processing: Literature review. *arXiv preprint arXiv:1906.08976.*

Kellie Webster, Marta Recasens, Vera Axelrod, and Jason Baldridge. 2018. Mind the gap: A balanced corpus of gendered ambiguous pronouns. In *Transactions of the ACL,* page to appear.

Thomas Wolf, Lysandre Debut, Victor Sanh, Julien Chaumond, Clement Delangue, Anthony Moi, Pierric Cistac, Tim Rault, R'emi Louf, Morgan Funtowicz, and Jamie Brew. 2019. Huggingface's transformers: State-of-the-art natural language processing. *ArXiv,* abs/1910.03771.

Jieyu Zhao, Tianlu Wang, Mark Yatskar, Ryan Cotterell, Vicente Ordonez, and Kai-Wei Chang. 2019. Gender bias in contextualized word embeddings. *arXiv preprint arXiv:1904.03310.*

Pei Zhou, Weijia Shi, Jieyu Zhao, Kuan-Hao Huang, Muhao Chen, Ryan Cotterell, and Kai-Wei Chang. 2019. Examining gender bias in languages with grammatical gender. *arXiv preprint arXiv:1909.02224.*

Ran Zmigrod, Sebastian J Mielke, Hanna Wallach, and Ryan Cotterell. 2019. Counterfactual data augmentation for mitigating gender stereotypes in languages with rich morphology. *arXiv preprint arXiv:1906.04571.*

Appendix

This Appendix contains the detailed list of all professions used in this paper in Tables 6, 7, and 8. The professions were chosen from a list of professions provided by the U.S. Bureau of Labor Statistics (2020) based on the percentage of women employed, shortened and subsequently translated into German masculine and feminine forms. Tables 6-8 are referred in Section 3.2, where we describe how our template-based BEC-Pro was created.

Additionally, we provide an illustration of the associations for the German individual professions of the three profession groups in Figure 6. Figure 6 is referred in Section 5.3 when discussing that the associations do not capture gender bias for the German model due to grammatical agreement.

original profession	shortened profession	% women	German profession (masc./fem.)
Nursing, psychiatric, and home health aides	health aide	88.3	Gesundheitsberater/Gesundheitsberaterin
Bookkeeping, accounting, and auditing clerks	bookkeeper	88.5	Buchhalter/Buchhalterin
Registered nurses	registered nurse	88.9	staatlich geprüfter Krankenpfleger/ staatlich geprüfte Krankenpflegerin
Maids and housekeeping cleaners	housekeeper	89.0	Haushälter/Haushälterin
Receptionists and information clerks	receptionist	89.3	Rezeptionist/Rezeptionist
Phlebotomists	phlebotomist	89.3	Phlebologe/Phlebologin
Billing and posting clerks	billing clerk	89.5	Fakturist/Fakturistin
Paralegals and legal assistants	paralegal	89.6	Rechtsanwaltsgehilfe/Rechtsanwaltsgehilfin
Teacher assistants	teacher assistant	89.7	Betreuungslehrer/Betreuungslehrerin
Licensed practical and licensed vocational nurses	vocational nurse	90.8	Berufskrankenpfleger/Berufskrankenpflegerin
Dietitians and nutritionists	dietitian	92.1	Ernährungsberater/Ernährungsberaterin
Hairdressers, hairstylists, and cosmetologists	hairdresser	92.3	Friseur/Friseurin
Medical assistants	medical assistant	92.7	Arzthelfer/Arzthelferin
Secretaries and administrative assistants	secretary	93.2	Sekretär/Sekretärin
Medical records and health information technicians	medical records technician	93.3	Medizintechniker/Medizintechnikerin
Childcare workers	childcare worker	93.4	Kinderbetreuer/Kinderbetreuerin
Dental assistants	dental assistant	94.9	Zahnarzthelfer/Zahnarzthelferin
Speech-language pathologists	speech-language pathologist	95.8	Logopäde/Logopädin
Dental hygienists	dental hygienist	96.0	Dentalhygieniker/Dentalhygienikerin
Preschool and kindergarten teachers	kindergarten teacher	98.7	Kindergärtner/Kindergärtnerin

Table 6: Shortening and translation of English female-typical profession terms into German masculine and feminine forms

original profession	shortened profession	% women	German profession (masc./fem.)
Drywall installers, ceiling tile installers, and tapers	taper	0.7	Trockenbaumonteur/Trockenbaumonteurin
Structural iron and steel workers	steel worker	0.9	Stahlarbeiter/Stahlarbeiterin
Miscellaneous vehicle and mobile equipment mechanics, installers, and repairers	mobile equipment mechanic	1.3	Mechaniker für mobile Geräte/ Mechanikerin für mobile Geräte
Bus and truck mechanics and diesel engine specialists	bus mechanic	1.5	Busmechaniker/Busmechanikerin
Heavy vehicle and mobile equipment service technicians and mechanics + Automotive service technicians and mechanics	service technician	1.5	Kfz-Servicetechniker/ Kfz-Servicetechnikerin
Heating, air conditioning, and refrigeration mechanics and installers	heating mechanic	1.5	Heizungsmechaniker/ Heizungsmechanikerin
Electrical power-line installers and repairers	electrical installer	1.6	Elektroinstallateur/Elektroinstallateurin
Operating engineers and other construction equipment operators	operating engineer	1.7	Betriebsingenieur/Betriebsingenieurin
Logging workers	logging worker	1.8	Holzfäller/Holzfällerin
Carpet, floor, and tile installers and finishers	floor installer	1.9	Bodenleger/Bodenlegerin
Roofers	roofer	1.9	Dachedecker/Dachdeckerin
Mining machine operators	mining machine operator	2.0	Bergbaumaschinentechniker/ Bergbaumaschinentechnikerin
Electricians	electrician	2.2	Elektriker/Elektrikerin
Automotive body and related repairers	repairer	2.2	Kfz-Mechaniker/Kfz-Mechanikerin
Railroad conductors and yardmasters	conductor	2.4	Schaffner/Schaffnerin
Pipelayers, plumbers, pipefitters, and steamfitters	plumber	2.7	Klempner/Klempnerin
Carpenters	carpenter	2.8	Zimmermann/Zimmerin
Security and fire alarm systems installers	security system installer	2.9	Installateur von Sicherheitssystemen/ Installateurin von Sicherheitssystemen
Cement masons, concrete finishers, and terrazzo workers	mason	3.0	Maurer/Maurerin
Firefighters	firefighter	3.3	Feuerwehrmann/Feuerwehrfrau

Table 7: Shortening and translation of English male-typical profession terms into German masculine and feminine forms

original profession	shortened profession	% women	German profession (masc./fem.)
Retail salespersons	salesperson	48.5	Verkäufer/Verkäuferin
Directors, religious activities and education	director of religious activities	48.6	Leiter religiöser Aktivitäten/ Leiterin religiöser Aktivitäten
Crossing guards	crossing guard	48.6	Verkehrslotse/Verkehrslotsin
Photographers	photographer	49.3	Fotograf/Fotografin
Lifeguards and other recreational, and all other protective service workers	lifeguard	49.4	Bademeister/Bademeisterin
Lodging managers	lodging manager	49.5	Herbergsverwalter/Herbergsverwalterin
Other healthcare practitioners and technical occupations	healthcare practitioner	49.5	Heilpraktiker/Heilpraktikerin
Advertising sales agents	sales agent	49.7	Vertriebsmitarbeiter/Vertriebsmitarbeiterin
Mail clerks and mail machine operators, except postal service	mail clerk	49.8	Postbeamter/Postbeamtin
Electrical, electronics, and electromechanical assemblers	electrical assembler	50.4	Elektro-Monteur/Elektro-Monteurin
Insurance sales agents	insurance sales agent	50.6	Versicherungskaufmann/Versicherungskauffrau
Insurance underwriters	insurance underwriter	51.1	Versicherungsvermittler/Versicherungsvermittlerin
Medical scientists	medical scientist	51.8	medizinischer Wissenschaftler/ medizinische Wissenschaftlerin
Statisticians	statistician	52.4	Statistiker/Statistikerin
Training and development specialists	training specialist	52.5	Ausbilder/Ausbilderin
Judges, magistrates, and other judicial workers	judge	52.5	Richter/Richterin
Bartenders	bartender	53.1	Barkeeper/Barkeeperin
Dispatchers	dispatcher	53.1	Fahrdienstleiter/Fahrdienstleiterin
Order clerks	order clerk	53.3	Auftragssachbearbeiter/Auftragssachbearbeiterin
Postal service mail sorters, processors, and processing machine operators	mail sorter	53.3	Postsortierer/Postsortiererin

Table 8: Shortening and translation of English balanced profession terms into German masculine and feminine forms

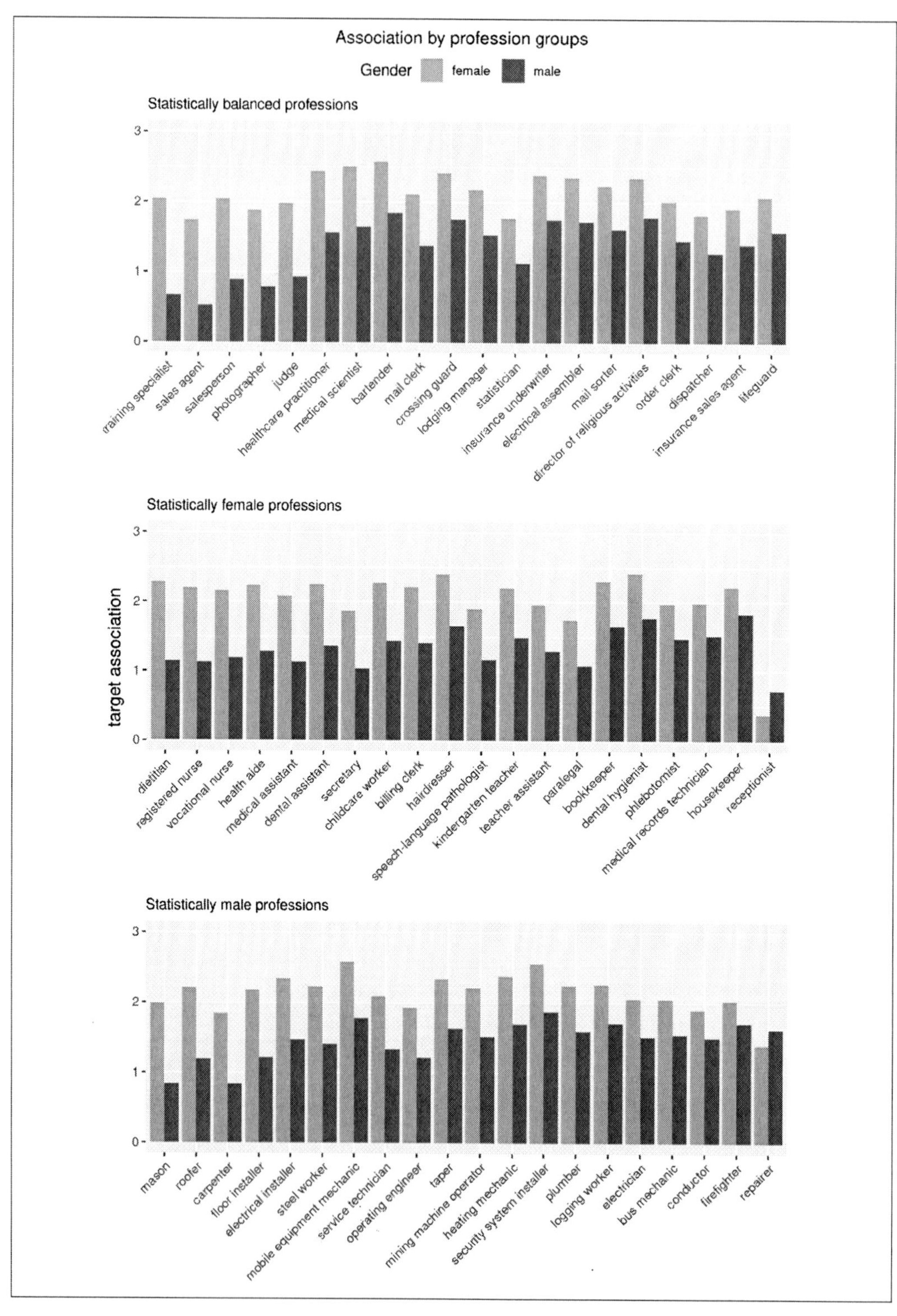

Figure 6: Mean associations for single professions of balanced, female and male profession groups for German BERT language model

Interdependencies of Gender and Race in Contextualized Word Embeddings

May Jiang
Computer Science
Princeton University
Princeton, NJ
mayjiang@princeton.edu

Christiane Fellbaum
Computer Science, Linguistics
Princeton University
Princeton, NJ
fellbaum@princeton.edu

Abstract

Recent years have seen a surge in research on the biases in word embeddings with respect to gender and, to a lesser extent, race. Few of these studies, however, have given attention to the critical intersection of race and gender. In this case study, we analyze the dimensions of gender and race in contextualized word embeddings of given names, taken from BERT, and investigate the nature and nuance of their interaction. We find that these demographic axes, though typically treated as physically and conceptually separate, are in fact interdependent and thus inadvisable to consider in isolation. Further, we show that demographic dimensions predicated on default settings in language, such as in pronouns, may risk rendering groups with multiple marginalized identities invisible. We conclude by discussing the importance and implications of intersectionality for future studies on bias and debiasing in NLP.

1 Introduction

In recent years, the rapid growth of natural language processing (NLP) has been accompanied by increasing attention to biases in NLP systems, with several studies investigating the demographic biases inherited by word embeddings from human text corpora. The vast majority of these studies have focused on measuring or mitigating bias with respect to gender, while fewer have concentrated on stereotypes with respect to race (Rozado, 2020). Even fewer of these studies have considered the intersection of gender and race.

Intersectionality, however, is a framework as critical as ever. Coined by black feminist scholar Kimberlé Crenshaw in 1989, intersectionality has since gained momentum as a vital framework to highlight and understand the powerful ways that different dimensions of an individual's identity combine and interact to create unique experiences of discrimination; Crenshaw elucidates the intersectional experience associated with race and sex as greater than the sum of racism and sexism, such that "any analysis that does not take intersectionality into account cannot sufficiently address the particular manner in which Black women are subordinated" (Crenshaw, 1989).

One consequence illuminated by this framework is that, because "people with multiple subordinate-group identities (e.g., ethnic minority women) do not fit the prototypes of their respective identity groups (e.g., ethnic minorities, women)," they and their unique experiences are often erased from the conversation – they experience 'intersectional invisibility' (Purdie-Vaughns and Eibach, 2008). In the field of psychology, due to systematic underrepresentation of certain groups in participant samples, "much of what is known about women in psychology is based on responses from women who are White and often middle class" (Cole, 2009). At an institutional level, "law enforcement, the government, and research institutions measure 'gender' as 'white women' and 'race' as 'African-American men'," and because of the prevalence of this "dualistic" approach in the social sciences, African-American women receive weaker attention in studies focusing solely on race or gender (Brown, 2010).

Proceedings of the Second Workshop on Gender Bias in Natural Language Processing, pages 17–25
Barcelona, Spain (Online), December 13, 2020.

We find this gap to be true of the social and linguistic properties characterizing contextual word embeddings as well. In this case study, we investigate the concepts of intersectionality inherent in the relationships and geometries of contextualized word embeddings. Specifically, this paper:

- examines the dimensions of gender and race in English-language BERT embeddings of European American and African American male and female names, finding that the concept of gender learned by the embeddings is closely dependent on race,

- explores the relationships between race and gender as captured by names and pronouns to show how default settings can contribute to the erasure of marginalized groups, and

- discusses the implications of these interdependencies and the vital importance of intersectionality for future studies on bias in NLP.

Bias Statement

In this work, we explore the intersection between race and gender, and our study of bias centers on the disparity between racial groups in the performance of the word embedding model on learning the concept of gender. If a system fails to recognize certain significant human and demographic characteristics of the non-prototypical members of a group, this results in a representational harm by which groups with multiple marginalized identities are erased. In particular, we draw on the description of 'coded exposure' given by sociologist Ruha Benjamin as the problematic phenomenon that "some technologies fail to see Blackness, while others render Black people hypervisible and expose them to systems of racial surveillance" – to be "watched, but not seen" (Benjamin, 2019). If gender and race are intertwined rather than independent, those at the intersection of marginalized racial and gender identities may be exposed to harmful biases related to the intersection and interaction of these identities, without being recognized for their identities themselves. Meanwhile, approaches that study, utilize, or debias these representations, but treat race and gender as orthogonal and isolated dimensions, would be poorly adapted for these groups.

Various studies have contended that because word embeddings are used as representations for text in a wide range of NLP tasks, any biases carried in the embeddings may be propagated to or even amplified in those downstream applications (Bolukbasi et al., 2016; Zhao et al., 2017; Bordia and Bowman, 2019). Certainly, this should be cause for concern, with the rising number of real-world applications and potential to impact lives. That said, we concur with Blodgett et al. (2020) that, independent of any allocational harms, the existence of these representational biases poses a critical problem in and of itself.

2 Related Work

The vast majority of studies of bias in word embeddings and contextual representations have focused on binary gender in isolation (Bolukbasi et al., 2016; Zhao et al., 2017; Zhao et al., 2019; Basta et al., 2019; Bordia and Bowman, 2019; Gonen and Goldberg, 2019). This is likely due to the advantage that gender pronouns are marked in language in a visible way that other demographic attributes are not. 'Bias', in these studies, is often measured as the similarity of words that are by definition gender-neutral – typically profession words – to words that are explicitly male or female gendered, such as pronouns. One popular method proposed for mitigating bias in word embeddings involves reducing the projection of gender-neutral words in the direction of a gender dimension vector defined by the difference between the vectors of 'he' and 'she' (Bolukbasi et al., 2016). Another measure of bias in word embeddings, the Word Embedding Association Test (WEAT), was introduced by Caliskan et al. (2017), adapted from the Implicit Association Test (IAT) of humans' reaction times to pairs of words (Greenwald et al., 1998).

More recently, studies have begun to factor intersectionality into their analyses of bias. Studying bias in sentence encoders, May et al. (2019) generalized the WEAT to sentence embeddings, using bleached sentence templates to test a number of hypotheses. Though several of their hypotheses are centered on gender, they also include a test of the "Angry Black Woman" stereotype and find significant evidence confirming its presence (May et al., 2019).

Tan and Celis (2019) similarly build on the WEAT, extending it to contextualized word embeddings and measuring intersectional bias as the association of European American and African American male

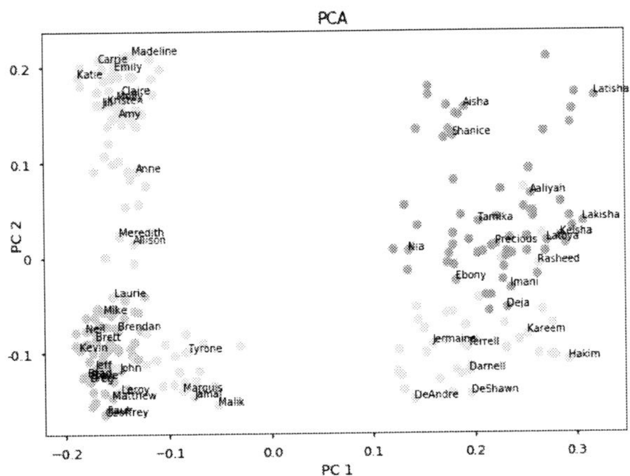

Figure 1: African American (AA) and European American (EA) male and female names projected onto their first and second principal components (AA female names in red, EA female names in yellow, AA male names in green, EA male names in blue)

and female names with pleasant and unpleasant words; they find significant evidence of bias, noting that the highest measured difference in bias is that between the names from the group with multiple privileged identities – European American men – against the names from the group with multiple marginalized identities – African American women. Further, Guo and Caliskan (2020) propose a method for identifying words that are unique to an intersectional group, and find numerous words pertaining to negative stereotypes associated significantly more strongly with an intersectional identity than with its constituent identities (Guo and Caliskan, 2020). To our knowledge, however, to date there has not been any systematic study or exploration of the conceptualization of gender and race learned by word embeddings, how these demographic dimensions relate or interact, or how bias may be embedded in gendered words such as pronouns themselves; the objective of this paper is to begin to fill in these gaps.

3 Learning Gender and Race in Word Embeddings from Names

To understand how and to what extent the concepts of gender and race are learned by contextualized word embeddings, in this case study we use contextualized embeddings of African American and European American male and female names from the pretrained BERT base-cased model (Devlin et al., 2019), with the sets of popular American given names borrowed from previous studies (Tan and Celis, 2019; May et al., 2019; Caliskan et al., 2017). These sets consist of 13 names for each race-gender pair, and were selected from Greenwald et al. (1998)'s original set of names used in introducing the IAT (Caliskan et al., 2017). We base our analysis on the principal component analysis (PCA) of these names, a common approach to identifying, visualizing, and understanding dimensions of gender and race in a word embedding vector space (Bolukbasi et al., 2016; Sedoc and Ungar, 2019; Manzini et al., 2019).

Figure 1 plots these names projected onto the first and second principal components of the PCA of all the names in the four sets. On inspection, the first principal component decidedly distinguishes the race of the names; all of the European American names have negative projections onto the component and all African American names, with the exception of a few male names for which racial association may have been more ambiguous, have positive projections. The second principal component appears to distinguish gender, cleanly separating the European American female names from the European American male names along the axis. However, though the PCA was performed on an equal number of name embeddings from each group, this gender component is significantly less successful in capturing the gender of African American names. African American female names, and male names to a lesser extent, have projections on this gender dimension close to zero, and there is substantial overlap in that region between the male and female names in a way that is in visible contrast to that of the European American names.

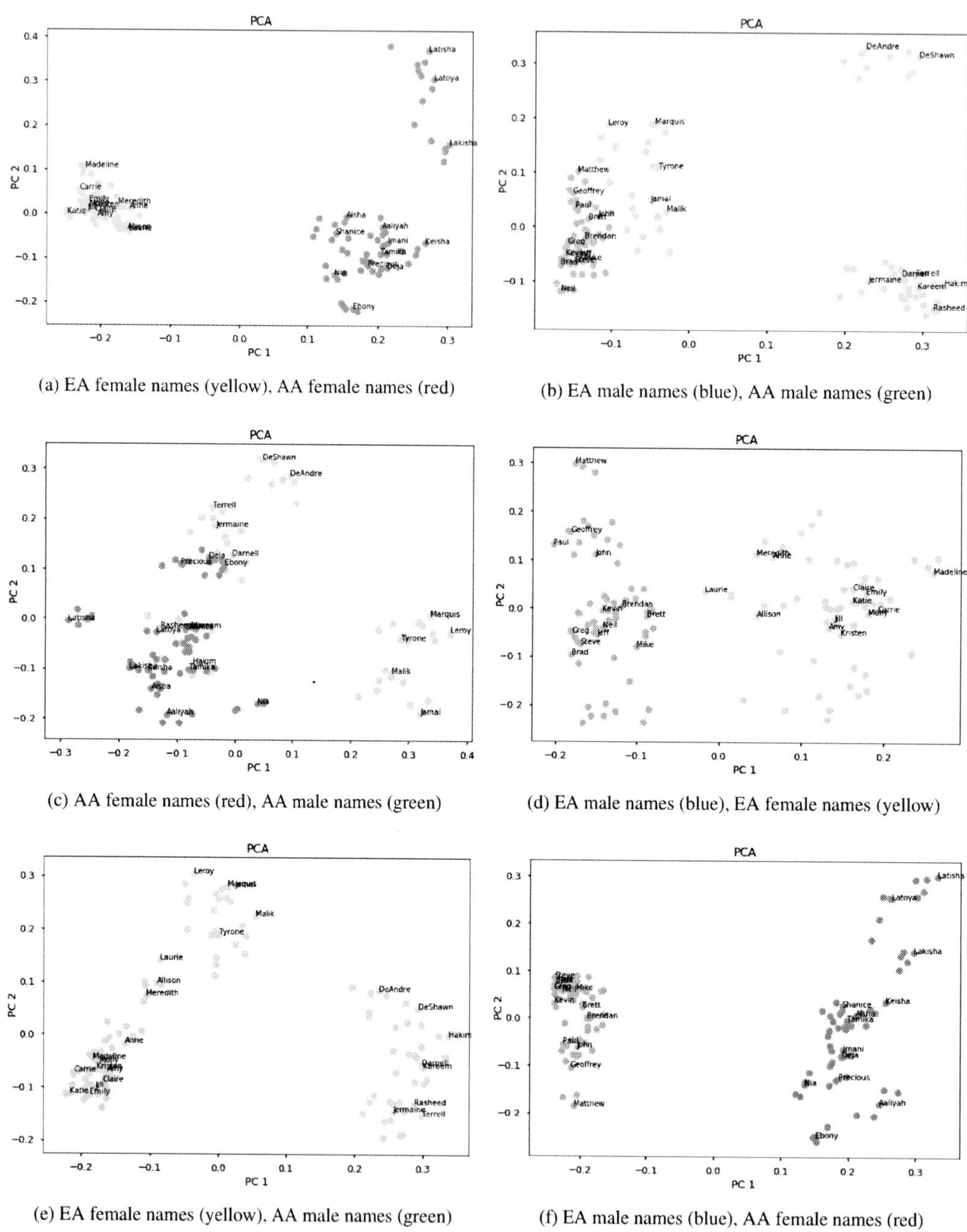

Figure 2: EA and AA male and female names projected onto their first and second principal components

Figure 2a plots the projections of the contextualized embeddings for the European American and African American female names on the first and second principal components of the PCA performed on names solely from those two sets, and the subsequent subfigures likewise plot the projections for European American and African American male names, African American male and female names, European American male and female names, African American male names and European American female names, and European American male names and African American female names.

Through the results of PCA on these subsets of the names, a few key themes emerge. First, it is immediately apparent that the concepts of gender and race are not learned uniformly across demographic groups; the juxtaposition of Figure 2c with Figure 2d illuminates this clearly, as the first principal component of the European American names linearly separates them by gender while neither the first nor the second principal component of the African American names results in a clean separation. To treat gender as a concept independent of race, then, risks the erasure of African Americans.

Further, we find that these concepts are not learned uniformly even within a single demographic group. That a small set of African American male names associate more closely with European American names as in Figure 2b is revealing of the heterogeneity of race, but even among the African American names that project onto the same direction of the first principal component – the race dimension – there is much more dispersion along that axis. It is worth noting that even given an equal number of names of each gender-racial group, the first principal components of the names' contextualized embeddings – the components that explain the most variance in the embeddings – are dimensions of race and gender that are better adapted to European American names.

Finally, across these experiments we find that the influence of race dominates that of gender in the embedding subspace. In Figure 1, the first principal component definitively distinguishes race, while the second principal component, more ambiguously for African American female names, distinguishes gender. Likewise, in Figure 2, the comparative ease with which the first principal components distinguish African American names from European American names is significant, as African American women's names associate much more closely with African American men's names than with European American women's names. This is striking, particularly in light of sociological studies on the centrality of race in understanding oppression, and the primacy of the role that race plays, even with the influence of factors such as race and class (Gillborn, 2015). Moreover, the weakness of the embedding model to recognize the femininity of African American women's names mirrors the biases in society that systematically marginalize African American women. Taken together, these themes underscore that the concepts and dimensions of race and gender in the BERT embedding space are not independent, and that ignoring their interaction may have harmful consequences for vulnerable populations.

4 Default Settings and Intersectional Invisibility

Studies of gender bias in word embeddings typically use either male and female names or pronouns for measurement and debiasing. As we have found, however, the understanding of gender learned by the model and applied to names depends significantly on the race of the names. In this section, we investigate whether pronouns – by definition neutral with respect to race – are, in fact, independent of race.

Figure 3a shows the PCA of the contextualized embeddings of the gender pronouns, visibly separated by gender along the first principal component axis. More illustratively, Figure 3b shows the European American and African American male and female names projected onto the first and second principal component dimensions obtained from the PCA of the gender pronouns in Figure 3a. We find that while European American names and African American men's names align definitively with the directions of their corresponding gendered pronouns, the names of African American women do not project significantly onto that gender dimension in the direction of the female pronouns. Since the default setting of race learned by the model is European American, 'she' is taken to mean European American women, and as the default setting of gender learned by the model is male, African American men become race-prototypical. However, because the race and gender dimensions are not independent, and the race dimension dominates the gender dimension such that the African American women's names associate more closely with the African American men's names, African American women – at the intersection of

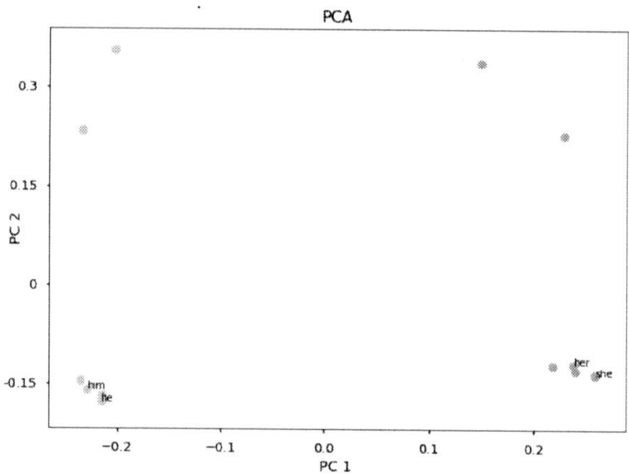

(a) Male (blue) and female (red) pronouns projected onto their first and second principal components

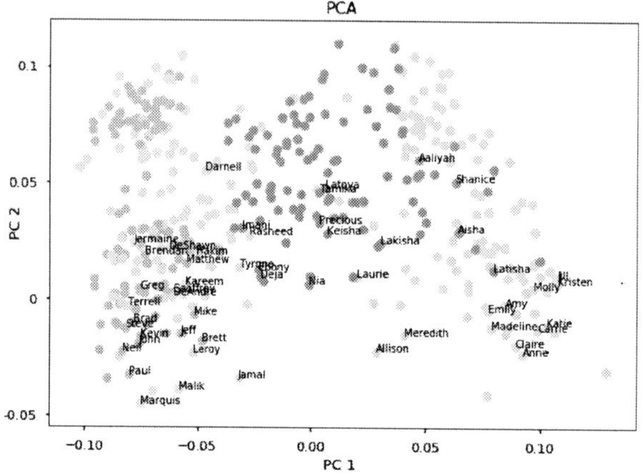

(b) AA and EA male and female names projected onto the first and second principal components of the gender pronouns from plot (a) above (AA female names in red, EA female names in yellow, AA male names in green, EA male names in blue)

Figure 3: Projections of pronouns and names on gender dimension from PCA of gender pronouns

marginalized gender and racial identities – experience intersectional invisibility to the language model as it is unable to associate their names with female pronouns.

Table 1 shows the cosine similarity between gender and race dimensions as identified using the first principal components of PCA on sets of names or pronouns. The gender dimension, for instance, is the first principal component of PCA on the words 'he', 'him', 'she', and 'her', with female pronouns' projections on that dimension in the positive direction. The race dimension using male names, analogously, is the first principal component of the PCA on the European American and African American male names, with African American names projecting on the component in the positive direction.

The dimensions sharing the highest similarity are the race dimensions for male and female names with a cosine similarity of 0.5536, which reinforces that race is the predominant demographic attribute captured by the word embeddings of the names. Likewise, there is a high cosine similarity of 0.5005 between the gender dimension derived from the gender pronouns and that derived from the European American male and female names. In contrast, the cosine similarity between the gender dimension derived from the pronouns and the gender dimension derived from the African American male and female names is close to zero. Further, while the gender dimension from the pronouns has a cosine similarity of only 0.036 with the race dimension from the European and African American male names, it shares a noticeable negative cosine similarity of -0.1461 with the race dimension derived from the European

Dimension	Dimension	Cosine similarity
Gender (male-female pronouns)	Gender (male-female EA names)	0.5005
Gender (male-female pronouns)	Gender (male-female AA names)	-0.0279
Gender (male-female pronouns)	Race (EA-AA male names)	0.0360
Gender (male-female pronouns)	Race (EA-AA female names)	-0.1461
Gender (male-female EA names)	Gender (male-female AA names)	-0.0177
Race (EA-AA female names)	Race (EA-AA male names)	0.5536

Table 1: Cosine similarity of gender and race dimensions identified by PCA using pronouns and names

and African American female names. That is, the gender dimension vector in the direction male-female has a negative relationship with the race dimension vector in the direction European American-African American, with the ultimate result that the names of African American women are marginalized from both the perspective of invisibility to the concept of gender as determined by pronouns, and conversely from the erroneous and unwanted exposure to the male direction of the gender dimension.

In sum, we find strong evidence that the concept and biases of race not only are not independent of the language model's understanding of gender as captured by pronouns, but are in fact embedded in that gender dimension itself.

5 Discussion and Conclusion

Above all, our findings reveal that language models cannot consider race and gender completely in isolation; since the word embedding space mirrors the reality of a society where racial and gender dimensions are intertwined, it is critically important to consider the significant interactive influences of gender and race. To fail to do so may be to fail to fully recognize both the unique experiences of those with intersecting identities and their positions as members of their constituent groups.

Further, the existing definitions, measures, and methods handling bias may be too narrow to encapsulate the nuances of diverse and multifaceted identities. We find that the human biases inherited by word embeddings are not merely manifested in the association of gendered words with gender-neutral terms relating to people, professions, or pleasantness and unpleasantness – as typically used in the measurement and analysis of bias – but are also able to fundamentally shape the relationships between the language, the labels, and the dimensions of identity themselves, as well as what these dimensions learn or fail to learn about groups of people.

This has profound implications for the way that bias is studied and measured, as well as mitigated. While previous studies have shown that the word embeddings for a set of names representing multiple marginalized identities are indeed shaped by biases in a unique and potentially more potent way compared to the embeddings for sets of names pertaining to each of their constituent identities, our finding that the racial and gender dimensions within word embedding subspaces are not independent implies that those most marginalized and vulnerable may be least seen and protected by methods that 'debias' by operating on isolated dimensions of race or gender built on default settings. Future work may extend our case study and analysis to specific demographic biases rooted in human studies, to other intersectional identities, considering potential biases with respect to demographic attributes such as religion, nationality, or age, to other words beyond proper names that may also carry biases, such as professions and adjectives, as well as to other embeddings and language models across different languages and cultures.

Ultimately, the weakness of word embeddings or language models to adequately, fairly, or uniformly learn the concept of gender for different racial groups and the dearth of research on intersecting identities and resulting biases concerning African American women and other multiply marginalized groups reveal an important blind spot in NLP. These manifestations of bias not only highlight the underlying complexities of inequality inherent in these models but also shed light on the parallel nuances of inequality in society and in the lived experiences of those individuals, further validating the intersectional framework as a crucial piece to understanding and unraveling the biases embedded in technology and society.

References

Christine Basta, Marta R. Costa-jussà, and Noe Casas. 2019. Evaluating the Underlying Gender Bias in Contextualized Word Embeddings. In *Proceedings of the First Workshop on Gender Bias in Natural Language Processing*, pages 33–39, Florence, Italy. Association for Computational Linguistics.

Ruha Benjamin. 2019. *Race after technology: abolitionist tools for the new Jim code*. Polity, Medford, MA.

Su Lin Blodgett, Solon Barocas, Hal Daumé III, and Hanna Wallach. 2020. Language (technology) is power: A critical survey of "bias" in NLP. In *Proceedings of ACL*, pages 5454–5476, Online, July. Association for Computational Linguistics.

Tolga Bolukbasi, Kai-Wei Chang, James Y Zou, Venkatesh Saligrama, and Adam T Kalai. 2016. Man is to computer programmer as woman is to homemaker? debiasing word embeddings. In *Advances in Neural Information Processing Systems 29*, pages 4349–4357. Curran Associates, Inc.

Shikha Bordia and Samuel R. Bowman. 2019. Identifying and Reducing Gender Bias in Word-Level Language Models. In *Proceedings of the 2019 Conference of the North*, pages 7–15, Minneapolis, Minnesota. Association for Computational Linguistics.

Geneva Brown. 2010. The intersectionality of race, gender, and reentry: Challenges for african-american women. *Issue Brief.. Washington, DC: American Constitution Society*.

Aylin Caliskan, Joanna J Bryson, and Arvind Narayanan. 2017. Semantics derived automatically from language corpora contain human-like biases. *Science*, 356(6334):183–186.

Elizabeth R. Cole. 2009. Intersectionality and research in psychology. *American Psychologist*, 64(3):170–180.

Kimberlé Crenshaw. 1989. Demarginalizing the intersection of race and sex: A black feminist critique of antidiscrimination doctrine, feminist theory and antiracist politics. *u. Chi. Legal f.*, page 139.

Jacob Devlin, Ming-Wei Chang, Kenton Lee, and Kristina Toutanova. 2019. BERT: Pre-training of deep bidirectional transformers for language understanding. In *Proceedings of NAACL-HLT*, pages 4171–4186, Minneapolis, Minnesota, June. Association for Computational Linguistics.

David Gillborn. 2015. Intersectionality, critical race theory, and the primacy of racism: Race, class, gender, and disability in education. *Qualitative Inquiry*, 21(3):277–287.

Hila Gonen and Yoav Goldberg. 2019. Lipstick on a pig: Debiasing methods cover up systematic gender biases in word embeddings but do not remove them. In *Proceedings of NAACL-HLT*, pages 609–614, Minneapolis, Minnesota, June. Association for Computational Linguistics.

Anthony G Greenwald, Debbie E McGhee, and Jordan LK Schwartz. 1998. Measuring individual differences in implicit cognition: the implicit association test. *Journal of personality and social psychology*, 74(6):1464.

Wei Guo and Aylin Caliskan. 2020. Detecting emergent intersectional biases: Contextualized word embeddings contain a distribution of human-like biases. *arXiv preprint arXiv:2006.03955*.

Thomas Manzini, Lim Yao Chong, Alan W Black, and Yulia Tsvetkov. 2019. Black is to Criminal as Caucasian is to Police: Detecting and Removing Multiclass Bias in Word Embeddings. In *Proceedings of the 2019 Conference of the North*, pages 615–621, Minneapolis, Minnesota. Association for Computational Linguistics.

Chandler May, Alex Wang, Shikha Bordia, Samuel R. Bowman, and Rachel Rudinger. 2019. On Measuring Social Biases in Sentence Encoders. In *Proceedings of the 2019 Conference of the North*, pages 622–628, Minneapolis, Minnesota. Association for Computational Linguistics.

Valerie Purdie-Vaughns and Richard P. Eibach. 2008. Intersectional invisibility: The distinctive advantages and disadvantages of multiple subordinate-group identities. *Sex Roles*, 59:377–391.

David Rozado. 2020. Wide range screening of algorithmic bias in word embedding models using large sentiment lexicons reveals underreported bias types. *PLOS ONE*, 15(4):1–26, 04.

João Sedoc and Lyle Ungar. 2019. The role of protected class word lists in bias identification of contextualized word representations. In *Proceedings of the First Workshop on Gender Bias in Natural Language Processing*, pages 55–61, Florence, Italy, August. Association for Computational Linguistics.

Yi Chern Tan and L Elisa Celis. 2019. Assessing social and intersectional biases in contextualized word representations. In *Advances in Neural Information Processing Systems*, pages 13230–13241.

Jieyu Zhao, Tianlu Wang, Mark Yatskar, Vicente Ordonez, and Kai-Wei Chang. 2017. Men Also Like Shopping: Reducing Gender Bias Amplification using Corpus-level Constraints. In *Proceedings of EMNLP*, pages 2979–2989, Copenhagen, Denmark. Association for Computational Linguistics.

Jieyu Zhao, Tianlu Wang, Mark Yatskar, Ryan Cotterell, Vicente Ordonez, and Kai-Wei Chang. 2019. Gender Bias in Contextualized Word Embeddings. In *Proceedings of the 2019 Conference of the North*, pages 629–634, Minneapolis, Minnesota. Association for Computational Linguistics.

Fine-tuning Neural Machine Translation on Gender-Balanced Datasets

Marta R. Costa-jussà* and Adrià de Jorge*
TALP Research Center
Universitat Politècnica de Catalunya, Barcelona
marta.ruiz@upc.edu, adria.de.jorge@estudiantat.upc.edu

Abstract

Misrepresentation of certain communities in datasets is causing big disruptions in artificial intelligence applications. In this paper, we propose using an automatically extracted gender-balanced dataset parallel corpus from Wikipedia. This balanced set is used to perform fine-tuning techniques from a bigger model trained on unbalanced datasets to mitigate gender biases in neural machine translation.

1 Introduction

Misrepresentation of individual communities in current datasets is causing severe disruptions in artificial intelligence applications. Examples of this are a lower performance of speech recognizers for women than for men (Tatman, 2017), a lower accuracy in face recognition for Asian faces than American or European ones (Xiong et al., 2018) and an amplification of stereotypes in Neural Machine Translation (NMT) (Font and Costa-jussà, 2019). These challenges are at the core of natural language processing applications, and, in particular, many works are focusing on trying to solve gender biases (Costa-jussà, 2019). With this objective in mind, and in the specific context of NMT, we propose the use of balanced data sets to mitigate gender biases in a standard NMT system taking advantage of domain adaptation techniques.

Previous research in the area of NMT has proposed to either mitigate biases using debiased word embeddings (Font and Costa-jussà, 2019) and using contextual information (Basta et al., 2020) or evaluating and measuring the amount of bias present in the translation (Stanovsky et al., 2019). The closest work to ours is the one by Saunders and Byrne (2020) where authors generate a small gender-balanced dataset and use Elastic Weight Consolidation techniques to perform transfer learning and mitigate the consequences of training with unbalanced datasets. Differently from this one, we use a larger non-synthetic balanced dataset to perform fine-tuning on an unbalanced-dataset and evaluate the reduction of gender bias in the final translation.

2 Bias statement

As proposed in previous work (Blodgett et al., 2020), we formulate the bias statement of our work. Our work consists of studying the effects of using a gender-balanced dataset to mitigate gender biases in NMT. In the NMT context, we can define gender bias as incorrectly translating a gendered source word into a target word opposite gender, when no ambiguity exists. We can attribute this to datasets that are over-represented with a particular gender. As shown in previous work (Bolukbasi et al., 2016b), there are representational harms in word embeddings such as demeaning women's ability to work in tech, e.g., *man is to computer programmer as woman is to homemaker*. The main concern is that training a system on unbalanced data will perpetuate these biases: first, on the methods built on top of these datasets, and second, people that use these systems will learn incorrect associations between words, unknowingly perpetuating these social biases. A system trained on balanced data is a first step in eliminating this representational harm, as there is the same number of instances between genders.

---

* Equal contribution

Proceedings of the Second Workshop on Gender Bias in Natural Language Processing, pages 26–34
Barcelona, Spain (Online), December 13, 2020.

To avoid stereotypical bias in professions, the next step would be to have the same professional distribution between genders, which can be achieved by gender-swapping the initial dataset. That way, the model will equally represent genders. Beyond this, we point out the limitation of doing a binary representation of gender, not reflecting the LGTBQ+ community. Note that our work trains a word embedding and NMT model and does not aim to reflect reality. In the end, mitigating gender bias in artificial intelligence systems is a short-term solution that needs to be combined with higher-level long-term projects in challenging current social power, among other principles (D'Ignazio and Klein, 2018).

3 Gender Balanced Dataset

This section explains the procedure followed to obtain an English-Spanish gender-balanced dataset, which uses the available Gebiotoolkit (Costa-jussà et al., 2019), and it extracts (multi-)parallel corpus at the sentence level from the Wikipedia Biographies. The toolkit consists of 3 blocks: a corpus extractor, which provides a layer to transform, collect and select entries in the desired languages; (2) a corpus aligner, which finds the parallel sentences within a text and provides a quality check of the parallel sentences given a few restrictions; (3) a gender classifier which includes a filtering module that classifies the gender of the entry and outputs the final parallel corpus. Hereinafter, we refer to this dataset as Balanced. We quantify the amount of gender bias in the collected dataset due to gender bias in word embeddings. This quantification of bias is also compared to the case of word embeddings computed on the EuroParl corpus (Koehn, 2005).

3.1 Balanced Dataset Generation

We used the available Gebiotoolkit (Costa-jussà et al., 2019) to extract the Balanced dataset. Gebiotoolkit is a tool for extracting multilingual parallel corpora at the sentence level, together with document and gender information from Wikipedia biographies. In this sense, the collected data set is not synthetic. We can generate this dataset from any of the languages available on Wikipedia. In our case, we have selected the English-Spanish language pair, which have considerable differences at the morphological level, and exhibit gender bias issues in NMT (Font and Costa-jussà, 2019).

After extraction, the biographies dataset has approximately 27,000 female-related sentences and 47,000 male-related sentences. To have an equal probability of finding a male or female related sentence, we balanced the dataset by removing male-related samples until having the same amount of masculine and feminine instances. In total, we end up with 54,000 parallel sentences, and the word embedding model has a vocabulary size of 17,277 English words.

Similarly, the Europarl corpus has 2,007,758 parallel sentences, and its word embedding model has a vocabulary size of 87,033 English words.

3.2 Gender bias Analysis for the dataset

To evaluate the amount of bias in the Balanced dataset, we build word embeddings, which is a vectorization of words following the Word2Vec (Mikolov et al., 2013) technique, and we assume that the presence of bias in word embeddings is a kind of reflection of the biases in the dataset (Caliskan et al., 2017). We use 128 as the number of dimensions for these vectors, a minimum count of 5 to remove poorly represented words and a bidirectional window of 3 words, that is, given a word $x[n]$, its "context" is

$$x[n-3], \ldots, x[n], \ldots, x[n+3]$$

To perform the gender bias analysis of these words embeddings, we use the measures proposed in previous works (Bolukbasi et al., 2016b; Gonen and Goldberg, 2019a). Inspired by these previous studies, we make use of the following lists of words:

- Definitional List 8 pairs (he/she; boy/girl; father/mother; male/female; his/her; himself/herself; man/woman; son/daughter)

- Biased List, which contains 1000 words, 500 female-biased, and 500 male-biased. (e.g., diet for female and hero for male)

- Extended Biased List, extended version of Biased List (5000 words, 2500 female-biased, and 2500 male-biased)

- Professional List 319 tokens (e.g., accountant, surgeon)

3.2.1 Gender Direction and Direct Bias

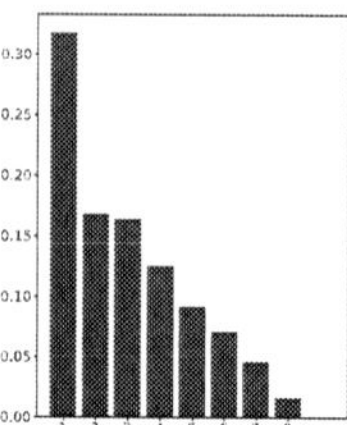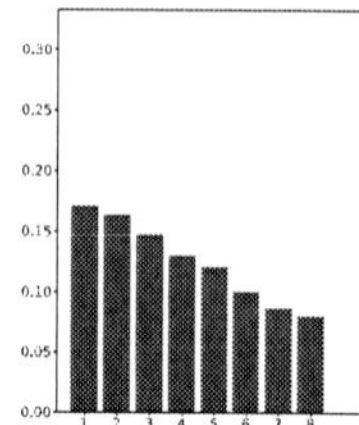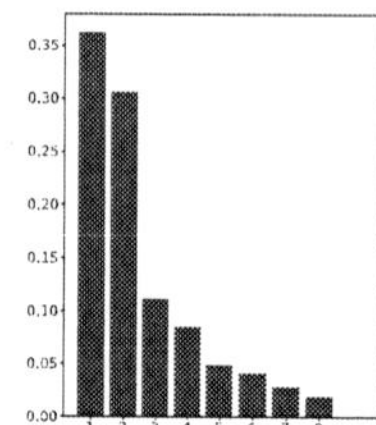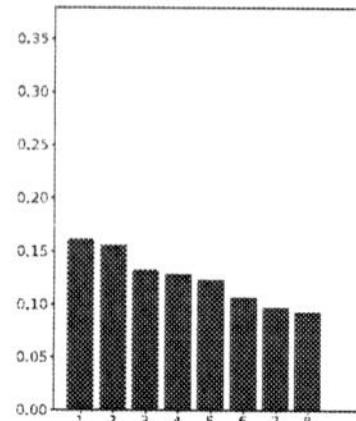

Figure 1: PCA Comparison between the gender base and a randomly generated base of 128 dimensions from Europarl (two graphs on the left) and Balanced (two graphs on the right) datasets.

Following the previous study (Bolukbasi et al., 2016a), we took the M gender pair difference vectors (Definitional List) and computed its principal components (PCs) to identify the gender subspace. We then generate a random base of M unit vectors of 128 dimensions for comparison. Figure 1 shows the PCA plots in both the gendered and the random vectors. In the EuroParl dataset, there is a clear dominance of one gender direction in the PCA from gender vectors. In the Balanced datasets, the supremacy is lower, but we can see that the 2 PCs from the left image (our gender base) explain almost 65% of the variance (information).

We take the definition of gender bias (Bolukbasi et al., 2016b), where they define the gender bias of a word $\overrightarrow{w}$ by its projection on the gender direction g. The higher the magnitude of the projection onto the previously defined base, the more biased the word is. We use the lists of neutral professions in (Zhao et al., 2018) to compute the direct bias of our Balanced dataset as follows.

$$\frac{1}{|N|} \sum_{w \in N} |cos(\overrightarrow{w}, g)| \tag{1}$$

After filtering by words in our word embeddings model, we get N=147 for the Europarl dataset and N=140 for the Balanced dataset. Direct bias is 0.23 for the EuroParl, and 0.10 for the Balanced dataset[1]. This measure confirms that most words still have some of its information alongside the gender direction. These results are higher of what is reported in Bolukbasi's work (although it is not directly comparable). Having a lower N may interfere in the direct bias measure. We use the PCA analysis to measure the gender bias in the word embeddings. The extracted PCs could be used to debias such embeddings (Bolukbasi et al., 2016b), but we are not using them in current work.

3.2.2 Clustering

The clustering measure wants to evaluate if stereotypically-gendered words (Biased List) are easy to cluster based on their word embedding representations. The higher the clustering accuracy, the more bias the words embeddings have. We use *Scikit learn* (Pedregosa et al., 2011) toolkit to perform an unsupervised k-means clustering classification (with 2 clusters).

Figures 2a and 2b show the tSNE projections of the vectors for both Europarl and Balanced datasets, respectively. The clustering model trained with the Europarl aligns with gender with an accuracy of

---

[1] Find words used in https://github.com/adridjs/thesis2020/tree/master/genderbias/data. Files with *pca_professions* suffix.

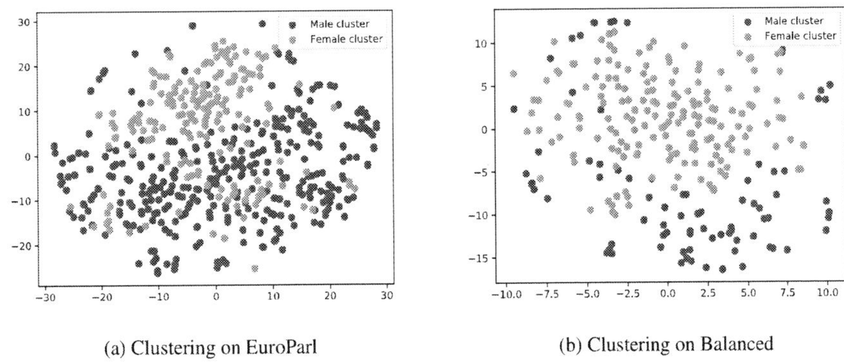

(a) Clustering on EuroParl   (b) Clustering on Balanced

Figure 2: tSNE projection after K-means clustering on Balanced and EuroParl datasets.

77.67% and Balanced dataset word embeddings aligns with gender with an accuracy of 68.47%. Note that not all the words in the Biased List appear in fact, we were only able to use 512 words and 263 words[2] (out of 1000) from the original Biased List, in the Europarl and Balanced cases, respectively,

3.2.3 Classification

We want to know if we can classify stereotypically-gendered words (Extended Biased List) into masculine or feminine based solely on their word embedding representations. We build an RBF-kernel SVM classifier to discover if the model can generalize its predictions into other stereotypically-gendered words. We evaluate on the EuroParl and Balanced corpus.

We start from the Extended Biased List of the 5000 most-biased words in (Gonen and Goldberg, 2019b) according to the original bias (2,500 from each gender). As in previous experiments, in our datasets, this list is reduced to 1277[3], which are the words that we can find in both of our datasets. We then split these into train and test sets, drawing a 20% (255 words) for the train set and 1022 for testing the model's performance. The classifier's accuracy for the Europarl dataset is 80.59%, and the Balanced dataset is 73.28%.

3.2.4 Discussion

The accuracy reported in Europarl, and Balanced datasets are not comparable since both have different total and vocabulary words. We know that the word embedding representation changes when having more word repetitions. The results in absolute terms tend to report less bias in the Balanced dataset compared to the Europarl dataset. Moreover, clustering and classification results in absolute terms are lower than the ones noted in previous studies (Gonen and Goldberg, 2019b).

4 Use of Domain Adaptation techniques for Gender Bias Mitigation

In this section we use the gender-balanced dataset described in the previous section to mitigate the gender bias present in a standard MT system. We build the NMT system using the standard Transformer (Vaswani et al., 2017) on a large dataset. Our idea is to use fine-tuning techniques with the balanced dataset on this baseline system.

4.1 Methodology

The idea is that we have a parent translation model trained with unbalanced data, and we want to learn a child model taking advantage of the balanced dataset. To avoid catastrophic forgetting, where the child model forgets everything learned from the parent, we use the mix fine tunning strategy. This strategy, which consists of initializing the child model with the parent model and train it on a percentage of the

---

[2] Words used can be found in https://github.com/adridjs/thesis2020/tree/master/$gender_bias/dataFiles with clustering\_words suffix$.

[3] Words used can be found in https://github.com/adridjs/thesis2020/blob/master/$gender_bias/data/svm_words.txt$

unbalanced data set concatenated with the entire balanced data set, has been proven to mitigate the catastrophic forgetting problem (Chu and Dabre, 2019).

We train the parent model with large datasets. We then fine-tune it with 3 types of datasets: Balanced, a Mix of the Large and Balanced dataset, having different proportions of the large dataset into it, and Concat, which contains the entire Large and Balanced datasets (see Figure 3).

4.2 Experimental Framework

Generic Training Data   To train the parent model, we used the English-Spanish EuroParl corpus (Koehn, 2005), which contains parallel data from the European Parliament's proceedings. We extract a part of the corpus that consists of 2 million parallel sentences. We applied a preprocessing step that consisted of tokenizing, truecasing, and filtering. We performed all these steps using scripts from the well-known Moses (Koehn et al., 2007) scripts.

Parameters   We train the network for an undefined number of epochs until convergence with an early stopping policy. That policy consists of setting a *patience*, which means that if the validation loss does not improve in *patience* epochs, stop the training. We established that to 5 as it gives good results empirically. We used 512 embeddings dimension, 6 layers in the encoder and decoder, 8 attention heads. We used a batch size of 16, a dropout of 0.1, and a learning rate of 0.001. We optimized with Adam.

Architecture   We use the Transformer (Vaswani et al., 2017) as baseline NMT model architecture, an encoder-decoder architecture based on attention-based mechanisms that boost the performance in NMT tasks compared to RNNs or CNNs architectures.

4.3 Fine-tuning

The baseline model is fine-tuned with a dropout to 0.3. This is used as a regularization technique together with the mixed fine-tuning approach to handle the catastrophic forgetting problem. This is the only modified hyperparameter between the baseline training and fine-tuning steps.

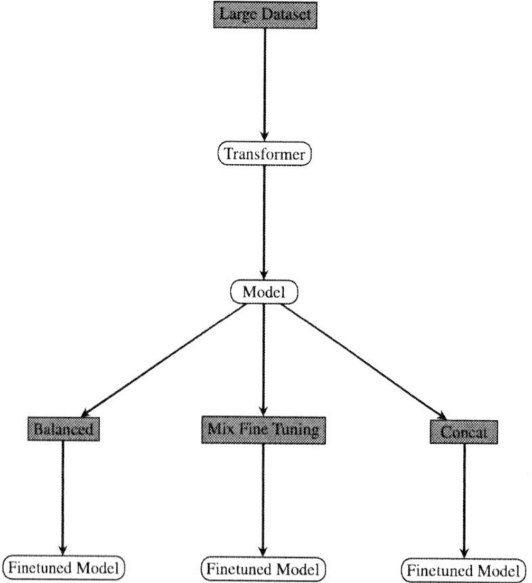

Figure 3: NMT training pipeline. The gray boxes represent the corpus used to train the model that they are pointing to.

Balanced   We hypothesize that fine-tuning on a corpus balanced in gender will improve the accuracy in gendered translations. We use the corpus extracted by Gebiotoolkit as reported in Section 3 - balanced in gender - to test this hypothesis. Note that the Balanced data is from a different domain than the training and test data.

Mix   This approach is building a dataset based on a mix of EuroParl and Balanced datasets. We study the influence on gender bias and NMT performance by having more or less in-domain data fed in the fine-tuning step. More percentage means more EuroParl data.

Concat   This approach consists of concatenating the whole EuroParl corpus with the Gender-Balanced biographies dataset.

Note that Balanced and Concat could also lie into the mix fine-tuning strategy, being 0% and 100%, respectively, the percentage of sentences from the Europarl corpus.

4.4   Results

Our findings are presented from Table 1 to 4. We report two baseline models: one trained with the EuroParl corpus and another trained with the concatenated dataset (Base-Concat) composed by EuroParl and Gebiotoolkit dataset. We report an evaluation in terms of translation performance and an evaluation in terms of gender bias accuracy.

4.4.1   Translation Evaluation

We use BLEU (Papineni et al., 2002) to evaluate the performance of our translation models on the WMT13 test set (*newstest2013*)[4]. The second baseline shows an increment of 1.5 points in the English-to-Spanish model and almost the same increment in the reversed model.

Translation Performance		
Corpus	en2es	es2en
EuroParl	26.87	25.50
Base-Concat	28.37	26.91
FT-Balanced	27.51	27.80
FT-Mix 5%	28.51	28.71
FT-Mix 10%	28.52	28.76
FT-Mix 20%	28.72	28.78
FT-Mix 30%	**28.76**	28.95
FT-Mix 40%	28.61	**29.05**
FT-Concat	28.68	28.29

Table 1: BLEU results for the different trained systems.

All the fine-tuned models surpass these two baselines, except the Balanced in the English-to-Spanish model. The best performance achieved in the English-to-Spanish model is the one where 30% of EuroParl data is present, while in the Spanish-English model the proportion is of 40%. We get final improvements over the best baseline system (Base-Concat) of up to 2 BLEU points.

4.4.2   Gender Bias Evaluation

We use the gender bias evaluation pipeline from (Stanovsky et al., 2019), also known as WinoMT, to evaluate the gender bias in these models. The dataset consists of 3,888 sentences. In each of these sentences, a primary entity that is coreferent with a pronoun, and a secondary entity tries to trick the translation system. The scripts provided by the authors extracted the grammatical gender of the primary entity from each translation by automatic word alignment and followed by morphological analysis. Then, it compares the translated primary entity with the annotated gender. The objective is to have a translation where the primary entity's gender matches the gold annotated one.

---

[4]http://www.statmt.org/wmt13/

General Bias   For the general bias measures, the best performance is achieved with FT-Concat, getting 49.8% accuracy at identifying the correct gender when translating into Spanish, which is an improvement of 2.5% points concerning the highest baseline, which is the Base-Concat.

General Gender Bias				
Corpus	Acc.	F-Score		Δ_g
		M	F	
EuroParl	46.6%	59.8%	31.3%	28.5
Base-Concat	47.3%	60.3%	32.4%	27.9
FT-Balanced	48.3%	60.4%	33.8%	26.6
FT-Mix 5%	47.5%	60.2%	32.0%	28.2
FT-Mix 10%	47.9%	60.4%	32.6%	27.8
FT-Mix 20%	48.2%	60.7%	33.3%	27.4
FT-Mix 30%	48.8%	60.8%	35.2%	25.6
FT-Mix 40%	49.0%	**61.1%**	35.5%	25.6
FT-Concat	**49.8%**	59.9%	**41.7%**	**18.2**

Table 2: Accuracy in the General WinoMT test set. F1-Score for masculine and feminine scores, and difference in performance between masculine and feminine scores (Δ_g)

Pro-Stereotypical Bias   In this setup, FT-Concat performs much better than any other model. Its accuracy is 10 points higher than the best baseline system. Its F-score differences are also the lowest, meaning less bias than in any different trained model.

Pro-stereotypical Gender Bias				
Corpus	Acc.	F-Score		Δ_g
		M	F	
EuroParl	53.5%	67.7%	35.9%	31.8
Base-Concat	56.2%	69.1%	38.8%	30.3
FT-Balanced	59.3%	70.0%	47.7%	22.3
FT-Mix 5%	57.3%	69.3%	43.2%	26.1
FT-Mix 10%	57.8%	69.4%	44.1%	25.3
FT-Mix 20%	58.2%	69.9%	44.6%	25.3
FT-Mix 30%	58.9%	70.3%	46.0%	24.3
FT-Mix 40%	59.0%	70.8%	45.5%	25.3
FT-Concat	**66.3%**	**74.1%**	**62.0%**	**12.1**

Table 3: Accuracy in the WinoMT test set. Pro-Stereotypical translations.

Anti-Stereotypical Bias   Lastly, the best model performance is obtained on the FT-Mix40% model, which has an accuracy of 45% (lowest for all the setups). The minimum F-score difference is 28,9%, which is very high (also competitive to the commercial reference systems reported in the original paper (Stanovsky et al., 2019). In general, we can see that in this setup, the models do not perform very well. This reveals that the systems are still biased, as we have low anti-stereotypical and high pro-stereotypical translation performance.

5   Conclusions

The motivation of our work lies in the hypothesis that the use of a gender-balanced dataset can diminish the gender bias in NMT systems.

For doing so, we first report an analysis of this Balanced dataset in terms of gender bias by using a word embedding evaluation set of measures. This analysis shows that this Balanced dataset only encodes

Anti-stereotypical Gender Bias			
Corpus	Acc,	F-Score	Δ_g
		M	F	
EuroParl	44.3%	57.1%	28.2%	28.9
Base Concat	39.0%	52.3%	21.5%	30.8
FT-Balanced	43.1%	56.7%	22.9%	33.8
FT-Mix 5%	43.1%	56.6%	23.5%	33.1
FT-Mix 10%	43.4%	57.1%	23.2%	33.9
FT-Mix 20%	44.1%	**57.4%**	24.7%	32.7
FT-Mix 30%	44.3%	57.1%	26.6%	30.5
FT-Mix 40%	**45.0%**	**57.4%**	**28.6%**	**28.8**
FT-Concat	44.5%	57.0%	26.3%	30.7

Table 4: Accuracy in the WinoMT test set. Anti-Stereotypical translations.

a small amount of bias when compared in absolute terms with other more massive datasets. Note that we can use these representations by downstream applications with the ability to have little gender bias.

Then, after this analysis, we use fine-tuning techniques to reduce gender bias in a standard MT system. Results show that even if our balanced dataset is from a different domain than the training and the test of the MT system, it does improve the translation quality (up to 2 BLEU points), and it can mitigate the gender bias in a significant amount (up to a 12.5% accuracy).

Acknowledgments

This work is supported in part by the Catalan Agency for Management of University and Research Grants (AGAUR) through an Industrial Ph.D. Grant, the Spanish Ministerio de Ciencia e Innovación and by the Agencia Estatal de Investigación, through the postdoctoral senior grant Ramón y Cajal and by the European Research Council (ERC) under the European Union's Horizon 2020 research and innovation programme (grant agreement No. 947657).

References

Christine Basta, Marta R. Costa-jussà, and José A. R. Fonollosa. 2020. Towards mitigating gender bias in a decoder-based neural machine translation model by adding contextual information. In *Proceedings of the The Fourth Widening Natural Language Processing Workshop*, pages 99–102, Seattle, USA, July. Association for Computational Linguistics.

Su Lin Blodgett, Solon Barocas, Hal Daumé III, and Hanna Wallach. 2020. Language (technology) is power: A critical survey of "bias" in NLP. In *Proceedings of the 58th Annual Meeting of the Association for Computational Linguistics*, pages 5454–5476, Online, July. Association for Computational Linguistics.

Tolga Bolukbasi, Kai-Wei Chang, James Y. Zou, Venkatesh Saligrama, and Adam Kalai. 2016a. Man is to computer programmer as woman is to homemaker? debiasing word embeddings. *CoRR*, abs/1607.06520.

Tolga Bolukbasi, Kai-Wei Chang, James Y Zou, Venkatesh Saligrama, and Adam T Kalai. 2016b. Man is to computer programmer as woman is to homemaker? debiasing word embeddings. In *Proceedings of Advances in Neural Information Processing Systems 29*, pages 4349–4357.

Aylin Caliskan, Joanna J. Bryson, and Arvind Narayanan. 2017. Semantics derived automatically from language corpora necessarily contain human biases. *Science*, 356:183–186.

Chenhui Chu and Raj Dabre. 2019. Multilingual multi-domain adaptation approaches for neural machine translation. *CoRR*, abs/1906.07978.

Marta R. Costa-jussà, Pau Li Lin, and Cristina España-Bonet. 2019. Gebiotoolkit: Automatic extraction of gender-balanced multilingual corpus of wikipedia biographies. In *Proceedings of 12th Language Resources and Evaluation Conference (LREC)*.

Marta R. Costa-jussà. 2019. An analysis of gender bias studies in natural language processing. *Nature Machine Intelligence*, 1(11):495–496.

Catherine D'Ignazio and Lauren Klein. 2018. Data feminism. MIT Press.

Joel Escudé Font and Marta R. Costa-jussà. 2019. Equalizing gender bias in neural machine translation with word embeddings techniques. In *Proceedings of the First ACL Workshop on Gender Bias in Natural Language Processing*, pages 147–154, Florence, Italy, August.

Hila Gonen and Yoav Goldberg. 2019a. Lipstick on a pig: Debiasing methods cover up systematic gender biases in word embeddings but do not remove them. In Jill Burstein, Christy Doran, and Thamar Solorio, editors, *NAACL-HLT (1)*, pages 609–614. Association for Computational Linguistics.

Hila Gonen and Yoav Goldberg. 2019b. Lipstick on a pig: Debiasing methods cover up systematic gender biases in word embeddings but do not remove them. *CoRR*, abs/1903.03862.

Philipp Koehn, Hieu Hoang, Alexandra Birch, Chris Callison-Burch, Marcello Federico, Nicola Bertoldi, Brooke Cowan, Wade Shen, Christine Moran, Richard Zens, Chris Dyer, Ondřej Bojar, Alexandra Constantin, and Evan Herbst. 2007. Moses: Open source toolkit for statistical machine translation. In *Proceedings of the 45th Annual Meeting of the Association for Computational Linguistics Companion Volume Proceedings of the Demo and Poster Sessions*, pages 177–180, Prague, Czech Republic, June. Association for Computational Linguistics.

Philipp Koehn. 2005. Europarl: A parallel corpus for statistical machine translation. In *MT summit*, volume 5, pages 79–86. Citeseer.

Tomas Mikolov, Ilya Sutskever, Kai Chen, Greg S Corrado, and Jeff Dean. 2013. Distributed representations of words and phrases and their compositionality. In C. J. C. Burges, L. Bottou, M. Welling, Z. Ghahramani, and K. Q. Weinberger, editors, *Advances in Neural Information Processing Systems 26*, pages 3111–3119. Curran Associates, Inc.

Kishore Papineni, Salim Roukos, Todd Ward, and Wei-Jing Zhu. 2002. Bleu: a method for automatic evaluation of machine translation. In *Proceedings of the 40th Annual Meeting of the Association for Computational Linguistics*, pages 311–318, Philadelphia, Pennsylvania, USA, July. Association for Computational Linguistics.

Fabian Pedregosa, Gaël Varoquaux, Alexandre Gramfort, Vincent Michel, Bertrand Thirion, Olivier Grisel, Mathieu Blondel, Peter Prettenhofer, Ron Weiss, Vincent Dubourg, et al. 2011. Scikit-learn: Machine learning in python. *Journal of machine learning research*, 12(Oct):2825–2830.

Danielle Saunders and Bill Byrne. 2020. Reducing gender bias in neural machine translation as a domain adaptation problem. In *Proceedings of the 58th Annual Meeting of the Association for Computational Linguistics*, pages 7724–7736, Online, July. Association for Computational Linguistics.

Gabriel Stanovsky, Noah A. Smith, and Luke Zettlemoyer. 2019. Evaluating gender bias in machine translation. In *Proceedings of the 57th Annual Meeting of the Association for Computational Linguistics*, pages 1679–1684, Florence, Italy, July. Association for Computational Linguistics.

Rachael Tatman. 2017. Gender and dialect bias in YouTube's automatic captions. In *Proceedings of the First ACL Workshop on Ethics in Natural Language Processing*, pages 53–59, Valencia, Spain, April. Association for Computational Linguistics.

Ashish Vaswani, Noam Shazeer, Niki Parmar, Jakob Uszkoreit, Llion Jones, Aidan N Gomez, Łukasz Kaiser, and Illia Polosukhin. 2017. Attention is all you need. In *Advances in neural information processing systems*, pages 5998–6008.

Zhangyang Xiong, Zhongyuan Wang, Changqing Du, Rong Zhu, Emily Xiao, and Tao Lu, 2018. *An Asian Face Dataset and How Race Influences Face Recognition: 19th Pacific-Rim Conference on Multimedia, Hefei, China, September 21-22, 2018, Proceedings, Part II*, pages 372–383. 09.

Jieyu Zhao, Yichao Zhou, Zeyu Li, Wei Wang, and Kai-Wei Chang. 2018. Learning gender-neutral word embeddings. *CoRR*, abs/1809.01496.

Neural Machine Translation Doesn't Translate Gender Coreference Right Unless You Make It

Danielle Saunders and **Rosie Sallis** and **Bill Byrne**
Department of Engineering, University of Cambridge, UK
{ds636, rs965, wjb31}@cam.ac.uk

Abstract

Neural Machine Translation (NMT) has been shown to struggle with grammatical gender that is dependent on the gender of human referents, which can cause gender bias effects. Many existing approaches to this problem seek to control gender inflection in the target language by explicitly or implicitly adding a gender feature to the source sentence, usually at the sentence level.

In this paper we propose schemes for incorporating explicit word-level gender inflection tags into NMT. We explore the potential of this gender-inflection controlled translation when the gender feature can be determined from a human reference, or when a test sentence can be automatically gender-tagged, assessing on English-to-Spanish and English-to-German translation.

We find that simple existing approaches can over-generalize a gender-feature to multiple entities in a sentence, and suggest effective alternatives in the form of tagged coreference adaptation data. We also propose an extension to assess translations of gender-neutral entities from English given a corresponding linguistic convention, such as a non-binary inflection, in the target language.

1 Introduction

Translation into languages with grammatical gender involves correctly inferring the grammatical gender of all entities in a sentence. In some languages this grammatical gender is dependent on the social gender of human referents. For example, in the Spanish translation of the sentence 'This is the doctor', 'the doctor' would be either 'el médico', masculine, or 'la médica', feminine. Since the noun refers to a person the grammatical gender inflection should be correct for a given referent.

In practice many NMT models struggle at generating such inflections correctly (Sun et al., 2019), often instead defaulting to gender-based social stereotypes (Prates et al., 2019) or masculine language (Hovy et al., 2020). For example, an NMT model might always translate 'This is the doctor' into a sentence with a masculine inflected noun: 'Este es el médico'.

Such behaviour can be viewed as translations exhibiting gender bias. By 'bias' we follow the definition from Friedman and Nissenbaum (1996) of behaviour which 'systematically and unfairly discriminate[s] against certain individuals or groups of individuals in favor of others.' Specifically, translation performance favors referents fitting into groups corresponding to social stereotypes, such as male doctors.

Such systems propagate the representational harm of erasure to referents – for example, a non-male doctor would be incorrectly gendered by the above example translation. Systems may also cause allocational harms if the incorrect translations are used as inputs to other systems (Crawford, 2017). System users also experience representational harms via the reinforcement of stereotypes associating occupations with a particular gender (Abbasi et al., 2019). Even if they are not the referent, the user may not wish for their words to be translated in such a way that they appear to endorse social stereotypes. Users will also experience a lower quality of service in receiving grammatically incorrect translations.

A common approach to this broad problem in NMT is the use of gender features, implicit or explicit. The gender of one or more words in a test sentence is determined from external context (Vanmassenhove

Proceedings of the Second Workshop on Gender Bias in Natural Language Processing, pages 35–43
Barcelona, Spain (Online), December 13, 2020.

et al., 2018; Basta et al., 2020) or by reliance on 'gender signals' from words in the source sentence such as gendered pronouns. That information can then be used when translating. Such approaches combine two distinct tasks: identifying the gender inflection feature, and then applying it to translate words in the source sentence. These feature-based approaches make the unstated assumption that if we *could* correctly identify that, e.g., the doctor in the above example should be female, we could inflect entities in the sentence correctly, reducing the effect of gender bias.

Our contribution is an exploration of this assumption. We propose a scheme for incorporating an explicit gender inflection tag into NMT, particularly for translating coreference sentences *where the reference gender label is known*. Experimenting with translation from English to Spanish and English to German, we find that simple existing approaches overgeneralize from a gender signal, incorrectly using the same inflection for every entity in the sentence. We show that a tagged-coreference adaptation approach is effective for combatting this behaviour. Although we only work with English source sentences to extend prior work, we note that our approach can be extended to source languages without inherent gender signals like gendered pronouns, unlike approaches that rely on those signals.

Intuitively, if gender tagging does not perform well when it can use the label determined by human coreference resolution, it will be even less useful when a gender label must be automatically inferred. Conversely, gender tagging that is effective in this scenario may be beneficial when the user can specify the gendered language to use for the referent, such as Google Translate's translation inflection selection (Johnson, 2018), or for translations where the grammatical gender to use for all human referents is known. We also find that our approach works well with RoBERTa-based gender tagging for English test sentences.

Existing work in NMT gender bias has focused on the translation of sentences based on binary gender signals, such as exclusively male or female personal pronouns. This excludes and erases those who do not use binary gendered language, including but not limited to non-binary individuals (Zimman, 2017; Cao and Daumé III, 2020). As part of this work we therefore explore applying tagging to indicate gender-neutral referents, and produce a WinoMT set to assess translation of coreference sentences with gender-neutral entities.

1.1 Related work

Variations on a gender tag or signal for machine translation have been proposed in several forms. Vanmassenhove et al. (2018) incorporate a 'speaker gender' tag into training data, allowing gender to be conveyed at the sentence level. However, this does not allow more fine-grained control, for example if there is more than one referent in a sentence. Similar approaches from Voita et al. (2018) and Basta et al. (2020) infer and use gender information from discourse context. Moryossef et al. (2019) also incorporate a single explicit gender feature for each sentence at inference. Miculicich Werlen and Popescu-Belis (2017) integrate coreference links into machine translation reranking to improve pronoun translation with cross-sentence context. Stanovsky et al. (2019) propose NMT gender bias reduction by 'mixing signals' with the addition of pro-stereotypical adjectives. Also related to our work is the very recent approach of Stafanovičs et al. (2020), who train their NMT models from scratch with all source language words annotated with target language grammatical gender.

In Saunders and Byrne (2020) we treat gender bias as a domain adaptation problem by adapting to a small set of synthetic sentences with equal numbers of entities using masculine and feminine inflections. We also interpret this as a gender 'tagging' approach, since the gendered terms in the synthetic dataset give a strong signal to the model. In this work we extend the synthetic datasets from this work to explore this effect further.

Other approaches to reducing gender bias effects involve adjusting the word embeddings either directly (Escudé Font and Costa-jussà, 2019) or by training with counterfactual data augmentation (Zhao et al., 2018; Zmigrod et al., 2019). We view these approaches as orthogonal to our proposed scheme: they have similar goals but do not directly control inference-time gender inflection at the word or sentence level.

2 Assessing and controlling gender inflection

We wish to investigate whether a system can translate into inflected languages correctly correctly given the reference gender label of a certain word. Our proposed approach involves fine-tuning a model on a very small, easily-constructed synthetic set of sentences which have gender tags. At test time we assign the reference gender label to the words whose gender inflection we wish to control.

2.1 Gender bias assessment

WinoMT (Stanovsky et al., 2019) is a test set for assessing the presence of gender bias in translation from English to several gender-inflected languages. Each of 3888 test sentence contains two human entities, one of which is coreferent with a pronoun. 1826 of these sentences have male primary entities, 1822 female and 240 neutral. The first test sentence in WinoMT is:

The developer argued with the designer because she did not like the design.

The gender label for this sentence is 'female' and the primary entity label is 'the developer'. The same sentence with a gender tag would be:

The developer $<$F$>$ argued with the designer because she did not like the design.

We only tag the primary entity in test sentences. During evaluation WinoMT extracts the hypothesis translation for 'the developer' by automatic word alignment and assesses its gender inflection in the target language. The main objective is high overall accuracy – the percentage of correctly inflected primary entities.

We note a comment by Rudinger et al. (2018), who develop a portion of the English WinoMT source sentences, that such schemas 'may demonstrate the presence of gender bias in a system, but not prove its absence.' In fact high WinoMT accuracy can be achieved by using the labeled inflection for *both* entities in a WinoMT test sentence, even though only one is specified by the sentence.

We therefore produce[1] a test set for the WinoMT framework to track the gender inflection of the secondary entity in each original WinoMT sentence (e.g. 'the designer' in the above example). We measure second-entity inflection correspondence with the gender label, which we refer to as **L2**. High L2 suggests that 'the designer' would also have feminine inflection in a translation of the above example, despite not being coreferent with the pronoun.

We are particularly interested in cases where L2 increases over a baseline, or high Δ**L2**. Many factors may contribute to a baseline system's L2, but we are specifically interested in whether *adding* gender features affects only the words they are intended to affect. High ΔL2 indicates a system learning to over-generalize from available gender features. We consider this as erasing the secondary referents, and therefore as undesirable behaviour.

2.2 Adaptation to gender-feature datasets

Name	English source	German target	Spanish target
S&B	the trainer finished his work the trainer finished her work the trainer finished their work	der Trainer beendete seine Arbeit die Trainerin beendete ihre Arbeit DEF TrainerW_END beendete PRP Arbeit	el entrenador terminó su trabajo la entrenadora terminó su trabajo DEF entrenadorW_END terminó su trabajo
V1	the trainer $<$M$>$ finished his work	der Trainer beendete seine Arbeit	el entrenador terminó su trabajo
V2	the trainer $<$F$>$ finished the work	die Trainerin beendete die Arbeit	la entrenadora terminó el trabajo
V3	the trainer $<$N$>$ and the choreographer $<$M$>$ finished the work	DEF TrainerW_END und der Choreograf beendeten die Arbeit	DEF entrenadorW_END y el coreógrafo terminaron el trabajo
V4	the trainer $<$F$>$, the choreographer $<$N$>$	die Trainerin, DEF ChoreografW_END	la entrenadora, DEF coreógrafW_END

Table 1: Examples of the tagging schemes explored in this paper. Adjective-based sentences (e.g. 'the tall woman finished her work') are never tagged. For neutral target sentences, we define synthetic placeholder articles DEF and noun inflections W_END, as well as a placeholder possessive pronoun for German PRP

---

[1]Our new adaptation and evaluation sets can be found at `https://github.com/DCSaunders/tagged-gender-coref`

In Saunders and Byrne (2020) we propose reducing gender bias effects quickly by model adaptation to sets of 388 simple synthetic sentences with equal numbers of male and female entities. A gendered-alternative-lattice rescoring scheme avoids catastrophic forgetting. The sentences follow a template:

The [entity] finished [his|her] work.

In one set the *entity* is always a profession (e.g. 'doctor'). In the other it is either '*[adjective] [man|woman]*' (e.g. 'tall man') or a profession that does not occur in WinoMT source sentences (e.g. 'trainer'.) We use the latter set to minimize the confounding effects of vocabulary memorization.

It is possible to extract natural text with gendered entities, for example using GeBioToolkit (Costa-jussà et al., 2020). The synthetic dataset is more suited to our work for two reasons: it has been shown to allow strong accuracy improvements on WinoMT, and it has a predictable format that can easily be augmented with gender tags. We leave the more complicated scenario of extracting and tagging natural adaptation data to future work.

As well as the unchanged **S&B** synthetic adaptation set, we propose four gender-tagged variations, which we illustrate in Table 1. In the first, **V1**, we add a gender tag following professions only (we do not tag adjective-based sentences since 'man' and 'woman' are already distinct words in English).

For the second, **V2**, we use the same tagging scheme but note that the possessive pronoun offers a gender signal that may conflate with the tag, so change all examples to '... finished *the* work'.

The third, **V3**, is the same as **V2** but in each profession-based sentence a second profession-based entity with a different gender inflection tag is added. This is intended to discourage systems from over-generalizing one tag to all sentence entities.

In the final scheme, **V4**, we simplify **V3** to a minimal, lexicon-like pattern:

The [entity1], the [entity2].

Both entities are tagged. We remove all adjective-based sentences, leaving only tagged coreference profession entities for adaptation. This set has the advantage of using simpler language than other sets, making it easier to extend to new target languages.

2.3 Exploring gender-neutral translation

We wish to extend previous machine translation coreference research to the translation of gender-neutral language, which may be used by non-binary individuals or to avoid the social impact of using gendered language (Zimman, 2017; Misersky et al., 2019). Recently Cao and Daumé III (2020) have encouraged inclusion of non-binary referents in NLP coreference work. Their study focuses heavily on English, which has minimal gender inflection and where gender-neutral language such as singular *they* is in increasingly common use (Bradley et al., 2019); the authors acknowledge that 'some extensions ... to languages with grammatical gender are non-trivial'.

In particular, existing NMT gender bias test sets typically analyse behaviour in languages with grammatical gender that corresponds to a referent's gender. Translation into these languages effectively highlights differences in translation between masculine and feminine referents, but these languages also often lack widely-accepted conventions for gender-neutral language (Ackerman, 2019; Hord, 2016). In some languages with binary grammatical gender it is possible to avoid gendering referents by using passive or reflexive grammar, but such constructions can themselves invalidate individual identities (Auxland, 2020).

We therefore explore a proof-of-concept scheme for translating tagged neutral language into inflected languages by introducing synthetic gender-neutral placeholder articles and noun inflections in the target language. For example, we represent the gender-neutral inflection of 'el entrenador' (the trainer) as 'DEF entrenadorW_END'

A variety of gender-neutral inflections have been proposed for various grammatically gendered languages, such as *e* or *x* Spanish (Papadopoulos, 2019) and Portuguese (Auxland, 2020) noun inflections instead of masculine *o* and feminine *a*. These language-specific approaches may develop in various forms across social groups and networks, and can shift over time (Shroy, 2016). Our intent is not to prescribe which should be used, but to explore an approach which in principle could be extended to various real inflection schemes.

We construct additional 'neutral-augmented' versions of the adaptation sets described in 2.2, adding
'*The [adjective] person finished [their|the] work*' sentences to the adjective-based sets and sentences
like '*The trainer <N> finished [their|the] work*' to the profession-based sets, with synthetic placeholder
articles DEF and inflections W_END on the target side of profession sentences. We give examples for
Spanish and German in Table 1. We also construct a neutral-label-only version of WinoMT containing the
1826 unique binary templates filled with they/them/their. We report results adapting to the original and
neutral-augmented sets separately for ease of comparison with prior work.

3 Experiments

We use baseline Transformer models, BPE vocabularies, synthetic datasets and baseline rescoring
gendered-alternative lattices from Saunders and Byrne (2020)[2] and follow the same adaptation scheme,
assessing on English-to-German and English-to-Spanish translation. We define gender tags as unique
vocabulary items which only appear in the source sentence. We adapt to synthetic data with mini-
batches of 256 tokens for 64 training updates, which we found gave good results when fine-tuning on
the S&B datasets. The V3 sets have about 30% more tokens, the V4 sets about 30% fewer and the
neutral-augmented sets about 50% more: we adjust the adaptation steps accordingly for these cases.

For all results we rescore the baseline system gendered-alternative lattices with the listed model. This
constrains the output hypothesis to be a gender-inflected version of the original baseline hypothesis.
Lattice rescoring allows minimal degradation in BLEU while letting gender inflections in the hypothesis
translation be varied for potentially large WinoMT accuracy increases. For the gender-neutral experiments
we add synthetic inflections and articles to the lattices.

When assessing automatic test set tagging we use the RoBERTa (Liu et al., 2019) pronoun disambiguation function tuned on Winograd Schema Challenge data as described in Fairseq documentation[3].

We wish to improve coreference without loss of general translation quality, and so assess BLEU on
a separate, untagged general test set. For ease of comparison with previous work, we report general
translation quality on the test sets from WMT18 (en-de) and WMT13 (en-es), reporting cased BLEU
using SacreBLEU[4] (Post, 2018).

3.1 Measured improvements in gender accuracy are often accompanied by over-generalization

Table 2 gives BLEU score and primary-entity accuracy for the original, binary versions of synthetic
adaptation sets described in section 2.2. WinoMT test sentences have primary entities tagged with their
gender label if the adaptation set had tags, and are unlabeled otherwise. We note that lattice rescoring
keeps the general test set score within 0.3 BLEU of the baseline for all adaptation sets, and focus on the
variation in WinoMT performance.

Primary-entity accuracy increases significantly over the baseline for all adaptation schemes. V3 and
V4, which contain coreference examples, are most effective for en-es, while V2, which contains a single
entity, is slightly more effective for en-de. This may reflect the difference in baseline quality: the stronger
en-de baseline is more likely to have already seen multiple-entity sentences.

We also report ΔL2, the change in the secondary entity's label correspondence compared to the baseline.
High ΔL2 implies that the model is over-generalizing a gender signal intended for the primary entity to
the secondary entity. In other words, the gender signal intended for the primary entity has a very strong
influence on the translation of the secondary entity. ΔL2 does indeed increase strongly from the baseline
for the S&B and V1 systems, confirming our suspicion that these models trained on sentences with a
single entity simply learn to apply any gender feature to both entities in the test sentences indiscriminately.

Remarkably, for adaptation to S&B and V1 datasets we found that the secondary entity is inflected to
correspond with the pronoun more often than the primary entity which is labeled as coreferent with it. A
possible explanation is that the secondary entity occurs at the start of the sentence in about two thirds of

---

[2]https://github.com/DCSaunders/gender-debias
[3]https://github.com/pytorch/fairseq/tree/master/examples/roberta/wsc
[4]BLEU+case.mixed+numrefs.1+smooth.exp+tok.13a+v.1.4.8

System	Labeled WinoMT	en-de			en-es		
		BLEU	Acc	ΔL2	BLEU	Acc	ΔL2
Baseline	×	42.7	60.1	-	27.8	49.6	-
S&B	×	42.4	82.3	27.4	27.7	66.3	29.7
V1	✓	42.5	81.7	26.6	27.7	69.0	26.4
V2	✓	42.5	**84.1**	24.2	27.5	70.9	13.2
V3	✓	42.6	77.4	**1.1**	27.5	80.6	**0.3**
V4	✓	42.6	80.6	2.0	27.6	**83.1**	8.7

Table 2: Test BLEU, WinoMT primary-entity accuracy (Acc), and change in second-entity label correspondence ΔL2. We adapt the baseline to a set without tags (S&B), or to one of the binary gender-inflection tagging schemes (V1-V4). 'Labeled WinoMT' indicates whether WinoMT primary entities are tagged with their reference gender label. All results are for rescoring the baseline system gendered-alternative lattices with the listed model.

System	en-de						en-es					
	Unlabeled		Auto-labeled		Reference labeled		Unlabeled		Auto-labeled		Reference labeled	
	Acc	ΔL2	Acc	ΔL2	Acc	ΔL2	Acc	ΔL2	Acc	ΔL2	Acc	ΔL2
Baseline	60.1	-	-	-	-	-	49.6	-	-	-	-	-
S&B	**82.3**	27.4	-	-	-	-	66.3	29.7	-	-	-	-
V1	81.5	26.6	81.7	26.5	81.7	26.6	**67.3**	29.6	68.5	31.2	69.0	26.4
V2	71.2	9.2	**83.6**	24.8	**84.1**	24.2	52.1	3.5	69.7	18.4	70.9	13.2
V3	57.5	-5.8	79.9	**3.7**	77.4	**1.1**	47.9	-2.5	77.7	6.4	80.6	**0.3**
V4	60.5	**-2.0**	79.2	4.6	80.6	2.0	48.5	**-0.6**	**80.6**	12.6	**83.1**	8.7

Table 3: WinoMT accuracy and change in second-entity label correspondence for the adaptation schemes in Table 2 when changing how tags are determined for **WinoMT source sentences**. The primary entity's gender label in each test sentence is either unlabeled, auto-labeled with RoBERTa, or labeled with the reference gender.

test sentences, compared to about one third for the primary entity. Adapting to single-entity test sets may encourage the model to simply inflect the first entity in the sentence using the gender signal.

For V2, where the source possessive pronoun is removed and the tag is the only gender signal, ΔL2 still increases significantly, although less than for V1. This indicates that even if the only signal is a gender tag applied directly to the correct word, it may be wrongly taken as a signal to inflect other words. The V3 scheme is the most promising, with a 17% increase in accuracy for en-de and a 30% increase for en-es corresponding to very small changes in L2, suggesting this model minimizes over-generalization from gender features beyond the tagged word. V4 performs similarly to V3 for en-de but suffers from an L2 increase for en-es. It is possible that a lexicon-style set with tags in every example may cause undesirable over-generalisation.

3.2 Reference labeled, auto-labeled and unlabeled test sentences

Table 3 lists accuracy and ΔL2 with and without WinoMT source sentence labeling for the same systems as Table 2. We also experiment with labeling WinoMT sentences automatically, using RoBERTa to predict the antecedent of the single pronoun in each test sentence – we note this would not necessarily be as effective in sentences with multiple pronouns.

V1 gives similar performance to S&B with and without WinoMT labeling. Removing the possessive pronoun as in V2 decreases accuracy compared to V1 without labeling and slightly increases it with labeling, suggesting removing the source pronoun forces the model to rely on the gender tag.

Accuracy under V2, V3 and V4 improves dramatically when gender labels are added to WinoMT primary entities. Without labels the accuracies for these systems improve far less or not at all. This is unsurprising, since in these datasets the gender tag is the only way to infer the correct target inflection. Nevertheless some accuracy improvement is still possible for V2 with neither tags nor possessive pronouns, possibly because the model 'sees' more examples of profession constructions in the target language.

Without test set labels, the V3 and V4 systems have negative ΔL2, implying that the second entity's inflection corresponds to the primary entity label less often than for the baseline. This is not necessarily

System	Labeled WinoMT	en-de		en-es	
		Acc	ΔL2	Acc	ΔL2
Baseline	$\times$	2.7	-	4.2	-
S&B	$\times$	13.5	28.8	6.4	3.9
V1	$\checkmark$	**27.3**	28.2	25.4	25.1
V2	$\checkmark$	23.0	39.6	32.1	27.5
V3	$\checkmark$	20.2	18.7	38.8	10.0
V4	$\checkmark$	19.4	**4.4**	**56.5**	**0.7**

Table 4: Primary-entity accuracy and second-entity label correspondence ΔL2 on a neutral-label-only WinoMT version. Adaptations sets and lattices are augmented with synthetic neutral articles and nouns. 'Labeled WinoMT' indicates whether sentences are tagged with their reference (neutral) gender label.

bad, as they are still low absolute values. Small absolute ΔL2 indicates that added primary-entity gender signals have little impact on the secondary entity relative to the baseline, which is the desired behaviour. Small negative values are therefore better than large positive values.

Auto-labeling WinoMT source sentences performs only slightly worse than using reference labels. We find that the automatic tags agree with human tags for 84% of WinoMT sentences, with no difference in performance between masculine- and feminine-labeled sentences, or pro- and anti-stereotypical sentences. This is encouraging, and suggests that the tagged inflection approach may also be applicable to natural text, for which manual labeling is often impractical.

3.3 Gender-neutral translation

In Table 4 we report on systems adapted to the neutral-augmented synthetic sets, evaluated on the neutral-only WinoMT set. We use test labeling for all cases where models are trained with tags – as with the binary experiments we found that performance was otherwise poor.

Unsurprisingly, the baseline model is unable to generate the newly defined gender-neutral articles or noun inflections – the non-zero accuracy is a result of existing WinoMT sentences with neutral entities like 'someone'. Adapting on the neutral-augmented S&B set does little better for en-es, although it gives a larger gain for en-de. This discrepancy may be because the only neutral gender signal in the S&B source sentences is from the possessive pronoun *their*. In Spanish, which has one gender-neutral third-person singular possessive pronoun, *their* has the same Spanish translation as *his* or *her* and therefore does not constitute a strong gender signal. By contrast in German we add a synthetic singular gender-neutral pronoun, which indicates neutral gender even without tags. This may also explain why V3 and V4 give weaker performance than V1 for German, as these sets no longer contain singular pronouns.

Adding a gender tag significantly improves primary entity accuracy. As with Table 2, there is little difference in labeled-WinoMT performance when the possessive pronoun is removed. Also as previously, the V3 and V4 'tagged coreference' sets shows far less over-generalization in terms of ΔL2 than the other tagged schemes, although V4 significantly outperforms V3 for en-es on this set.

We note that primary-entity accuracy is relatively low compared to results for the original WinoMT set, with our best-performing system reaching 56.5% accuracy. We consider this unsurprising since the model has never encountered most of the neutral-inflected occupation terms before, even during adaptation, due to the lack of overlap between the adaptation and WinoMT test sets. However, it does suggest that more work remains for introducing novel gender inflections for NMT.

4 Conclusions

Tagging words with target language gender inflection is a powerful way to improve accuracy of translated inflections. This could be applied in cases where the correct grammatical gender to use for a given referent is known, or as monolingual coreference resolution tools improve sufficiently to be used for automatic tagging. It also has potential application to new inflections defined for gender-neutral language.

However, there is a risk that gender features will be used in an over-general way. Providing a strong gender signal for one entity has the potential to harm users and referents by erasing other entities in the same sentence, unless a model is specifically trained to translate sentences with multiple entities. In particular we find that our V3 system, which is trained on multiple-entity translation examples, allows good performance while minimizing peripheral effects.

We conclude by emphasising that work on gender coreference in translation requires care to ensure that the effects of interventions are as intended, as well as testing scenarios that capture the full complexity of the problem, if the work is to have an impact on gender bias.

Acknowledgments

This work was supported by EPSRC grants EP/M508007/1 and EP/N509620/1 and has been performed using resources provided by the Cambridge Tier-2 system operated by the University of Cambridge Research Computing Service[5] funded by EPSRC Tier-2 capital grant EP/P020259/1. Work by R. Sallis during a research placement was funded by the Humanities and Social Change International Foundation.

References

Mohsen Abbasi, Sorelle A Friedler, Carlos Scheidegger, and Suresh Venkatasubramanian. 2019. Fairness in representation: Quantifying stereotyping as a representational harm. In *Proceedings of the 2019 SIAM International Conference on Data Mining*, pages 801–809. SIAM.

Lauren Ackerman. 2019. Syntactic and cognitive issues in investigating gendered coreference. *Glossa: a journal of general linguistics*, 4(1).

Morrigan Auxland. 2020. Para Todes: A Case Study on Portuguese and Gender-Neutrality. *Journal of Languages, Texts and Society*, 4:1–23.

Christine Basta, Marta R. Costa-jussà, and José A. R. Fonollosa. 2020. Towards mitigating gender bias in a decoder-based neural machine translation model by adding contextual information. In *Proceedings of the The Fourth Widening Natural Language Processing Workshop*, pages 99–102, Seattle, USA, July. Association for Computational Linguistics.

Evan D Bradley, Julia Salkind, Ally Moore, and Sofi Teitsort. 2019. Singular 'they' and novel pronouns: Gender-neutral, nonbinary, or both? *Proceedings of the Linguistic Society of America*, 4(1):36–1.

Yang Trista Cao and Hal Daumé III. 2020. Toward gender-inclusive coreference resolution. In *Proceedings of the 58th Annual Meeting of the Association for Computational Linguistics*, pages 4568–4595, Online, July. Association for Computational Linguistics.

Marta R Costa-jussà, Pau Li Lin, and Cristina España-Bonet. 2020. GeBioToolkit: Automatic extraction of gender-balanced multilingual corpus of Wikipedia biographies. In *Proceedings of The 12th Language Resources and Evaluation Conference*, pages 4081–4088.

Kate Crawford. 2017. The trouble with bias. In *Conference on Neural Information Processing Systems, invited speaker*.

Joel Escudé Font and Marta R. Costa-jussà. 2019. Equalizing gender bias in neural machine translation with word embeddings techniques. In *Proceedings of the First Workshop on Gender Bias in Natural Language Processing*, pages 147–154, Florence, Italy, August. Association for Computational Linguistics.

Batya Friedman and Helen Nissenbaum. 1996. Bias in computer systems. *ACM Trans. Inf. Syst.*, 14(3):330–347, July.

Levi CR Hord. 2016. Bucking the linguistic binary. *Western Papers in Linguistics*, 3(1).

Dirk Hovy, Federico Bianchi, and Tommaso Fornaciari. 2020. "You sound just like your father" Commercial machine translation systems include stylistic biases. In *Proceedings of the 58th Annual Meeting of the Association for Computational Linguistics*, pages 1686–1690, Online, July. Association for Computational Linguistics.

Melvin Johnson. 2018. Providing gender-specific translations in Google Translate. (accessed: Aug 2020).

Yinhan Liu, Myle Ott, Naman Goyal, Jingfei Du, Mandar Joshi, Danqi Chen, Omer Levy, Mike Lewis, Luke Zettlemoyer, and Veselin Stoyanov. 2019. RoBERTa: A robustly optimized BERT pretraining approach. *arXiv preprint arXiv:1907.11692*.

---

[5]http://www.hpc.cam.ac.uk

Lesly Miculicich Werlen and Andrei Popescu-Belis. 2017. Using coreference links to improve Spanish-to-English machine translation. In *Proceedings of the 2nd Workshop on Coreference Resolution Beyond OntoNotes (COR-BON 2017)*, pages 30–40, Valencia, Spain, April. Association for Computational Linguistics.

Julia Misersky, Asifa Majid, and Tineke M Snijders. 2019. Grammatical gender in German influences how role-nouns are interpreted: Evidence from ERPs. *Discourse Processes*, 56(8):643–654.

Amit Moryossef, Roee Aharoni, and Yoav Goldberg. 2019. Filling gender & number gaps in neural machine translation with black-box context injection. In *Proceedings of the First Workshop on Gender Bias in Natural Language Processing*, pages 49–54, Florence, Italy, August. Association for Computational Linguistics.

Benjamin Papadopoulos. 2019. *Innovaciones al género morfológico en el Español de hablantes genderqueer (Morphological gender innovations in Spanish of genderqueer speakers)*. eScholarship, University of California.

Matt Post. 2018. A call for clarity in reporting BLEU scores. In *Proceedings of the Third Conference on Machine Translation: Research Papers*, pages 186–191, Belgium, Brussels, October. Association for Computational Linguistics.

Marcelo OR Prates, Pedro H Avelar, and Luís C Lamb. 2019. Assessing gender bias in machine translation: a case study with Google Translate. *Neural Computing and Applications*, pages 1–19.

Rachel Rudinger, Jason Naradowsky, Brian Leonard, and Benjamin Van Durme. 2018. Gender bias in coreference resolution. In *Proceedings of the 2018 Conference of the North American Chapter of the Association for Computational Linguistics: Human Language Technologies, Volume 2 (Short Papers)*, pages 8–14, New Orleans, Louisiana, June. Association for Computational Linguistics.

Danielle Saunders and Bill Byrne. 2020. Reducing gender bias in neural machine translation as a domain adaptation problem. In *Proceedings of the 58th Annual Meeting of the Association for Computational Linguistics*, pages 7724–7736, Online, July. Association for Computational Linguistics.

Alyx J Shroy. 2016. Innovations in gender-neutral French: Language practices of nonbinary French speakers on Twitter. *Ms., University of California, Davis*.

Artūrs Stafanovičs, Toms Bergmanis, and Mārcis Pinnis. 2020. Mitigating gender bias in machine translation with target gender annotations. In *Proceedings of the Fifth Conference on Machine Translation (WMT)*.

Gabriel Stanovsky, Noah A. Smith, and Luke Zettlemoyer. 2019. Evaluating gender bias in machine translation. In *Proceedings of the 57th Annual Meeting of the Association for Computational Linguistics*, pages 1679–1684, Florence, Italy, July. Association for Computational Linguistics.

Tony Sun, Andrew Gaut, Shirlyn Tang, Yuxin Huang, Mai ElSherief, Jieyu Zhao, Diba Mirza, Elizabeth Belding, Kai-Wei Chang, and William Yang Wang. 2019. Mitigating gender bias in natural language processing: Literature review. In *Proceedings of the 57th Annual Meeting of the Association for Computational Linguistics*, pages 1630–1640, Florence, Italy, July. Association for Computational Linguistics.

Eva Vanmassenhove, Christian Hardmeier, and Andy Way. 2018. Getting gender right in neural machine translation. In *Proceedings of the 2018 Conference on Empirical Methods in Natural Language Processing*, pages 3003–3008, Brussels, Belgium, October-November. Association for Computational Linguistics.

Elena Voita, Pavel Serdyukov, Rico Sennrich, and Ivan Titov. 2018. Context-aware neural machine translation learns anaphora resolution. In *Proceedings of the 56th Annual Meeting of the Association for Computational Linguistics (Volume 1: Long Papers)*, pages 1264–1274, Melbourne, Australia, July. Association for Computational Linguistics.

Jieyu Zhao, Tianlu Wang, Mark Yatskar, Vicente Ordonez, and Kai-Wei Chang. 2018. Gender bias in coreference resolution: Evaluation and debiasing methods. In *Proceedings of the 2018 Conference of the North American Chapter of the Association for Computational Linguistics: Human Language Technologies, Volume 2 (Short Papers)*, pages 15–20, New Orleans, Louisiana, June. Association for Computational Linguistics.

Lal Zimman. 2017. Transgender language reform: Some challenges and strategies for promoting trans-affirming, gender-inclusive language. *Journal of Language and Discrimination*, 1(1):83–104.

Ran Zmigrod, Sabrina J. Mielke, Hanna Wallach, and Ryan Cotterell. 2019. Counterfactual data augmentation for mitigating gender stereotypes in languages with rich morphology. In *Proceedings of the 57th Annual Meeting of the Association for Computational Linguistics*, pages 1651–1661, Florence, Italy, July. Association for Computational Linguistics.

Can Existing Methods Debias Languages Other than English?
First Attempt to Analyze and Mitigate Japanese Word Embeddings

Masashi Takeshita, **Yuki Katsumata**, **Rafal Rzepka**, and **Kenji Araki**

Graduate School of Information Science and Technology
Hokkaido University, Sapporo, Japan
{takeshita.masashi, katsumata, rzepka, araki}@ist.hokudai.ac.jp

Abstract

It is known that word embeddings exhibit biases inherited from the corpus, and those biases reflect social stereotypes. Recently, many studies have been conducted to analyze and mitigate biases in word embeddings. Unsupervised Bias Enumeration (UBE) (Swinger et al., 2019) is one of approach to analyze biases for English, and Hard Debias (Bolukbasi et al., 2016) is the common technique to mitigate gender bias. These methods focused on English, or, in smaller extent, on Indo-European languages. However, it is not clear whether these methods can be generalized to other languages. In this paper, we apply these analyzing and mitigating methods, UBE and Hard Debias, to Japanese word embeddings. Additionally, we examine whether these methods can be used for Japanese. We experimentally show that UBE and Hard Debias cannot be sufficiently adapted to Japanese embeddings.

1 Introduction

Word embeddings are widely used in natural language processing tasks, and they have been reported to inherit social stereotypes, e.g. gender and racial stereotypes (Bolukbasi et al., 2016; Caliskan et al., 2017). For example, "programmer" and "homemaker" should be gender neutral by definition, but the analogy of "man is to programmer as woman is to homemaker" holds as observed by Bolukbasi et al. (2016). Such biases cause differences in F1 scores between the pro- and anti-stereotypical conditions. For example in the coreference resolution task, it is difficult to correctly link "physician:she" and "secretary:he" for systems which use gender-biased word embeddings, because "physician:he" and "secretary:she" are strongly related more than "physician:she" and "secretary:he" in the word embeddings (Zhao et al., 2018a). Therefore, in recent years, research has been conducted to mitigate the bias in word embeddings (Bolukbasi et al., 2016; Zhao et al., 2018b; Wang et al., 2020). However, to the authors' best knowledge, most of them have focused on English (Sun et al., 2019; Blodgett et al., 2020), and no study has addressed word embeddings of languages other than Indo-European languages about bias analysis and mitigation.

We hypothesize that it is not obvious that the method developed for English can be easily adapted to other languages for two following reasons. First is due to various grammatical features which do not exist in English. Embeddings can have different characteristics depending on language, for example Spanish words have gender which leads to the grammatical gender bias (Zhou et al., 2019). There is a substantial risk that we cannot adapt the bias mitigation methods meant for English while working on such a language. Secondly, especially when the language family differs, not only the characteristics of a given language but also the cultural background of its users changes, which in turn influences further the bias in the embeddings (Raijmakers, 2020). Therefore, it may not be possible to directly apply bias analysis and mitigation methods developed for English to other languages.

Bias statement Following categorization of Crawford (2017), we focus on representational bias, especially stereotyping one, which means that a system "propagates negative generalisations about particular

Proceedings of the Second Workshop on Gender Bias in Natural Language Processing, pages 44–55
Barcelona, Spain (Online), December 13, 2020.

social groups" (Blodgett et al., 2020, p.5456). Stereotyping happens in natural language processing tasks when an unfair association of words represents a particular social group with other concepts (not included in its definition), like an analogy of "man is to programmer as woman is to homemaker". If an AI agent has such stereotypes, they can appear in its output as reported in works on dialogue systems (Liu et al., 2019), possibly harming users.

There are several works on stereotypes in word embeddings for English (Bolukbasi et al., 2016; Zhao et al., 2018b; Wang et al., 2020) and some other languages (Sahlgren and Olsson, 2019; Pujari et al., 2019), but to the authors' best knowledge, research regarding Japanese word embeddings does not exist.

In this paper, we analyze the representational bias in Japanese word embeddings, and attempt to mitigate gender bias by using existing methods designed for English. We also show that those methods are difficult to generalize to Japanese.

2 Related work

2.1 Bias in word embeddings and its mitigation for English

This section describes bias analysis and gender bias mitigation for English word embeddings.

2.1.1 Bias analysis

Caliskan et al. (2017) proposed the Word Embedding Association Test (WEAT) to evaluate the inherent social biases in embedding. WEAT measures the difference of semantic similarity with a word embedding between two sets of target words (e.g. "male" and "female" names) and attribute words (e.g. "career" and "family" terms). This metric was used to show that social biases of embeddings are correlated with social stereotypes and the proportion of gender of workers in each occupation.

Swinger et al. (2019) adapted WEAT and proposed Unsupervised Bias Enumeration (UBE) to discover the biases in embedding by unsupervised clustering using first names. They asked crowdworkers to evaluate the results of WEATs which are outputted by UBE and confirm if these results capture social stereotypes, such as gender as well as religion and race.

2.1.2 Approaches to bias mitigation

Bolukbasi et al. (2016) confirmed the existence of the gender bias in English word embeddings, and proposed a method called Hard Debias to mitigate the gender bias. Hard Debias uses words that should be neutral to gender, such as "doctor" and "programmer", and reduces the bias by subtracting the vector components of gender directions from gender neutral words. Gender directions are defined by the first principal component of a word vector of each word consisting of a gender definition word pairs, such as "she" and "he".

However, Gonen and Goldberg (2019) proved experimentally that Hard Debias could not sufficiently remove gender bias and that it can be recovered from embeddings after mitigation.

In the work of Mu and Viswanath (2018), the most statistically dominant principal components are encoding the frequency of words. Their method improves performance of embedding by subtracting the common mean vector from each word vector and removing the dominant principal components. Wang et al. (2020) proposed Double-Hard Debias which was inspired by work of Mu and Viswanath (2018). They improved Hard Debias by deciding the dominant principal component of gender bias before performing Hard Debias. Experiments on English embeddings, including the neighborhood metric (Gonen and Goldberg, 2019), showed improved results.

All of the above-mentioned research examples work on English language. Next, we present studies on the bias inherent in non-English embeddings.

2.2 Word embedding biases in languages other than English

There are two major directions of research on non-English word embedding bias. The first is a bias study of multilingual embeddings, which compares what biases exist in embeddings available in both English and other languages, e.g. Spanish and French, and how they differ depending on language (Zhou et al., 2019; Zhao et al., 2020). The second direction is to address biases in monolingual embeddings of languages other than English (Zhou et al., 2019; Sahlgren and Olsson, 2019; Pujari et al., 2019;

Raijmakers, 2020). For example, the gender bias has been found and mitigated in Swedish (Sahlgren and Olsson, 2019) and Hindi (Pujari et al., 2019). Both used Hard Debias for gender bias mitigation – Sahlgren and Olsson (2019) could not mitigate the gender bias but Pujari et al. (2019) were able to achieve that goal. However, (Sahlgren and Olsson, 2019) analyzed their results only partially. The problem in the Pujari et al. (2019) method is that they used Support Vector Machine (SVM) trained on gender-biased embeddings during Hard Debias evaluation for Hindi. Raijmakers (2020) proposed a WEAT-extended method to investigate gender bias in monolingual embeddings of 26 languages, including Japanese, but did not attempt to mitigate any of them. This work also lacks a detailed analysis, as it only investigates the overall gender bias of embeddings and does not assess whether gender neutral words have gender bias.

In this paper, we examine biases in Japanese monolingual embeddings and attempt to mitigate gender bias as a case study.

3 Specificity of Japanese language

Japanese and Western languages use different types of characters. There are three types of characters in Japanese language: phonetic *hiragana*[*], *katakana*, and ideographic *kanji*. Embeddings of *kanji* may capture not only the meaning of the word but also the meaning of the characters. For example word 数学 ("maths") consists of two ideograms: 数 ("number") and 学 ("learning"). *Katakana* often represents a foreign word プログラマ ("programmer"), while words written in rounded shape of *hiragana* like ふわ ふわ (*fuwafuwa*, "fluffy") are often associated with a feminine image (Iwahara et al., 2003).

4 Experiments

In this section we explain word embeddings we used, describe UBE (Swinger et al., 2019) used in the bias analysis experiment, and two other methods (Hard Debias (Bolukbasi et al., 2016), Double-Hard Debias (Wang et al., 2020)) used in the bias mitigation experiment. Finally, we explain our evaluation methodology.

4.1 Word embeddings for experiments

As the target of our analysis we use two publicly available embeddings: word2vec (Mikolov et al., 2013) trained on Japanese Wikipedia (Suzuki et al., 2018)[†] and fastText (Bojanowski et al., 2016) trained on the Wikipedia text and Common Crawl. Number of dimensions in these embeddings is 200 and 300, respectively.

We use 50,000 most frequent words (Bolukbasi et al., 2016) and also limit the words to be assessed for bias to nouns, verbs, adjectives, adjectival verbs and adverbs in their dictionary forms using morphological analyzer Juman++ (Morita et al., 2015).

4.2 Bias analysis experiment

Unsupervised Bias Enumeration (UBE) In this subsection, we introduce procedural steps of UBE which is a method to detect various biases in embeddings using names.

As the first step, we filter out possibly problematic first names. In many languages there are polysemous first names such as "May" in English (name of a month). Also in Japanese first names that have other meaning, such as *Hoshi* (star), can be found. We filter them out because of the ambiguity they tend to bring. Identically to Caliskan et al. (2017), we remove 20% of names with the lowest mean of cosine similarity between a name and all other names. Then, after filtering, the names are clustered with k-means++ (Arthur and Vassilvitskii, 2006) included in scikit-learn library (Pedregosa et al., 2011). Female and male first names data is borrowed from JMnedict[‡]. Names being used for both genders are treated as neutral. The number of clusters was experimentally set to 10 in both embeddings (word2vec and fastText). JMnedict also includes foreign surnames. Initially, we were going to exclude them, but we thought that we might be able to find social stereotypes regarding foreigners, so we eventually included their names in the dataset. The results of the filtering are shown in Table 1.

---

[*]An italic represents romanization of Japanese words.
[†]`http://www.cl.ecei.tohoku.ac.jp/~m-suzuki/jawiki_vector/` (2017.2.2 version)
[‡]`https://www.edrdg.org/enamdict/enamdict_doc.html`

Embeddings	Neutral first name	Female first name	Male first name	Foreign surname	Total
word2vec	302	7,750	2,714	717	11,483
fastText	319	8,439	2,585	558	11,901

Table 1: The number of names after filtering

Secondly, we cluster the words which are included in the most frequent M tokens into clusters of m words. In work of Swinger et al. (2019), occupation and food-related clusters were generated for English. We set m to 64 as in their setup, but increase M from 30,000 to 50,000 in order to match the bias mitigation experiment of (Bolukbasi et al., 2016).

Thirdly, each m cluster is further divided into Voronoi sets with a high degree of dot product between a word vector and the vector mean of each name cluster. In this step, all word vectors and name vectors are normalized to size 1. After that, the most relevant words were chosen as t in each Voronoi set, and we set $t = 3$, following Swinger et al. (2019). However, if the number of elements in each Voronoi set generated after Voronoi partitioning is smaller than t, all elements are used.

Finally, in the fourth step, we compute the WEAT score and p-value. First, we calculate the WEAT score for each cluster of names and the t words included in Voronoi sets and chosen in order of relevance. Next, we calculate the p-value. Following Swinger et al. (2019), we use "rotational null hypothesis" for p-value. We multiply each name vector by an uniform Haar random orthogonal matrix and perform the above-described third step identically to how the WEAT score is computed. This is done $R = 10,000$ times, and the percentage of times the score is higher than the original score becomes the p-value. Finally, the statistically significant WEATs are outputted. For determining the critical p-value, we follow Swinger et al. (2019), who utilized method of Benjamini and Hochberg (1995) to guarantee an α bound on false discovery rate. The α is set to 0.05 as in Swinger et al. (2019).

Our hypothesis is that the use of first names in Japanese does not reflect social stereotypes. As mentioned in Section 3, *kanji* ideograms have their own specific meanings, and Japanese first names are sometimes given with the intention of expressing the meaning of the *kanji*. In the case of a name consisting of a single *kanji* character, its meaning may have a significant impact on the information conveyed by embeddings. Additionally, as mentioned in Section 3, since the usage of embeddings may differ depending on a character type, we assume that such types may have an influence on Japanese embeddings. Therefore, we presume that embeddings of names are unlikely to reflect social stereotypes and that clusters are formed by the character type and the meaning of ideograms.

4.3 Gender bias mitigation

We target bias mitigation for gender bias in Japanese embeddings by using Hard Debias (Bolukbasi et al., 2016) and Double-Hard Debias (Wang et al., 2020).

4.3.1 Mitigating methods

Hard Debias   Hard Debias is a method for bias mitigation by removing gender direction from gender neutral words. Gender direction is defined in advance as the first principal component of gender definition word pairs. Original Hard Debias (Bolukbasi et al., 2016) normalizes a word vector to size 1, but we do not so, because its length can contain important information as pointed out by Ethayarajh et al. (2019).

Double-Hard Debias   Double-Hard Debias follows Mu and Viswanath (2018), before doing Hard Debias, first centralizing the entire embedding and then removing the dominant principal component of the gender bias. Hard Debias was improved by performing these steps.

4.3.2 Gender Definition and Specific Words

Bolukbasi et al. (2016) defines gender specific words in advance, then uses them in the training data and extends the gender specific words with SVM. However, it has been pointed out that searching for gender specific words using embeddings of the bias mitigation targets poses the problem of not being able to

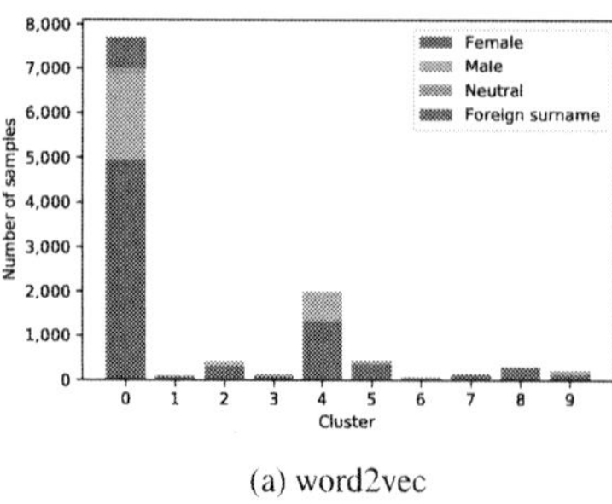

(a) word2vec

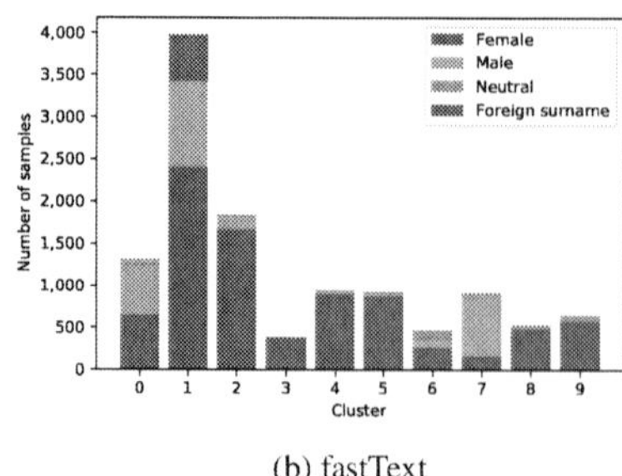

(b) fastText

Figure 1: Results of clustering names by first names and foreign surnames with $n = 10$

properly classify truly gender specific words (Ethayarajh et al., 2019; Kumar et al., 2020). For that reason we collect gender specific words using Knowledge Based Classifier (KBC) proposed by Kumar et al. (2020).

The KBC has been implemented as follows. First we translate the definition words used by Bolukbasi et al. (2016) and use them as gender definition words for Japanese. However, since "herself" and other words they utilized do not exist in Japanese embeddings, we instead use, for example, synonyms of "mother" to match the number of pairs[§]. Then, for any word w, we check whether the definition of w contains gender definition words or not by using Wordnet (Bond et al., 2012) and ConceptNet (Speer and Havasi, 2013). If the gender word is present in a definition or node, w is treated as a gender specific word, and if not, it is labelled as a gender neutral word. However, our preliminary experiments showed that some relationships in ConceptNet contained gender bias themselves, so we chose edges for which effects of gender bias were not significant: IsA, PartOf, HasA, Synonym, Antonym, DefinedAs, and MannerOf.

4.4 Evaluation methods

Experiment 1: bias analysis We select the top 12 WEATs with the highest WEAT scores among the output WEATs in the bias analysis experiment and check whether these WEATs reflect social stereotypes. Five illustrative names for each name cluster were used for the evaluation. They are selected using a simple greedy heuristic presented in the original paper (Swinger et al., 2019). To evaluate whether the output WEATs reflected social stereotypes, we asked seven native Japanese speakers (5 males and 2 females, 19-29 years old) to associate statistically significant cluster of words with one most stereotypically related cluster of names. If WEATs represent a social stereotype, there should be high agreement between WEATs and annotators. Pairs of names/words clusters selected by more than 50% annotators were treated as correct associations (annotation guideline follows Swinger et al. (2019) but no rewards were given to annotators).

Experiment 2: mitigating gender bias We evaluate gender bias of the Japanese word embeddings using the neighborhood metric (Gonen and Goldberg, 2019).

The neighborhood metric is a measure of bias, which clusters $n \times k$ words with the largest bias in embedding before mitigation into k clusters by using k-means++, and then evaluates bias level providing the percentage of words belonging to each cluster that is consistent with the original bias. Higher percentage indicates that the word embedding includes a bias. We use the difference in cosine similarity between the word vectors of "woman" and "man" and between "she" and "he" as the magnitude of the gender bias. After compressing the data into two dimensions using tSNE (van der Maaten and Hinton, 2008), we perform further clustering also using k-means++. For this experiment, we set $k = 2$ to evaluate the gender bias related to females and males. We conduct experiments setting n to 100, 500, and 1,000, following Wang et al. (2020).

[§]Definitional word pairs we used are: ["woman", "man"], ["female", "male" (gender)], ["female", "male" (sex)], ["girl", "boy"], ["little girl", "little boy"], ["mother", "father"], ["mother parent", "father parent"], ["daughter", "son"], ["she", "he"],["*Hanako*", "*Taro*"]

w2v F0	w2v F1	w2v F2	w2v F3	w2v F4	w2v F5	w2v F6	w2v F7	w2v F8	w2v F9
Hiroji	*Shinzaemon*	*Kyoko*	***Kasumi***	*Kotaro*	***Yomogi***	***Yu***	*Rie* (h)	*Yukino* (h)	***Etsu***
Akiko	*Ikurumi*	*Mai*	***Suzu***	*Akari*	***Mari***	***Syu***	*Chika* (h)	*Juri* (h)	***Ryo***
Asuka	*Noriaki*	*Sachiko*	***Mine***	*Tomihisa*	***Satsuki***	*Shichiro*	*Akio* (h)	*Yae* (h)	***Itsuki***
Shigetaka	*Toriha*	*Sekiko*	***Usagi***	*Zyotaro*	*Sachi*	***Sada***	*Ura* (h)	*Ao* (h)	***Atsushi***
Sachino	*Ayame*	*Kazuki*	***Midori***	*Kiyono* (h)	*Kuon*	***Hisao***	*Kaoru* (h)	*Atsumi* (h)	***Kou***
+7,712	*+97*	*+417*	*+113*	*+1,993*	*+419*	*+52*	*+134*	*+290*	*+206*
64% F	*72% F*	*77% F*	*92% F*	*67% F*	*85% F*	*54% F*	*96% F*	*98% F*	*64% F*

Table 2: Clustering results of the first names and the foreign surnames using word2vec (w2v) with $n = 10$ and the illustrative names of each cluster. (h) indicates a *hiragana* word, and **bold** font represents single kanji names. "% F" in the last row indicates female name ratio in the cluster.

ft F0	ft F1	ft F2	ft F3	ft F4	ft F5	ft F6	ft F7	ft F8	ft F9
Sachio	*Yumie*	*Fuyu*	*Mitsuki*	*Kaede*	*Mana*	***Hiro***	*Masato*	*Ayano*	*Miyoko*
Katsuyo	*Kikue*	*Akiho*	*Yoshino*	*Teruka*	*Kaori*	***Akira***	*Eiichi*	*Matsue*	*Harue*
Takashige	*Mitsuki* (k)	*Raiko*	*Arisu*	*Kikyou*	*Ena*	***Kei***	*Yoshihiro*	*Nao*	*Kazuko*
Yoshimi	*Jewison* (k)	*Takie*	*Yuuki*	*Midori*	*Yuki*	***Akane***	*Kenji*	*Hiroyasu*	*Akie*
Sukeichi	*Yurie*	*Ruuku*	*Ebiko*	*Tsukuyo*	*Nana*	***Ken***	*Kano*	*Chiho*	*Katsuko*
+1,301	*+3,978*	*+1827*	*+377*	*+940*	*+913*	*+456*	*+901*	*+522*	*+636*
50% F	*61% F*	*92% F*	*98% F*	*95% F*	*96% F*	*61% F*	*19% F*	*93% F*	*91% F*

Table 3: Clustering results for the first names and the foreign surnames using fastText (ft) with $n = 10$ and the illustrative names of each cluster. (k) indicates a *katakana* word, and **bold** font represents single kanji names. "% F" in the last row indicates female name ratio in the cluster.

5 Results

5.1 Experiment 1: bias analysis

The results of clustering names are shown in Figure 1a for word2vec, Figure 1b for fastText, and in Tables 2, 3, correspondingly. There are several possible readings of *kanji* ideograms for a single Japanese name, but we use only one reading in the tables. Figures 1a and 1b show the overall results of clustering names. Tables 2 and 3 list the illustrative names of each cluster.

In work of Swinger et al. (2019), distinct clusters are generated for both genders. However, as shown in the Figure 1a and Table 2, in the case of Japanese, no clusters of male names are formed from word2vec embedding and most of the names are clustered in cluster 0. Names in *hiragana* gathered in clusters 7 and 8. On the other hand, as shown in Figure 1b and Table 3, male names are grouped in cluster 7 when fastText is used. In both word embeddings, clusters of single *kanji* ideograms (3, 5, 6 and 9 on word2vec and 6 on fastText) and female names ending with "-ko" (cluster 2 on word2vec, cluster 9 on fastText) were formed. We can observe that each cluster captures some distinctive characteristics, but all of them are formed rather by the character type or number of characters, not by features that reflect social stereotypes.

The top 12 WEATs outputted by UBE are shown in Tables 4, 5. Table 4 illustrates the results of UBE on word2vec and Table 5 on fastText. The fastText lexicon contains a number of uninterpretable parts of words that could not be removed by the morphological analyzer Juman++, and we enclosed them in quotes. The colored background indicates cases where the annotators agreed with WEATs that the words reflect social stereotypes of the names. As far as Tables 4 and 5 are concerned, we can observe that most WEATs fail to capture social stereotypes (15% agreement for word2vec, 24% for fastText).

5.2 Experiment 2: mitigating gender bias

The results of experiments using the neighborhood metric are shown in Tables 6 and 7. The tSNE visualization is shown in Figures 2 and 3.

Regardless of which pair ("she/he" or "women/men") is used to evaluate the size of the gender bias in Japanese word2vec embedding, neither Hard Debias nor Double-Hard Debias come close to sufficient

w2v F0	w2v F1	w2v F2	w2v F3	w2v F4	w2v F5	w2v F6	w2v F7	w2v F8	w2v F9
investigate, grow old, warp	escape safely, betray, patrol	meet, be irritated, be enthusiastic	disperse, lithography, burn		offer devoutly, deify, funeral	in time, good offices, assault	'boru' (h), keep (h), some (h)	'nosu' (h), 'noku', pain (h)	stupid, salvation of country, yin-yang
	Chikugo, Kofu, Komoro (places)	*Keisuke, Hiro, Sekine*	astringent, white horse, Mt.Fuji	country club (k), *Kissho-ji* (place), Japanese old ordinary high school	*Asama* (place), imperial capital, Mt.Yae	*Nagai, Akamatsu, Nabeshima*		*Tochigi*(h), *Saitama* (h), *Nanba* (places) (h)	*shogi*, northern seas, Konan (place in China)
	Chikuzen (place), *Shimofusa* (place), Edo shogunate	*Chube*	tray, folding screen, the Healing Buddha		devine sprit, deify, dedication	family of shogunate, *Yoshinori, Harunobu*			trick, Toi (ancient China class), Buddhist priest
		pleasure, *Zyunichi*, boy friend	beautiful, many, *kirakira* (glitter) (k)				'yo' (h), 'sun' (h), irresponsible	adult (h), guy (h), No.1 (h)	pain, intelligent person, captivation
		buddy, *Shinji*, transfer student	frog, spider, fang		emperor, sanctuary, superiority	stratagem, revenge, assassin		rat (h), life (h), original title	die out, hollow, thief
Venezuela (k), Slovakia (k), Croatia (k)	dukedom, Ruthenia (k), Netherland (k)	American, Britisher, Japanese diaspora			Arabia (k), Hindu (k), Jerusalem				Guangzhou, Yunnan, Fujian (places in China)
	castle town, villa, the main enclosure of a castle	apartment (k), one house, *manshon* (k) (rich apartment)	giant tree, fountain, stone pillar		tomb, mosque (k), royal palace				study (room), warehouse
	direct line of descent, relative, collateral line	childhood friend, childhood friend (only *kanji*), same age				eldest son, successor, father and son			princess, empress dowager, mother-in-law
general education college, graduate school of letters, department of sociology		classmate, upperclass-man, pupil				study of Chinese classics, assistant professor, school principal			academy, degree, pass an examination
	topography, ancient manuscript, genealogy	conversation, story of one's experience, recollection	scroll, collection of haikus, iconography		inscription, series of publication, hymn	history book, historical material, transcription			word, anthology, national history
		fullname (k), family name, initial (k)	seal, character used as a phonetic symbol, Greek		free translation, Greek, original meaning			*hiragana* (h), word (h), written in English	translation into classical Chinese, classical Chinese, translitera-tion
		confess, go around together, meet	dance, light up, plant		divine, praise, protect	ask, look after, beg			do, bestow, destroy

Table 4: The top 12 highest-scoring WEATs output (statistically significant) by UBE on word2vec. 'w2v F' indicate the cluster in Table 2. (h) indicates a *hiragana* word, (k) stands for a *katakana*. All other words are written in *kanji* ideograms except ones in quotation – they are uninterpretable parts of words (noise). Orange cells indicate the clusters of names and words selected by more than 50% annotators matches the generated WEAT.

ft F0	ft F1	ft F2	ft F3	ft F4	ft F5	ft F6	ft F7	ft F8	ft F9
director, investigate, assistant professor	sweet novel comic (k), comedian, *Kaiseisha* (company)	go (h), get up (h), feel (h)	Iceland (k), Toulouse (k), America (k)	orange (k), leaf, the Milky Way	bikini model (k), girl, idol (k)		*Yukio, Yuji* (h), factory	Nuremberg (k) (place), *Hitachi-naka* (h) (place), Okhotsk (k)	career woman (k), wife, lady (k)
		dry, be dazzled, mold	enough, very (h), excellent	somehow, all year round, *hirahira* (h) (fluttering)	erotic (k), cute, look like a grown-up	split, I (*ware*), too much	leading person, go through (h), plan		
	Joseph (k), Norman (k), Harry (k)		aurora (k), Laguna (k), acacia (k)		Erina (k), Emily (k), Lilly (k)		*Hiroshi* (k), *Kenji* (k), Ministry of Transport	*Yawatahama, Dazaifu, Wakayama* (places)	*Toru* (k), Susan (k), *Takeshi* (k)
			stone wall, imperial guards, *Chika-matsu*	enjoyment of the moon, wild cherry tree, Japanese apricot with red blossoms		Horse (old orthography), stipend, vivid		equator, *Okinawa* (place), *Kyushu* (place)	
			Ito (h), *Hida* (h) (place), 'koji' (h)	kid (h), crab (h), burnt (h)	'koru' (h), 'ri' (h), 'puri' (h)	connection, detail, cut off	'rero' (h), line (h), feeling (h)		
						to (old unit of volume), disaster, I (*onore*)	hero, expert, primeval man		royal princess, imperial princess, princess
			very, a bit, first	various, other place, this way			tax included, immediately after, pipe (h)		
successor, third son, eldest son							sworn friend, brother, family		mother, ex-wife, married couple
			particular, multiple, diverse-ness			little, slant, error		the whole country, rising, neighbor-hood	
family name, brief history, pen name						meaning, abbreviation, character (letter)	omitted letter, name, one's title		old name, favorite phrase, speech
raise, explain, be granted	distribute, compare, return						prompt one to do, neglect, receive		
						price, side, measure			

Table 5: The top 12 highest-scoring WEATs output (statistically significant) by UBE on fastText. 'ft F' indicate the cluster in Table 3. (h) indicates a *hiragana* word, (k) stands for a *katakana*. All other words are written in *kanji* ideograms except ones in quotation – they are uninterpretable parts of words (parser noise). Orange cells indicate the clusters of names and words selected by more than 50% annotators matches the generated WEAT.

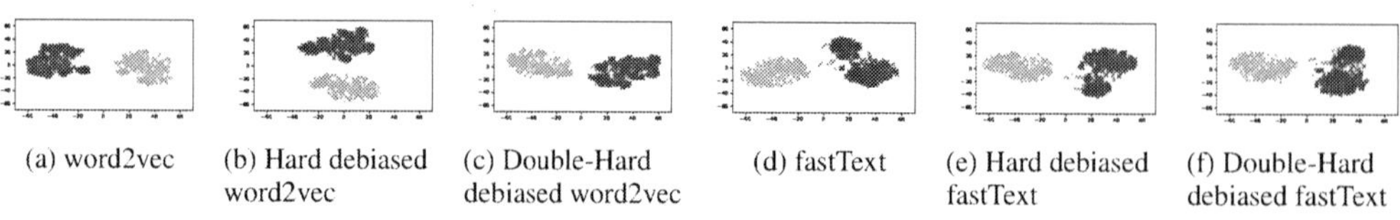

<table>
<tr><td>(a) word2vec</td><td>(b) Hard debiased word2vec</td><td>(c) Double-Hard debiased word2vec</td><td>(d) fastText</td><td>(e) Hard debiased fastText</td><td>(f) Double-Hard debiased fastText</td></tr>
</table>

Figure 2: tSNE visualisation of the top 500 words in the case of "she" and "he". Graphs (a-c) show the results for word2vec. Graphs (d-f) show the results for fastText.

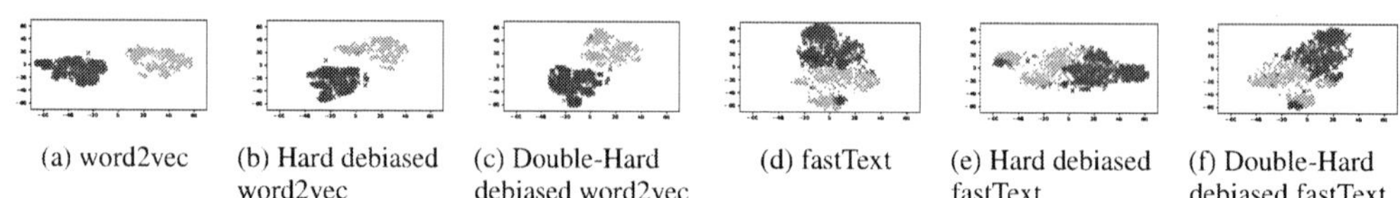

<table>
<tr><td>(a) word2vec</td><td>(b) Hard debiased word2vec</td><td>(c) Double-Hard debiased word2vec</td><td>(d) fastText</td><td>(e) Hard debiased fastText</td><td>(f) Double-Hard debiased fastText</td></tr>
</table>

Figure 3: tSNE visualisation of the top 500 words in the case of "women" and "men". Graphs (a-c) show the results for word2vec, (d-f) for fastText. Clusters in 3d-3f are not separated, so gender bias is not visible.

mitigation of the gender bias. Also when fastText is used, neither of the bias mitigation methods is able to effectively mitigate the gender bias in the "she/he" case. However, when "woman/man" were used, gender bias could not be confirmed even before mitigating bias using the neighborhood metric.

6 Discussion

6.1 Experiment 1: bias analysis

Based on our experimental results, it is difficult to say that WEATs reflect social stereotypes. This supports our hypothesis that Japanese first name embeddings do not reflect social stereotypes. However, Ethayarajh et al. (2019) noticed that WEAT systematically overestimates the bias. We need to examine their findings in the future.

As mentioned in Section 5.2, each cluster of names is formed by the character type, which also supports our hypothesis that clusters are formed by the surface characteristics of Japanese language, not by the meaning. However, clusters are not formed by the meaning of *kanji* included in the names themselves. Particularly, our hypothesis that the clustering would be affected by a single *kanji* character was not supported by the experimental results. Rather than single ideograms, the single *kanji* character names are grouped, and we were able to confirm that clusters were not formed by the meaning of these characters. We also confirmed that clusters of three or more character names were created ("ft F1" cluster in Table 3). Foreign surnames also did not form their own clusters, but were grouped into the element-richest clusters. Therefore, our experimental results show that name embeddings form concentric circles of names merely from superficial information of character type and number of characters rather than meaning, gender or nationality.

Based on the above considerations, it can be said that Japanese first name embeddings do not contain much of social stereotypes, and the similarity between name and word vectors are affected by character types of a word rather than the meaning of the word itself. We think that the fact that WEATs failed to reflect social stereotypes is because the main information conveyed by name and word embeddings is mostly superficial. Swinger et al. (2019) express their concern about the difficulty of applying UBE with respect to groups that cannot be significantly distinguished by name. The results of our experiment support that speculation.

6.2 Experiment 2: mitigating gender bias

Gonen and Goldberg (2019) showed experimentally that Hard Debias fails to mitigate the gender bias when the neighborhood metric is used. We replicated this phenomenon in Japanese word embeddings. According to Wang et al. (2020), Double-Hard Debias can mitigate gender bias with the neighborhood

Embedding	Method	Top 100	Top 500	Top 1000
word2vec	Original	1.00 (1.00)	1.000 (0.994)	1.000 (0.999)
	Hard Debias	1.00 (1.00)	0.995 (0.992)	0.993 (0.988)
	Double-Hard Debias	1.00 (1.00)	**0.960 (0.978)**	**0.933 (0.967)**
fastText	Original	1.0 (1.00)	0.753 (0.972)	0.594 (0.959)
	Hard Debias	**0.99** (1.00)	**0.607** (0.974)	0.593 (0.976)
	Double-Hard Debias	**0.99** (1.00)	**0.607** (0.973)	**0.592 (0.958)**

Table 6: Experimental results on the neighborhood metric in the case of "she" and "he". The accuracy of the metric after dimensionality reduction with tSNE is shown in parentheses.

Embedding	Method	Top 100	Top 500	Top 1000
word2vec	Original	1.00 (0.99)	1.000 (0.982)	0.996 (0.945)
	Hard Debias	1.00 (1.00)	0.993 (0.965)	0.993 (0.971)
	Double-Hard Debias	1.00 (**0.98**)	**0.966 (0.937)**	**0.916 (0.940)**
fastText	Original	**0.64 (0.51)**	0.585 (0.622)	0.645 (**0.643**)
	Hard Debias	0.64 (0.68)	**0.583 (0.598)**	0.647 (0.652)
	Double-Hard Debias	**0.64 (0.51)**	**0.583** (0.647)	**0.573** (0.662)

Table 7: Experimental results on the neighborhood metric in the case of "women" and "men". The accuracy of the metric after dimensionality reduction by tSNE is shown in parentheses.

metric when targeting English GloVe and word2vec (results of the latter only shown in their Appendix). However, the bias could not be sufficiently mitigated in Japanese embeddings by using their method[¶].

One of the reasons might be related to the way how the gender definition words are predefined in those methods. Ethayarajh et al. (2019) comment on the results of Gonen and Goldberg (2019) stating that Hard Debias removes only the components of the predefined gender direction, and that it is impossible to remove other undefined components of the gender direction. Their conclusion is that even if one mitigates the bias with non-exhaustive gender definition word pairs, potential gender directions remain (Ethayarajh et al., 2019, p.1699).

We think this is true even if we remove the dominant principal components and make the embedding space isotropic, so the same criticism applies to Double-Hard Debias. In our opinion, the experimental results presented in this paper indicate that the list of gender definition word pairs we used was not sufficient to mitigate the gender bias. This poses the following problem. The number and types of words for gender naturally vary from language to language. Depending on the language, the exhaustive set of gender definition word pairs will differ. Also, the gender direction affecting the downstream task is not guaranteed to be identifiable or known a priori by simply using gender definition words translated from English. Therefore, it will be generally difficult to provide a comprehensive set of gender definition word pairs, suitable for downstream tasks, especially working with languages of a small NLP research population and limited resources.

7 Conclusion

In this paper, we analyzed the representational bias of Japanese word embeddings and attempted to mitigate the gender bias in these embeddings with previous methods developed for English. The experimental results showed that Japanese first name embeddings do not include social stereotypes and that the similarity of word vectors is influenced by the superficial information of character type. And, the existing gender

---

[¶]Unfortunately, there is no pre-trained GloVe model available for Japanese, so we were not able to investigate the influence of the embedding type.

bias mitigation methods did not sufficiently mitigate the gender bias in Japanese embeddings. These results suggest that it is difficult to generalize the previous methods for English to Japanese. This, in turn, may be suggesting that it could be difficult to apply those methods not only to Japanese, therefore it is important to consider whether and how they can be used to analyze and mitigate bias in other languages.

In the future, we will develop methods for bias analysis and of bias mitigation specifically dedicated to Japanese language. We will also examine the generalizability of other existing methods, and try to answer remaining question: what are the meta-conditions for a method to be independent of a language.

References

David Arthur and Sergei Vassilvitskii. 2006. k-means++: The advantages of careful seeding. Technical Report 2006-13, Stanford InfoLab, June.

Yoav Benjamini and Yosef Hochberg. 1995. Controlling the False Discovery Rate: A Practical and Powerful Approach to Multiple Testing. *Journal of the Royal Statistical Society: Series B (Methodological)*, 57(1):289–300.

Su Lin Blodgett, Solon Barocas, Hal Daumé III, and Hanna Wallach. 2020. Language (technology) is power: A critical survey of "bias" in NLP. In *Proceedings of the 58th Annual Meeting of the Association for Computational Linguistics*, pages 5454–5476, Online, July. Association for Computational Linguistics.

Piotr Bojanowski, Edouard Grave, Armand Joulin, and Tomas Mikolov. 2016. Enriching word vectors with subword information. *arXiv preprint arXiv:1607.04606*.

Tolga Bolukbasi, Kai-Wei Chang, James Zou, Venkatesh Saligrama, and Adam Kalai. 2016. Man is to computer programmer as woman is to homemaker? debiasing word embeddings. In *Proceedings of the 30th International Conference on Neural Information Processing Systems*, NIPS'16, page 4356–4364, Red Hook, NY, USA. Curran Associates Inc.

Francis Bond, Timothy Baldwin, Richard Fothergill, and Kiyotaka Uchimoto. 2012. Japanese semcor: A sense-tagged corpus of japanese. In *Proceedings of the 6th global WordNet conference (GWC 2012)*, pages 56–63. Citeseer.

Aylin Caliskan, Joanna J Bryson, and Arvind Narayanan. 2017. Semantics derived automatically from language corpora contain human-like biases. *Science*, 356(6334):183–186.

Kate Crawford. 2017. The trouble with bias. Keynote at Neural Information Processing Systems (NIPS'17).

Kawin Ethayarajh, David Duvenaud, and Graeme Hirst. 2019. Understanding undesirable word embedding associations. In *Proceedings of the 57th Annual Meeting of the Association for Computational Linguistics*, pages 1696–1705, Florence, Italy, July. Association for Computational Linguistics.

Hila Gonen and Yoav Goldberg. 2019. Lipstick on a pig: Debiasing methods cover up systematic gender biases in word embeddings but do not remove them. In *Proceedings of the 2019 Conference of the North American Chapter of the Association for Computational Linguistics: Human Language Technologies, Volume 1 (Long and Short Papers)*, pages 609–614, Minneapolis, Minnesota, June. Association for Computational Linguistics.

Akihiko Iwahara, Takeshi Hatta, and Aiko Maehara. 2003. The effects of a sense of compatibility between type of script and word in written japanese. *Reading and Writing*, 16(4):377–397.

Vaibhav Kumar, Tenzin Singhay Bhotia, Vaibhav Kumar, and Tanmoy Chakraborty. 2020. Nurse is closer to woman than surgeon? mitigating gender-biased proximities in word embeddings.

Haochen Liu, Jamell Dacon, Wenqi Fan, H. Liu, Zhiwei Liu, and Jiliang Tang. 2019. Does gender matter? towards fairness in dialogue systems. *arXiv*, abs/1910.10486.

Tomas Mikolov, Ilya Sutskever, Kai Chen, Greg Corrado, and Jeffrey Dean. 2013. Distributed representations of words and phrases and their compositionality. In *Proceedings of the 26th International Conference on Neural Information Processing Systems - Volume 2*, NIPS'13, page 3111–3119, Red Hook, NY, USA. Curran Associates Inc.

Hajime Morita, Daisuke Kawahara, and Sadao Kurohashi. 2015. Morphological analysis for unsegmented languages using recurrent neural network language model. In *Proceedings of the 2015 Conference on Empirical Methods in Natural Language Processing*, pages 2292–2297, Lisbon, Portugal, September. Association for Computational Linguistics.

Jiaqi Mu and Pramod Viswanath. 2018. All-but-the-top: Simple and effective post-processing for word representations. In *6th International Conference on Learning Representations, ICLR 2018*.

F. Pedregosa, G. Varoquaux, A. Gramfort, V. Michel, B. Thirion, O. Grisel, M. Blondel, P. Prettenhofer, R. Weiss, V. Dubourg, J. Vanderplas, A. Passos, D. Cournapeau, M. Brucher, M. Perrot, and E. Duchesnay. 2011. Scikit-learn: Machine learning in Python. *Journal of Machine Learning Research*, 12:2825–2830.

Arun K. Pujari, Ansh Mittal, Anshuman Padhi, Anshul Jain, Mukesh Jadon, and Vikas Kumar. 2019. Debiasing gender biased hindi words with word-embedding. In *Proceedings of the 2019 2nd International Conference on Algorithms, Computing and Artificial Intelligence*, ACAI 2019, page 450–456, New York, NY, USA. Association for Computing Machinery.

Thijs Raijmakers. 2020. Gender bias in word embeddings of different languages.

Magnus Sahlgren and Fredrik Olsson. 2019. Gender bias in pretrained Swedish embeddings. In *Proceedings of the 22nd Nordic Conference on Computational Linguistics*, pages 35–43, Turku, Finland, September–October. Linköping University Electronic Press.

Robert Speer and Catherine Havasi. 2013. Conceptnet 5: A large semantic network for relational knowledge. In *The People's Web Meets NLP*, pages 161–176. Springer.

Tony Sun, Andrew Gaut, Shirlyn Tang, Yuxin Huang, Mai ElSherief, Jieyu Zhao, Diba Mirza, Elizabeth Belding, Kai-Wei Chang, and William Yang Wang. 2019. Mitigating gender bias in natural language processing: Literature review. In *Proceedings of the 57th Annual Meeting of the Association for Computational Linguistics*, pages 1630–1640, Florence, Italy, July. Association for Computational Linguistics.

Masatoshi Suzuki, Koji Matsuda, Satoshi Sekine, Naoaki Okazaki, and Kentaro Inui. 2018. A joint neural model for fine-grained named entity classification of wikipedia articles. *IEICE Transactions on Information and Systems*, E101.D(1):73–81.

Nathaniel Swinger, Maria De-Arteaga, Neil Thomas Heffernan IV, Mark DM Leiserson, and Adam Tauman Kalai. 2019. What are the biases in my word embedding? In *Proceedings of the 2019 AAAI/ACM Conference on AI, Ethics, and Society*, AIES '19, page 305–311, New York, NY, USA. Association for Computing Machinery.

Laurens van der Maaten and Geoffrey Hinton. 2008. Visualizing data using t-SNE. *Journal of Machine Learning Research*, 9:2579–2605.

Tianlu Wang, Xi Victoria Lin, Nazneen Fatema Rajani, Bryan McCann, Vicente Ordonez, and Caiming Xiong. 2020. Double-hard debias: Tailoring word embeddings for gender bias mitigation. In *Proceedings of the 58th Annual Meeting of the Association for Computational Linguistics*, pages 5443–5453, Online, July. Association for Computational Linguistics.

Jieyu Zhao, Tianlu Wang, Mark Yatskar, Vicente Ordonez, and Kai-Wei Chang. 2018a. Gender bias in coreference resolution: Evaluation and debiasing methods. In *Proceedings of the 2018 Conference of the North American Chapter of the Association for Computational Linguistics: Human Language Technologies, Volume 2 (Short Papers)*, pages 15–20, New Orleans, Louisiana, June. Association for Computational Linguistics.

Jieyu Zhao, Yichao Zhou, Zeyu Li, Wei Wang, and Kai-Wei Chang. 2018b. Learning gender-neutral word embeddings. In *Proceedings of the 2018 Conference on Empirical Methods in Natural Language Processing*, pages 4847–4853, Brussels, Belgium, October-November. Association for Computational Linguistics.

Jieyu Zhao, Subhabrata Mukherjee, saghar Hosseini, Kai-Wei Chang, and Ahmed Hassan Awadallah. 2020. Gender bias in multilingual embeddings and cross-lingual transfer. In *Proceedings of the 58th Annual Meeting of the Association for Computational Linguistics*, pages 2896–2907, Online, July. Association for Computational Linguistics.

Pei Zhou, Weijia Shi, Jieyu Zhao, Kuan-Hao Huang, Muhao Chen, Ryan Cotterell, and Kai-Wei Chang. 2019. Examining gender bias in languages with grammatical gender. In *Proceedings of the 2019 Conference on Empirical Methods in Natural Language Processing and the 9th International Joint Conference on Natural Language Processing (EMNLP-IJCNLP)*, pages 5276–5284, Hong Kong, China, November. Association for Computational Linguistics.

Evaluating Bias In Dutch Word Embeddings

Rodrigo Alejandro Chávez Mulsa
Maastricht University
rodrigo.mulsa@outlook.com

Gerasimos Spanakis
Maastricht University
jerry.spanakis@
maastrichtuniversity.nl

Abstract

Recent research in Natural Language Processing has revealed that word embeddings can encode social biases present in the training data which can affect minorities in real world applications. This paper explores the gender bias implicit in Dutch embeddings while investigating whether English language based approaches can also be used in Dutch. We implement the Word Embeddings Association Test (WEAT), Clustering and Sentence Embeddings Association Test (SEAT) methods to quantify the gender bias in Dutch word embeddings, then we proceed to reduce the bias with Hard-Debias and Sent-Debias mitigation methods and finally we evaluate the performance of the debiased embeddings in downstream tasks. The results suggest that, among others, gender bias is present in traditional and contextualized Dutch word embeddings. We highlight how techniques used to measure and reduce bias created for English can be used in Dutch embeddings by adequately translating the data and taking into account the unique characteristics of the language. Furthermore, we analyze the effect of the debiasing techniques on downstream tasks which show a negligible impact on traditional embeddings and a 2% decrease in performance in contextualized embeddings. Finally, we release the translated Dutch datasets to the public along with the traditional embeddings with mitigated bias.

1 Introduction

In recent years language models have become more relevant in the field of Natural Language Processing (NLP). As word embeddings were shown to perform better in many tasks than many traditional techniques, the research community followed this direction and made further advancements resulting in another breakthrough - contextualized word embeddings (e.g. BERT Devlin et al. (2018), RoBERTa Liu et al. (2019)). As opposed to traditional (context-free) word embeddings that have a fixed representation vector, contextualized word embeddings change depending on the sentences (context) in which they are used. They have achieved state-of-the-art in NLP tasks and effectively replaced traditional word embeddings. Due to their outstanding performance, they are broadly adopted in many real-world applications (Wolf et al., 2019).

Models employing those embeddings often support decisions that strongly impact people's lives, so their fairness and correctness is critical. Unfortunately, previous research has shown that traditional and contextualized word embeddings can encode social biases present in the training data (Caliskan et al., 2017; Garg et al., 2018; May et al., 2019; Zhao et al., 2019).

The social biases in machine learning applications can have an impact on society, as the case in computer vision where three commercial gender classification systems reported higher error rates when recognizing women, specifically those with darker skin tones (Buolamwini, 2018). These biases can cause undesired effects in downstream NLP tasks (Zhao et al., 2018; Basta et al., 2019) where biased NLP models can amplify bias in real world applications and especially affect minorities which are misrepresented in the data. It has been shown that some minorities like people with disabilities are misrepresented and are associated with a negative sentiment (Hutchinson et al., 2020).

Proceedings of the Second Workshop on Gender Bias in Natural Language Processing, pages 56–71
Barcelona, Spain (Online), December 13, 2020.

This paper explores the existing gender bias in six traditional and two contextualized Dutch word embedding models by using a combination of state-of-the-art methods proposed in previous literature for English (Caliskan et al., 2017; Gonen and Goldberg, 2019). Then, we attempt to mitigate the gender bias in these models and analyze the effect of this step in an applicable downstream task. (Bolukbasi et al., 2016; Liang et al., 2019) Therefore we answer the following questions:

1. Are Dutch contextualized word embeddings sensitive to gender bias and if so how does the bias compares to traditional Dutch word embeddings?

2. Are measuring and mitigating gender bias methods created for English models compatible with Dutch models?

3. What impact does a bias mitigation method have on the models when used in downstream tasks?

2   Related Work

In social psychology the Implicit Association Test (IAT) (Greenwald et al., 1998) is used to measure the strength of implicit associations between concepts (e.g., black people, gay people) and evaluations (e.g., good, bad) or stereotypes (e.g., athletic, clumsy). When doing an IAT a participant is asked to quickly sort words into categories that are on the left and right hand side of the computer screen. The IAT has five main parts and the score is based on how long it takes a person, on average, to sort the words in the third part of the IAT versus the fifth part of the IAT. We would say that one has an implicit preference for thin people relative to fat people if they are faster to categorize words when Thin People and Good share a response key and Fat People and Bad share a response key, relative to the reverse.

Similarly to the IAT, research in traditional embeddings has proposed how to identify gender bias by measuring the distance between gendered words like pronouns and neutral nouns (Bolukbasi et al., 2016), while there has been some relevant work done towards mitigating the bias in the embeddings (Sun et al., 2019), it has been demonstrated that some of the methods are not enough and the bias can remain hidden within the embeddings. Regardless of the distances in the gender dimension, frequency of words are not taken into account (Wang et al., 2020) and biased words can remain clustered together (Gonen and Goldberg, 2019). Furthermore, these bias methods have to be modified when used on contextualized word embeddings because the embedding representation of every word changes depending on the context in the sentence.

A modified method is Sent-Debias (Liang et al., 2019) which relies heavily on the sentences used to reduce the bias and we hypothesise that due to the extensive use of the pronouns he and she in English, which are not used in Dutch due to their multiple meaning, the mitigation step encompasses a smaller gender subspace in comparison to English and thus the bias is reduced less.

A predisposition towards English word embeddings exists when researching bias, where the proposed mitigation techniques cannot be directly applied in non-genderless languages. Moreover, there is a lack of work in debiasing contextualized embeddings for other languages that contains characteristics that prohibits to simply import the original methods, like Dutch with *zij* meaning both *she* and *they* in English. While some work has been done in languages that contain grammatical gender like Spanish and French (Zhou et al., 2019), these proposed methods are restricted to traditional embeddings.

This paper looks into the intersection of the aforementioned techniques by analyzing and mitigating gender bias in traditional word embeddings and the state-of-the-art Dutch models BERTje (de Vries et al., 2019), RobBERT (Delobelle et al., 2020) while providing a version of the WEAT and SEAT data for this task in Dutch (Caliskan et al., 2017).

3   Bias Statement

Examples of English NLP models bringing negative consequences to misrepresented groups like an algorithm penalising job applications that contained words like "woman's" and "women's chess club captain." (Dastin, 2018), or high paying jobs advertisements being shown less to woman than to man (Datta et al.,

2015) are real world cases which could be repeated in Dutch speaking countries, if these Dutch models are deployed without considering the bias present in the word embeddings. In this paper we study the bias by means of embeddings cosine similarities showing that after applying a debiasing technique, other different forms of bias like clustering can remain by having gender stereotype words grouped together enforcing their association. A NLP recommendation system associating words as caring and artistic to girls while using mathematician and sportive to boys could enforce gendered roles and a gender unequal society when for example, recommending toys or books as it has been studied in psychology (Murnen, 2018).

The high usability of language models has allowed a broad adoption of these techniques in real world applications, by mitigating different types of bias in NLP models we could not only avoid amplifying these biases but shift the social balance in the long term by avoiding algorithms enforcing social biases against minorities.

4 Methods and Data

In the following section we explain the methods and data used in this research. Multiple sets of data (e.g. pairs of sentences, lists of gendered words and combinations of sentences of different categories), are needed as a means to analyze and mitigate bias in word embeddings, three algorithms are implemented to measure bias in embeddings; two being applicable to traditional embeddings and the third one is a method adapted for contextualized word embeddings.

Then we show the approaches we use to mitigate the bias in either type of embeddings and test the performance of the bias mitigation on downstream tasks. Furthermore we recall this research is done on Dutch embeddings, thus the data used is from the same language translated from the English data used on the methods original research.

4.1 Models

We perform experiments in six traditional word embeddings, the 300 dimensional Dutch FastText (Grave et al., 2018), the 320 dimensional small and big embeddings from CLIPS (Tulkens et al., 2016) trained on Corpora Of the Web (COW), the 160 and 320 dimensional embeddings from CLIPS trained on the Sonar corpus (Schäfer and Bildhauer, 2012) and the 100 dimensional Word2Vec from NLPL (Fares et al., 2017). Furthermore, we test the state-of-the-art 768 dimensional contextualized word embeddings BERTJe (de Vries et al., 2019) and RobBert (Delobelle et al., 2020) which are respectively the homologous versions to BERT (Devlin et al., 2018) and Roberta (Liu et al., 2019) in Dutch.

4.2 Bias Measuring Methods

4.2.1 Word Embedding Association Test

The Word Embeddings Association Test (WEAT), as proposed by Caliskan et al. (2017) is a statistical test, similar to the Implicit Association Test (IAT) (Greenwald et al., 1998), which helps to measure human bias in textual data. Both IAT and WEAT use two lists of target words and two lists of attribute words, the first pair of lists correspond to terms we want to compare and the second pair of lists represent the categories in which we believe bias can be present.

Caliskan et al. (2017) defined ten tests using WEAT to measure the bias in different categories[1]

In our research we translate the WEAT lists of words used in the tests to Dutch and modify them accordingly so words in these lists remain associated only to the corresponding category. Some of the modifications correspond to the different linguistic characteristics of the language and the lack of meaningful translations of certain words in the data (e.g. avoid using *zij/ ze* which they both can be used as what would be *she* and *they* in English making them not candidate words to represent gender since they can encode neutral plural too). We put special attention to Weat- *6, 7* and *8* since these tests measure the gender bias in three different lists[2] of attributes; Career vs Family, Mathematics vs Art, and Science

---

[1]Full list in Appendix including extra tests 11-16.

[2]The corresponding terms in Dutch are: *carriere vs gezinsactiviteiten, wiskunde vs kunst, and wetenschap vs kunst.*

vs Art. *Weat-6* uses male and female names used in English[3] while *weat 7 and 8* use gendered words for the target lists (e.g. grandpa, grandma).

WEAT consists of two parts, the p-values (p) and the effect size (d). The test statistic (3) indicates the significance where a p-value larger than 0.05 indicates the bias is insignificant, while the effect size (4) measures the magnitude of the associations representing how much bias is quantified.

With the purpose of measuring bias, we use the WEAT test statistic that measures the difference of the aggregated similarities between a target word list, with notation M or F, to the attribute word lists A and B. The target to attribute similarities are computed by getting the mean of the cosine similarity between the words in a target list (e.g. M) and the words in an attribute list (e.g. A) and then subtracting the mean of the same measurement of the second attribute list (e.g. B). The test statistic can be described as:

$$s(M, F, A, B) = [\sum_{m \epsilon M} s(m, A, B) - \sum_{f \epsilon F} s(f, A, B)] \tag{1}$$

where $s(w, A, B)$ corresponds to the cosine similarities between some word w and the attribute words a and b represented as:

$$s(w, A, B) = [\frac{\sum_{a \epsilon A} cos(w, a)}{|A|} - \frac{\sum_{b \epsilon B} cos(w, b)}{|B|}] \tag{2}$$

In order to compute the significance we first merge the M and F lists, then we generate $100,000$[4] permutations, denoted as $PERM$, of this combined list and split each of them in new pairs of M_i and F_i lists, we perform the test statistic (1) on every pair and calculate the test significance by looking at the amount of permutations where the result of the test statistic is higher than the result of the original tested lists, and divide this count by the total amount of permutations (single tail test). Described as:

$$p = \frac{\sum_{i \epsilon PERM} [s(Mi, Fi, A, B) > s(M, F, A, B)]}{|PERM|} \tag{3}$$

Furthermore, the amount of bias in WEAT is analyzed using the effect size d that is computed by obtaining the difference between the mean of the cosine similarities between the M and F lists to the attributes A and B, and normalizing them by dividing them with the standard deviation of both lists combined, which can be formulated as:

$$d = \frac{mean_{m \in M} s(m, A, B) - mean_{f \in F} s(f, A, B)}{\text{stddev}_{w \in M \cup F} s(w, A, B)} \tag{4}$$

4.2.2 Clustering accuracy

A different metric was introduced by Gonen and Goldberg (2019) showing that word embeddings with mitigated bias can remain clustered together even though the distance between attribute and target words (in WEAT) is insignificant. The clustering accuracy test requires to project the whole vocabulary into a male and female term to get the gender direction of each word in the vocabulary. Gonen and Goldberg (2019) used the pronouns *he* and *she* because they are widely used and the only difference between them is in the gender subspace. The homologous pronouns in Dutch are *hij* and *zij* which represent a problem in this research due to *zij* meaning both *she* and *they* thus adding extra meaning besides gender to the geometrical difference of the pronouns. We tested different[5] pairs of words that could better substitute the pronouns in the projection step and selected the pair *man* and *vrouw* to generate the gender direction of the words in the vocabulary. We implement this test for traditional word embeddings, first we compute the gender direction of every[6] word in the vocabulary W by getting the dot product of each word to a

---

[3]We created an alternative list of target words for seat-6 with a list of dutch female and male names, based on popularity retrieved from the Sociale Verzekeringsbank *(Social Insurance Bank in English)*, results are shown in the appendix.

[4]If there are more than $100k$ possible permutations, we sample $99,999$ and assume at least one of the permutations satisfied the inequality in (3) to account for the loss of precision.

[5]Some of the candidate pairs include [*jongen, meisje*] & [*mannelijk, vrouwelijk*].

[6]We limit the vocabulary in this test by skipping words where gender gives them part of its meaning (e.g. *grandma/grandpa*).

male and female word, 'man' and 'vrouw' in this case, and getting the difference of the scalars as the gender direction of each word. Then we sort the entire vocabulary based on this gender direction and retrieve the k most associated to the male and female direction[7].

We use this top $2k$ most biased words and create ground truth labels $l \in L$ where $l = 0$ if the word is from the k male words and $l = 1$ if the word is from the k female words. Next we run KMeans predictions to categorize the words giving to each word a predictive label $\hat{l}$.

$$a = \frac{1}{2k} \sum_{i=1}^{2k} 1[l_i == \hat{l}_i] \tag{5}$$

We use (5) to count how many of the words were clustered correctly according to the ground truth labels l and compare this metric with the traditional word embeddings before and after mitigating the bias. Then, set $a = max(a, 1 - a)$ to test if the words remain clustered after mitigating the bias. Given a, the closer it is to 1 the more biased the embeddings are, while a more random clustering is represented the closer its value is to 0.5, thus the least bias there is.

4.2.3 SEAT

Following from Caliskan et al. (2017), May et al. (2019) proposed a method adapted from WEAT that can be used in contextualized word embeddings like BERT, by converting every word in WEAT into multiple sentences using a set of semantically bleached sentence templates. Then the same formulas are used as in WEAT where the embeddings represent the entire sentence instead of only a word. This approach hypothesizes that the models that use context to get more accurate vector representations should not be tested on a word basis like WEAT, and by converting the original WEAT lists of words into sentences with multiple contexts the models can generalize better and therefore can be tested too for biases.

Similar to the WEAT lists of words, we translated and adjusted the sentences used in SEAT to Dutch. May et al. (2019) enriched the tests by adding b versions of the tests 3, 5, 6, 7 and 8 by replacing given names with group terms (e.g., male, son, female, daughter) and vice versa. Similar as with WEAT, in our results we focus on the tests 6, 6b, 7, 7b, 8 and 8b which are related to gender bias.

Examples of the sentences templates introduced by May et al. (2019) include: 'This is a *<WeatWord>*', 'That is a *<WeatWord>*'. We adapted all the SEAT templates to Dutch and this equivalent sentences become: 'Dit is een *<WeatWord>*', 'Dat is een *<WeatWord>*'.

4.3 Debiasing Methods

4.3.1 Hard-Debias

It was demonstrated with WEAT that there is bias in traditional word embeddings when comparing attributes and target words. Based on the WEAT mathematical definition of bias, Bolukbasi et al. (2016) hypothesized there is a gender direction encoded in these embeddings which can be subtracted from the word representations and by equalizing the distance between similar terms (e.g., *he* and *she*) it is possible to reduce the bias in the word embeddings.

Hard-Debias requires three lists of words, a gender specific list, a definitional list and an equalize list. The first list contains a broad list of gender related words that are not debiased since their meaning depends at least partially on the gender subspace, the second list correspond to the words used in the PCA to define the bias subspace and the third list contains words that should be equalized in opposite direction in the gender subspace with the same magnitude. We translated to Dutch the lists used in Hard-Debias and modified them similarly as with the previous data to adjust for the language differences.

Following the description by Wang et al. (2020), given a vocabulary W from some word embeddings, we can denote each word embedding in W as $\vec{w} \in \mathbb{R}^n$ per each $w \in W$. We define a subspace in W as B which is defined by k orthogonal unit vectors $B = \{b_1, ..., b_k\} \in \mathbb{R}^n$. We can describe a projection of some embedding $\vec{w}$ on B by:

We assume a predefined set of n (male, female) pairs of words $D_1, D_2, ..., D_n \subset W$, where the main difference between each pair of words is the gender (Bolukbasi et al., 2016). Let

---

[7]In our experiments we get the 500 most female and the 500 most male oriented words.

$$\vec{w}_B = \sum_{j=1}^{k} (\vec{w} \cdot b_j) b_j \qquad (6) \qquad\qquad \mu_i := \sum_{w \in D_i} \vec{w} / |D_i| \qquad (7)$$

Then we identify a gender subspace B that captures the gender bias. Following from (7) we can compute B as the first $k \geq 1$ components from the principal component analysis (PCA) (Abdi and Williams, 2010).

$$B = PCA_k(\bigcup_{i=1}^{n} \bigcup_{w \in D_i} (\vec{w} - \mu_i))$$
$$(8)$$

Then we neutralize the word embeddings corresponding to words that are neutral to gender by modifying each $\vec{w} \in \mathbb{R}^n$ such that every word $w \in N$ has a zero projection in the gender subspace.

$$\vec{w} = \vec{w} - \vec{w_B} \qquad (9)$$

Finally we equalize the gendered word pairs D_i (e.g. *man* and *vrouw*) such that they have a gender component in opposite directions but with the same magnitude. This ensure that the distance between neutral words to biased words is the same with respect to the bias subspace.

4.3.2   Sent-Debias

The added context in sentence embeddings and the unlikelihood of retraining models due to their increasing size like GPT2 (Radford et al., 2019), have made debiasing of these models even harder.

A modified Hard-Debias compatible with sentence representations was proposed by skipping the equalizing step from the original method, and studying the effect and performance of diverse sentence pairs that encode the bias subspace (Liang et al., 2019). We generate a new dataset of 30,000 gendered sentence pairs in order to compute the gender direction by using the Wikipedia Monolingual Corpora in Dutch from Linguatools (Kolb, 2018) and the Gensim library (Sojka, 2010). After processing the corpora into single sentences[8] we proceed to find k amount of sentences that contains one of the words from the gendered word list used in Hard-Debias, we save the sentence as a tuple with the new sentence created by swapping the gendered word in the original sentence by the same word of opposite gender from the gendered list, making them different only in the bias subspace (e.g. "*She* is the best friend of Obama" creates the pair: "*He* is the best friend of Obama").

We compute the gender subspace and mitigate the bias by making the sentence embedding orthogonal to this gender subspace. A major consideration we had to take when creating this Dutch dataset was that in this language, some of the pronouns that are gender related, like *zij/ze*, can be associated to the female gender or be used as plural (*she/they*), while the male pronoun *zij* is also used as a subjunctive with every pronoun, thus an unsupervised method to generate the dataset cannot include these words since it would bring noise to the subspace we want to generate. Similar as in Hard-Debias we use these pairs of sentences with the principal component analysis (PCA) to get the gender subspace made of the first k components of the PCA. We then project each sentence embedding into each of the components and use the sum of these vectors to subtract the gender subspace from every sentence embedding to mitigate the bias.

4.4   Downstream tasks

4.4.1   Relation Identification Task

Data for this Dutch task was created following a similar task used in the original *word2vec* toolkit[9] which contains approximately 20,000 relation identification questions, each of the form: "If A has a relation to B, which word has the same relation to D?. This Dutch dataset created by Tulkens et al. (2016) aims to replicate the original evaluation set as closely as possible, while also including some characteristics

---

[8]With a maximum length equal to the longest length of accepted inputs in BERTJe and RobBert (512).

[9]https://code.google.com/archive/p/word2vec/

of Dutch that are not present in English, such as the formation of diminutives, and thus being a more accurate evaluation task for the models in Dutch.

The task is described as approximately 20,000 relation identification questions, each of the form: "If A has a relation to B, which word has the same relation to D?". As such, it uses the fact that vectors are compositional. For example, given man, woman, and king, the answer to the question should be queen, the relation here being 'gender'.

4.4.2 Sentiment Analysis Task

In most real world applications the contextualized word embeddings will be fine-tuned to a specific task in which they are used, we proceed to finetune the models BERTJe and RobBERT, on the Sentiment Analysis task (van der Burgh and Verberne, 2019) using the 110k Dutch Book Reviews dataset (DBRD)[10] and test the performance difference when the model bias has been mitigated. The dataset has been used to compare the original performance of BERTJe and RobBERT, it is split in a balanced 10% test (2224 reviews) and 90% train split where each review is labeled as positive or negative.

WEAT test	Weat-6	Weat-7	Weat-8
FastText	$1.534^{**} \rightarrow 1.605^{**}$	$1.484^{**} \rightarrow \mathbf{1.260^{**}}$	$1.147^{**} \rightarrow \mathbf{0.672}$
COW-small	$1.866^{**} \rightarrow \mathbf{1.840^{**}}$	$1.759^{**} \rightarrow \mathbf{0.947^{*}}$	$1.339^{**} \rightarrow \mathbf{0.392}$
COW-big	$1.771^{**} \rightarrow \mathbf{1.738^{**}}$	$1.713^{**} \rightarrow \mathbf{1.100^{*}}$	$1.425^{**} \rightarrow \mathbf{0.506}$
Sonar-160	$0.726 \rightarrow \mathbf{0.578}$	$1.451^{**} \rightarrow \mathbf{0.410}$	$1.180^{**} \rightarrow \mathbf{0.271}$
Sonar-320	$0.528 \rightarrow \mathbf{0.526}$	$1.1716^{*} \rightarrow \mathbf{0.643^{*}}$	$0.995^{*} \rightarrow \mathbf{0.615}$
Model-NLPL	$1.748^{**} \rightarrow \mathbf{1.721^{**}}$	$1.443^{**} \rightarrow \mathbf{1.161^{**}}$	$0.766 \rightarrow 0.885^{*}$

Arrow indicates before to after mitigating bias; * indicates significant at 0.05, ** significant at 0.01.

Table 1: WEAT effect size on gender related test.

5 Experiments and Results

In this section we explain how we use the methods and data explained in previous sections to measure and mitigate the bias in Dutch embeddings. We demonstrate the existence of bias in traditional word embeddings and explain the bias mitigation process that has been used. Then we demonstrate that contextualized word embeddings show less bias than traditional ones while also determining that the bias mitigation is not as effective in contextualized word embeddings as in traditional word embeddings.

5.1 Results On Word Embeddings

5.1.1 WEAT

We performed the WEAT test on the 16^{11} adapted lists of words translated to Dutch. Among all the traditional word embeddings we see high effect sizes and multiple tests are significant at different levels.

The results of the WEAT effect sizes on gendered related tests are shown in table (1) where we see an overall high effect size across all the scores on the original models. Then we look into the results after the debiasing step (at the right of the arrow) where it shows that the bias mitigation is effective in almost every test for every model with just 2 cases where the score did not decrease. If the gender related results of the FastText model are compared to the rest of the tests in the appendix (8) for example, we can see how other types of bias are present, but the mitigation step mainly provides good results in the gender related tests by reducing the gender bias further than on other types of biases.

In the other models we also see a high amount of significant tests where the bias mitigation has a positive impact on every test effect size and some of the bias loses its significance. We note the models by Clips (COW and Sonar) contain significant bias with a relative high effect size specially in tests with gender words as target ($d > 1.0$). Furthermore, the results in table (1) for the Word2Vec NLPL model are also high and significant on Weat-6 and Weat-7.

---

[10]Dataset available at:
`https://github.com/benjaminvdb/110kDBRD`

[11]All the results are available in the appendix.

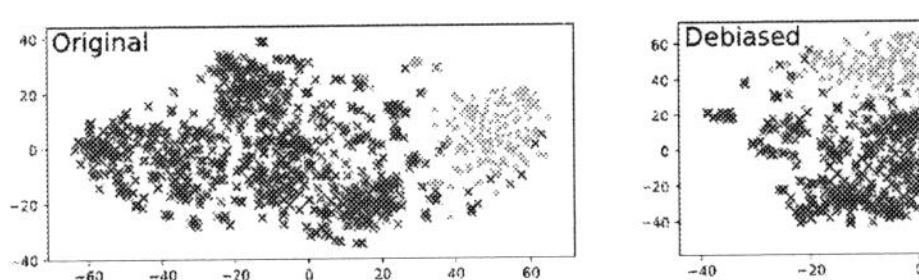

Figure 1: Example of clustered bias on FastText in dutch.

5.1.2 Clustering Accuracy Test

We perform the clustering accuracy test to compare if biased words remain clustered together even after performing the Hard-Debias method to mitigate the gender bias present in the embeddings. Our results matches the English results from Gonen and Goldberg (2019) which show that mitigating bias focusing only on WEAT can hide bias which is measured differently. On table 2, using formula (5) we compare the accuracy in which KMeans creates two clusters using the previously defined biased words before and after mitigating the bias. Since the goal is to have embeddings where there are no biased words, attempting to cluster the words should perform randomly and not create groups of male and female words, thus the closer the score to 0.5 the better.

Model	Original	Debiased
FastText	0.611	0.605
COW-small	1.0	1.0
COW-big	0.999	0.999
Sonar-160	1.0	1.0
Sonar-320	0.998	0.998
Model NLPL	0.999	0.995

Before and after the bias mitigation step.

Table 2: Cluster test results

The results in (2) show that after mitigating the bias on the FastText model the accuracy slightly decreases by 0.006 hence the Hard-Debias method can work in reducing the cluster bias, while the results also show there is no change in the predictions on the Clips models having an almost perfect accuracy, and in the case of the NLPL model the score decreases slightly by 0.004 like in the FastText case. Our results in this Dutch models are similar to the ones presented in English models (Gonen and Goldberg, 2019) which demonstrates that bias can be barely unaffected by some debiasing methods when analyzed with a different metric than WEAT.

We also provide an example in figure (1) of the 500 female and 500 male most biased words clustering together before and after the mitigation step, showing that even though their position changes, they remain grouped together.

5.1.3 SEAT

We use the Huggingface transformers library (Wolf et al., 2019) to load and use both BERTJe (de Vries et al., 2019) and RobBert (Delobelle et al., 2020). To retrieve the sentence embeddings we use the special tokens corresponding to each model, in BERTJe we use the [CLS] token while in RobBert we use the $< s >$ token.

We then load the bare models to compute the adapted SEAT test to BERTJe and RobBERT. In BERTJe we see that the tests like SEAT-1[12] has no significant bias but the gender oriented tests like SEAT-6, 6B, 7b and 8 show bias; although the effect size is less compared to the previously shown results in the word embeddings. This has been hypothesized as contextual embeddings are less susceptible to bias due to the context words influence, yet the results have proved these embeddings are not exempt of bias and a bias mitigation technique is needed.

We then modify the Huggingface transformers library to implement the mitigation step every time we generate an embedding. The following table (3) shows the SEAT results, where the bias mitigation

---

[12]Available in the appendix.

applied using Sent-Debias in both models, reduce the effect size in four out of six tests, but the change on the bias scores in this metric is minimal compared to the bias mitigation in traditional embeddings. This could be due to contextualized embeddings encoding the gender direction along with the bias in a more complex subspace than the one used in traditional embeddings.

5.2 Performance On Downstream Tasks

5.2.1 Relation Identification Task

We test the embeddings before and after mitigating the bias on a relation identification task in Dutch. We present in our results the accuracy in which the models find a word w in the vocabulary W which maximizes the similarity score with the vector $(A - B + D)$.

Our results are displayed in table 4 having mixed scores after the bias mitigation step where the biggest amount decreased is shown with the smallest model Sonar-160 by 0.01397 and the models Cow-big and NLPL show a small increase in their scores by 0.00225 and 0.00305 respectively.

5.2.2 Sentiment Analysis Task

For this task we report the accuracy score, the 95% confidence intervals[13] and F1 score. The results displayed in table (5) show that both of the models performance decreases approximately 2% in the downstream task after going through the bias mitigation, which correlates to similar results that have been presented in previous research (Liang et al., 2019). We hypothesize this could be due to the transformation the embeddings go through when mitigating the bias or because the dataset used in the downstream task is biased thus conflicting with the model training.

SEAT list	BERTJe	RobBERT
SEAT-06	$0.666^{**} \rightarrow \mathbf{0.614^{**}}$	$0.191 \rightarrow \mathbf{0.190}$
SEAT-06b	$0.349^{*} \rightarrow \mathbf{0.294^{*}}$	$0.552^{**} \rightarrow 0.5846^{**}$
SEAT-07	$0.6300^{**} \rightarrow \mathbf{0.588^{**}}$	$0.331^{*} \rightarrow \mathbf{0.252}$
SEAT-07b	$0.613^{**} \rightarrow \mathbf{0.605^{**}}$	$0.683^{**} \rightarrow \mathbf{0.669^{**}}$
SEAT-08	$0.089 \rightarrow 0.114$	$0.080 \rightarrow 0.105$
SEAT-08b	$0.286 \rightarrow 0.294$	$0.157 \rightarrow \mathbf{0.149}$

Arrow indicates before to after mitigating bias; * indicates significant at 0.05, ** significant at 0.01.

Table 3: SEAT effect size on gender related tests.

Model	Original	Debiased
FastText-320	0.67445	0.662
Cow-320	0.513	0.512
Cow-Big	0.516	0.518
Sonar-160	0.408	0.394
Sonar-320	0.429	0.421
Model-NLPL	0.430	0.433

Before and after the bias mitigation step.

Table 4: Relation identification task results

Model	Original		Debiased	
	ACC (95% CI) [%]	F1 [%]	ACC (95% CI) [%]	F1 [%]
BERTJe	0.952 (0.943,0.961)	0.952	0.946 (0.937,0.955)	0.946
RobBERT	0.935 (0.925,0.945)	0.935	0.913 (0.901,0.925)	0.913

Before and after the bias mitigation step.

Table 5: Sentiment analysis task results

6 Discussion

In the traditional word embeddings we see large effect sizes ($d > 1.0$) in every WEAT test that passes the significance statistic and we manage to decrease these scores with the Hard-Debias method. We also note that the bias mitigation on tests that uses names in either English or Dutch doesn't perform as well as in the other tests that terms of groups are used. We hypothesize that while names can encode bias, it could be in a different subspace than the group terms and if not enough names are used in the data of Hard-Debias to generate the gender subspace then the mitigation fails when dealing with names.

We point out that Hard-Debias has an equalizing step that depends in a list of gendered word pairs which should not be transformed by the bias direction and instead centralized where each pair is separated by the same distance. This can be a limitation on the method since it heavily relies in this list of gendered

---

[13]Confidence intervals are calculated using the normal approximation to the binomial distribution.

word pairs where having an incomplete list could translate into bad performance of the model if words that depend on the gender dimension for their meaning lose it.

The clustering metric shows that even if the bias is reduced using Hard-Debias and tested on WEAT, there can be other approaches to identify bias and some methods won't mitigate the bias from that point of view, therefore we suggest more research should be done in different ways to identify bias and mitigate it.

The results on the relation identification task showed that the bias mitigation step had a slight influence on the model results, but overall the method shows that Hard-Debias does not affect negatively in a remarkable amount the performance on the task.

As for the results of BERTJe and RobBert, they both show bias in the same tests associated to gender but present a smaller effect size overall ($d < 1.0$) compared to traditional embeddings on WEAT. When using Sent-Debias the effect sizes decreases along the significance statistic of the bias, yet the tests remain in the same statistical significance category ($p \leq 0.05 \vee p \leq 0.01$). This shows that the bias mitigation technique works but it does not completely eliminate the bias. A possible reason to this result is that contextualized words embeddings contain a more complex gender subspace and a stronger method might be necessary in order to mitigate the bias on it.

Moreover, we show on the sentiment analysis task that similarly to the English research (May et al., 2019), when mitigating the bias the accuracy on downstream tasks decreases by a small percentage, this demonstrates that methods built for English embeddings can also be used for Dutch ones and produce similar results on equivalent tasks.

One of our work's limitations is that while our methods are directly applied in Dutch, our test data was created in English and adapted for Dutch. That means that our tests do not specifically take into consideration some of the linguistic features in Dutch that are not present in English, such as the use of diminitives (e.g. *bier → biertje*) or the distinct styles of expressions in the Dutch dialects, regional languages (e.g. *Limburgish*) or the Afrikaans sister language.

We also highlight that both WEAT and SEAT don't test for the lack of bias, just test whether if in the test cases bias exist but there could be other non-tested cases where bias is present. An example of this is shown when computing the clustering accuracy test which demonstrates that if we measure bias from a different point of view, the bias remains and thus further research in different bias mitigation techniques is recommended.

7 Conclusion

With this research we show that among others, gender bias is present in Dutch traditional and contextualized word embeddings (as probably in other languages as well). We then show how methods used to measure and mitigate bias in English embeddings, can be used in Dutch embeddings by properly translating the data and taking into consideration the unique characteristics of the language (*e.g. zij/ze*). Furthermore, we analyze the effect of the mitigating techniques in downstream tasks showing negligible impact in traditional embeddings and approximately a 2% decrease of performance in contextualized embeddings, which can be considered detrimental if the embeddings used guarantee a more gender-neutral approach.

A promising future direction stemming from this research would be the development of extensive bias tests taking into consideration Dutch dialects and other language peculiarities. Moreover, more research is needed into the evaluation of different definitions of bias in contextual embeddings as we have shown in the findings that clustering bias persists regardless of the WEAT results in traditional embeddings. With this paper, we highlight the existence of bias in commonly used representation models, therefore, we advocate the use of mitigated bias models, especially in many industry applications (e.g. real-world NLP models) where bias existence can harm minorities.

Finally, we release the new Dutch datasets for all bias tests to the public[14] and the traditional embeddings with mitigated bias.

---

[14]Available at: `https://github.com/Noixas/Official-Evaluating-Bias-In-Dutch`

Acknowledgement

Authors would like to thank Visma Connect B.V. for providing the cloud resources that allowed carrying out this research and more specifically Yvo Keuter for his supervision and mentorship during Rodrigo's time at Visma Connect.

References

Hervé Abdi and Lynne J. Williams. 2010. Principal component analysis. *Wiley Interdisciplinary Reviews: Computational Statistics*, 2(4):433–459, 7.

Christine Basta, Marta R. Costa-jussà, and Noe Casas. 2019. Evaluating the Underlying Gender Bias in Contextualized Word Embeddings. Technical report.

Tolga Bolukbasi, Kai Wei Chang, James Zou, Venkatesh Saligrama, and Adam Kalai. 2016. Man is to computer programmer as woman is to homemaker? Debiasing word embeddings. Technical report.

Joy Buolamwini. 2018. Gender Shades: Intersectional Accuracy Disparities in Commercial Gender Classification *. Technical report.

Aylin Caliskan, Joanna J. Bryson, and Arvind Narayanan. 2017. Semantics derived automatically from language corpora contain human-like biases. *Science*, 356(6334):183–186, 4.

Jeffrey Dastin. 2018. Amazon scraps secret AI recruiting tool that showed bias against women - Reuters, 10.

Amit Datta, Michael Carl Tschantz, and Anupam Datta. 2015. Automated Experiments on Ad Privacy Settings. *Proceedings on Privacy Enhancing Technologies*, 2015(1):92–112.

Wietse de Vries, Andreas van Cranenburgh, Arianna Bisazza, Tommaso Caselli, Gertjan van Noord, and Malvina Nissim. 2019. BERTje: A Dutch BERT Model. 12.

Pieter Delobelle, Thomas Winters, and Bettina Berendt. 2020. RobBERT: a Dutch RoBERTa-based Language Model. 1.

Jacob Devlin, Ming-Wei Chang, Kenton Lee, and Kristina Toutanova. 2018. BERT: Pre-training of Deep Bidirectional Transformers for Language Understanding. 10.

Murhaf Fares, Andrey Kutuzov, Stephan Oepen, and Erik Velldal. 2017. Word vectors, reuse, and replicability: Towards a community repository of large-text resources. Technical report.

Nikhil Garg, Londa Schiebinger, Dan Jurafsky, and James Zou. 2018. Word embeddings quantify 100 years of gender and ethnic stereotypes. *Proceedings of the National Academy of Sciences of the United States of America*, 115(16):E3635–E3644, 4.

Hila Gonen and Yoav Goldberg. 2019. Lipstick on a Pig: Debiasing Methods Cover up Systematic Gender Biases in Word Embeddings But do not Remove Them. 3.

Edouard Grave, Piotr Bojanowski, Prakhar Gupta, Armand Joulin, and Tomas Mikolov. 2018. Learning Word Vectors for 157 Languages. Technical report.

Anthony G. Greenwald, Debbie E. McGhee, and Jordan L.K. Schwartz. 1998. Measuring individual differences in implicit cognition: The implicit association test. *Journal of Personality and Social Psychology*, 74(6):1464–1480.

Ben Hutchinson, Vinodkumar Prabhakaran, Emily Denton, Kellie Webster, Yu Zhong, and Stephen Denuyl. 2020. Social Biases in NLP Models as Barriers for Persons with Disabilities. pages 5491–5501, 5.

Peter Kolb. 2018. Wikipedia Monolingual Corpora – Linguatools.

Paul Pu Liang, Irene Li, Emily Zheng, Yao Chong Lim, Ruslan Salakhutdinov, and Louis-Philippe Morency. 2019. Towards Debiasing Sentence Representations. Technical report.

Yinhan Liu, Myle Ott, Naman Goyal, Jingfei Du, Mandar Joshi, Danqi Chen, Omer Levy, Mike Lewis, Luke Zettlemoyer, and Veselin Stoyanov. 2019. RoBERTa: A Robustly Optimized BERT Pretraining Approach. 7.

Chandler May, Alex Wang, Shikha Bordia, Samuel R. Bowman, and Rachel Rudinger. 2019. On Measuring Social Biases in Sentence Encoders. Technical report.

Sarah K. Murnen. 2018. Fashion or action? Gender-stereotyped toys and social behavior. In *Gender typing of children's toys: How early play experiences impact development.*, pages 189–211. American Psychological Association, 2.

Alec Radford, Jeffrey Wu, Rewon Child, David Luan, Dario Amodei, and Ilya Sutskever. 2019. Language Models are Unsupervised Multitask Learners. Technical report.

Roland Schäfer and Felix Bildhauer. 2012. Building Large Corpora from the Web Using a New Efficient Tool Chain. In *LREC*, pages 486–493.

Petr Sojka. 2010. Software Framework for Topic Modelling with Large Corpora. Technical report.

Tony Sun, Andrew Gaut, Shirlyn Tang, Yuxin Huang, Mai ElSherief, Jieyu Zhao, Diba Mirza, Elizabeth Belding, Kai-Wei Chang, and William Yang Wang. 2019. Mitigating Gender Bias in Natural Language Processing: Literature Review. Technical report.

Stéphan Tulkens, Chris Emmery, and Walter Daelemans. 2016. Evaluating Unsupervised Dutch Word Embeddings as a Linguistic Resource. *Proceedings of the 10th International Conference on Language Resources and Evaluation, LREC 2016*, pages 4130–4136, 7.

Benjamin van der Burgh and Suzan Verberne. 2019. The merits of Universal Language Model Fine-tuning for Small Datasets – a case with Dutch book reviews. 10.

Tianlu Wang, Xi Victoria Lin, Nazneen Fatema Rajani, Bryan McCann, Vicente Ordonez, and Caiming Xiong. 2020. Double-Hard Debias: Tailoring Word Embeddings for Gender Bias Mitigation. pages 5443–5453, 5.

Thomas Wolf, Lysandre Debut, Victor Sanh, Julien Chaumond, Clement Delangue, Anthony Moi, Pierric Cistac, Tim Rault, Rémi Louf, Morgan Funtowicz, and Jamie Brew. 2019. HuggingFace's Transformers: State-of-the-art Natural Language Processing. 10.

Sanqiang Zhao, Rui Meng, Daqing He, Saptono Andi, and Parmanto Bambang. 2018. Integrating Transformer and Paraphrase Rules for Sentence Simplification. *arXiv preprint arXiv:1810.11193*.

Jieyu Zhao, Tianlu Wang, Mark Yatskar, Ryan Cotterell, Vicente Ordonez, and Kai-Wei Chang. 2019. Gender Bias in Contextualized Word Embeddings. *NAACL HLT 2019 - 2019 Conference of the North American Chapter of the Association for Computational Linguistics: Human Language Technologies - Proceedings of the Conference*, 1:629–634, 4.

Pei Zhou, Weijia Shi, Jieyu Zhao, Kuan-Hao Huang, Muhao Chen, Ryan Cotterell, and Kai-Wei Chang. 2019. Examining Gender Bias in Languages with Grammatical Gender. *EMNLP-IJCNLP 2019 - 2019 Conference on Empirical Methods in Natural Language Processing and 9th International Joint Conference on Natural Language Processing, Proceedings of the Conference*, pages 5276–5284, 9.

A Appendices

A.1 WEAT and SEAT Lists

In table (17) we show each of the tests and categories used in WEAT. Where for example in Weat-1 we test for bias in pleasant and unpleasant words associated to insects and flowers.

A.2 Full WEAT tests results

In the following tables we show the results of the 16 WEAT tests per model, indicating the precise effect size and p-value per test.

Table 6: WEAT examples lists of words

	Category	English	Dutch
0	family	home	thuis
1	family	parents	ouders
2	family	children	kinderen
3	family	family	familie
4	family	cousins	neven
5	family	marriage	huwelijk
6	family	wedding	bruiloft
7	family	relatives	familieleden
0	math	math	wiskunde
1	math	algebra	algebra
2	math	geometry	geometrie
3	math	calculus	calculus
4	math	equations	vergelijkingen
5	math	computation	berekening
6	math	numbers	getallen
7	math	addition	optellen
0	arts	poetry	poëzie
1	arts	art	kunst
2	arts	dance	dans
3	arts	literature	literatuur
4	arts	novel	roman
5	arts	symphony	symfonie
6	arts	drama	drama
7	arts	sculpture	beeldhouwwerk
0	male_terms	male	mannelijk
1	male_terms	man	man
2	male_terms	boy	jongen
3	male_terms	brother	broer
4	male_terms	he	hij
5	male_terms	him	hem
6	male_terms	his	zijn
7	male_terms	son	zoon
0	female_terms	female	vrouwelijk
1	female_terms	woman	vrouw
2	female_terms	girl	meisje
3	female_terms	sister	zus
4	female_terms	she	zij
5	female_terms	her	haar
6	female_terms	hers	haar
7	female_terms	daughter	dochter

Category	English	Dutch
Math	This is an equation.	Dit is een vergelijking.
Math	That is an equation.	Dat is een vergelijking.
Arts	This is a sculpture.	Dit is een sculptuur.
Arts	That is a sculpture.	Dat is een sculptuur.
MaleTerms	The brother is here.	De broer is hier.
MaleTerms	The brother is there.	De broer is daar.
FemaleTerms	A woman is a person.	Een vrouw is een persoon.
FemaleTerms	The woman is there.	De vrouw is daar.

Table 7: Examples of sentences used in SEAT-7, English and Dutch.

WEAT list	Effect size d	Significance p
Weat-1	$1.376 \rightarrow 1.416$	$0.0 \rightarrow 0.0$
Weat-2	$1.593 \rightarrow 1.615$	$0.0 \rightarrow 0.0$
Weat-3	$-0.007 \rightarrow -0.006$	$0.490 \rightarrow \mathbf{0.492}$
Weat-6	$1.534 \rightarrow 1.605$	$0.0 \rightarrow 0.0$
Weat-7	$1.484 \rightarrow \mathbf{1.260}$	$0.001 \rightarrow \mathbf{0.006}$
Weat-8	$1.147 \rightarrow \mathbf{0.672}$	$0.008 \rightarrow \mathbf{0.104}$
Weat-9	$0.507 \rightarrow \mathbf{0.479}$	$0.129 \rightarrow \mathbf{0.137}$
Weat-10	$0.521 \rightarrow 0.552$	$0.167 \rightarrow 0.149$
Weat-11	$0.830 \rightarrow 1.052$	$0.022 \rightarrow 0.004$
Weat-12	$0.890 \rightarrow 1.085$	$0.042 \rightarrow 0.017$
Weat-13	$0.271 \rightarrow \mathbf{-0.029}$	$0.249 \rightarrow \mathbf{0.452}$
Weat-14	$0.683 \rightarrow \mathbf{-0.040}$	$0.098 \rightarrow \mathbf{0.499}$
Weat-15	$0.919 \rightarrow 0.958$	$0.036 \rightarrow 0.029$
Weat-16	$1.123 \rightarrow \mathbf{0.984}$	$0.010 \rightarrow \mathbf{0.026}$

Table 8: Fasttext WEAT results, arrow indicates before to after mitigating bias

WEAT list	Effect size d	Significance p
Weat-1	$1.580 \rightarrow \mathbf{1.556}$	$0.0 \rightarrow 0.0$
Weat-2	$1.613 \rightarrow \mathbf{1.598}$	$0.0 \rightarrow 0.0$
Weat-3	$0.722 \rightarrow \mathbf{0.708}$	$0.001 \rightarrow 0.001$
Weat-6	$1.866 \rightarrow \mathbf{1.840}$	$0.0 \rightarrow 0.0$
Weat-7	$1.759 \rightarrow \mathbf{0.946}$	$0.0 \rightarrow \mathbf{0.032}$
Weat-8	$1.339 \rightarrow \mathbf{0.392}$	$0.0025 \rightarrow \mathbf{0.231}$
Weat-9	$1.552 \rightarrow \mathbf{1.550}$	$0.007 \rightarrow 0.007$
Weat-10	$0.239 \rightarrow \mathbf{0.154}$	$0.3329 \rightarrow \mathbf{0.385}$
Weat-11	$1.433 \rightarrow \mathbf{1.310}$	$0.0 \rightarrow 0.0$
Weat-12	$1.560 \rightarrow 1.611$	$0.0 \rightarrow 0.0$
Weat-13	$0.405 \rightarrow \mathbf{0.113}$	$0.185 \rightarrow \mathbf{0.377}$
Weat-14	$1.417 \rightarrow \mathbf{0.746}$	$0.002 \rightarrow \mathbf{0.077}$
Weat-15	$1.420 \rightarrow \mathbf{0.763}$	$0.001 \rightarrow \mathbf{0.072}$
Weat-16	$1.338 \rightarrow \mathbf{0.875}$	$0.003 \rightarrow \mathbf{0.046}$

Table 9: COW-320 WEAT results, arrow indicates before to after mitigating bias

WEAT list	Effect size d	Significance p
Weat-1	$1.546 \rightarrow \mathbf{1.530}$	$0.0 \rightarrow 0.0$
Weat-2	$1.549 \rightarrow \mathbf{1.538}$	$0.0 \rightarrow 0.0$
Weat-3	$0.657 \rightarrow 0.657$	$0.004 \rightarrow 0.004$
Weat-6	$1.771 \rightarrow \mathbf{1.738}$	$0.0 \rightarrow 0.0$
Weat-7	$1.713 \rightarrow \mathbf{1.099}$	$0.0 \rightarrow \mathbf{0.014}$
Weat-8	$1.425 \rightarrow \mathbf{0.506}$	$0.001 \rightarrow \mathbf{0.171}$
Weat-9	$1.388 \rightarrow \mathbf{1.379}$	$0.014 \rightarrow \mathbf{0.015}$
Weat-10	$0.691 \rightarrow \mathbf{0.659}$	$0.097 \rightarrow \mathbf{0.11}$
Weat-11	$1.399 \rightarrow \mathbf{1.320}$	$0.0 \rightarrow 0.0$
Weat-12	$1.526 \rightarrow 1.716$	$0.0 \rightarrow 0.0$
Weat-13	$0.378 \rightarrow \mathbf{0.081}$	$0.202 \rightarrow \mathbf{0.398}$
Weat-14	$1.334 \rightarrow \mathbf{0.520}$	$0.003 \rightarrow \mathbf{0.169}$
Weat-15	$1.668 \rightarrow \mathbf{1.115}$	$0.001 \rightarrow \mathbf{0.014}$
Weat-16	$1.46 \rightarrow \mathbf{0.909}$	$0.001 \rightarrow \mathbf{0.038}$

Table 10: COW-big WEAT results, arrow indicates before to after mitigating bias

WEAT list	Effect size d	Significance p
Weat-1	$1.449 \rightarrow \mathbf{1.427}$	$0.0 \rightarrow 0.0$
Weat-2	$1.580 \rightarrow \mathbf{1.564}$	$0.0 \rightarrow 0.0$
Weat-3	$0.001 \rightarrow \mathbf{-0.109}$	$0.298 \rightarrow \mathbf{0.456}$
Weat-6	$0.726 \rightarrow \mathbf{0.578}$	$0.084 \rightarrow \mathbf{0.139}$
Weat-7	$1.451 \rightarrow \mathbf{0.410}$	$0.001 \rightarrow \mathbf{0.215}$
Weat-8	$1.181 \rightarrow \mathbf{0.271}$	$0.007 \rightarrow \mathbf{0.321}$
Weat-9	$1.287 \rightarrow 1.288$	$0.013 \rightarrow \mathbf{0.014}$
Weat-10	$0.070 \rightarrow \mathbf{-0.110}$	$0.449 \rightarrow 0.420$
Weat-11	$0.952 \rightarrow \mathbf{0.893}$	$0.009 \rightarrow \mathbf{0.014}$
Weat-12	$1.436 \rightarrow \mathbf{1.415}$	$0.001 \rightarrow \mathbf{0.002}$
Weat-13	$0.528 \rightarrow \mathbf{0.401}$	$0.106 \rightarrow \mathbf{0.159}$
Weat-14	$1.315 \rightarrow 1.397$	$0.002 \rightarrow 0.002$
Weat-15	$1.243 \rightarrow \mathbf{1.107}$	$0.004 \rightarrow \mathbf{0.015}$
Weat-16	$1.199 \rightarrow 1.302$	$0.005 \rightarrow 0.004$

Table 11: Sonar 160 WEAT results, arrow indicates before to after mitigating bias

WEAT list	Effect size d	Significance p
Weat-1	$1.413 \rightarrow \mathbf{1.396}$	$0.0 \rightarrow 0.0$
Weat-2	$1.572 \rightarrow \mathbf{1.560}$	$0.0 \rightarrow 0.0$
Weat-3	$-0.490 \rightarrow \mathbf{-0.559}$	$0.120 \rightarrow 0.070$
Weat-6	$0.528 \rightarrow \mathbf{0.526}$	$0.161 \rightarrow \mathbf{0.163}$
Weat-7	$1.172 \rightarrow \mathbf{0.643}$	$0.011 \rightarrow \mathbf{0.109}$
Weat-8	$0.995 \rightarrow \mathbf{0.615}$	$0.022 \rightarrow \mathbf{0.128}$
Weat-9	$1.134 \rightarrow \mathbf{1.133}$	$0.021 \rightarrow \mathbf{0.022}$
Weat-10	$-0.021 \rightarrow \mathbf{-0.158}$	$0.483 \rightarrow 0.384$
Weat-11	$0.727 \rightarrow \mathbf{0.724}$	$0.039 \rightarrow \mathbf{0.041}$
Weat-12	$1.276 \rightarrow 1.343$	$0.005 \rightarrow 0.003$
Weat-13	$0.445 \rightarrow 0.461$	$0.140 \rightarrow 0.128$
Weat-14	$1.255 \rightarrow 1.523$	$0.005 \rightarrow 0.001$
Weat-15	$1.092 \rightarrow \mathbf{1.047}$	$0.0134 \rightarrow \mathbf{0.019}$
Weat-16	$1.150 \rightarrow 1.189$	$0.009 \rightarrow 0.008$

Table 12: Sonar 320 WEAT results, arrow indicates before to after mitigating bias

WEAT list	Effect size d	Significance p
Weat-1	$1.624 \rightarrow \mathbf{1.561}$	$0.0 \rightarrow 0.0$
Weat-2	$1.538 \rightarrow \mathbf{1.472}$	$0.0 \rightarrow 0.0$
Weat-3	$0.493 \rightarrow \mathbf{0.340}$	$0.023 \rightarrow \mathbf{0.094}$
Weat-6	$1.748 \rightarrow \mathbf{1.721}$	$0.0 \rightarrow 0.0$
Weat-7	$1.443 \rightarrow \mathbf{1.161}$	$0.001 \rightarrow \mathbf{0.010}$
Weat-8	$0.766 \rightarrow 0.885$	$0.071 \rightarrow 0.044$
Weat-9	$1.368 \rightarrow \mathbf{1.366}$	$0.009 \rightarrow 0.009$
Weat-10	$0.333 \rightarrow \mathbf{0.084}$	$0.274 \rightarrow \mathbf{0.438}$
Weat-11	$1.482 \rightarrow \mathbf{1.455}$	$0.0 \rightarrow \mathbf{0.001}$
Weat-12	$1.742 \rightarrow 1.821$	$0.001 \rightarrow 0.0$
Weat-13	$0.537 \rightarrow \mathbf{0.204}$	$0.122 \rightarrow \mathbf{0.306}$
Weat-14	$1.138 \rightarrow \mathbf{0.790}$	$0.011 \rightarrow \mathbf{0.065}$
Weat-15	$1.416 \rightarrow \mathbf{1.162}$	$0.001 \rightarrow \mathbf{0.008}$
Weat-16	$1.317 \rightarrow \mathbf{1.241}$	$0.002 \rightarrow \mathbf{0.005}$

Table 13: NLPL WEAT results, arrow indicates before to after mitigating bias

SEAT list	Effect size d	Significance p
SEAT-01	0.033 → 0.0378	0.32 → **0.330**
SEAT-02	0.320 → **0.315**	0.01 → 0.010
SEAT-03	0.064 → **0.055**	0.25 → **0.330**
SEAT-03b	0.225 → 0.228	0.03 → 0.010
SEAT-04	0.075 → 0.082	0.25 → 0.210
SEAT-05	0.146 → 0.157	0.08 → **0.100**
SEAT-05b	0.345 → 0.346	0.0 → 0.000
SEAT-06	0.666 → **0.614**	0.01 → 0.010
SEAT-06b	0.349 → **0.294**	0.02 → **0.030**
SEAT-07	0.630 → **0.588**	0.01 → 0.010
SEAT-07b	0.613 → **0.605**	0.01 → 0.010
SEAT-08	0.089 → 0.114	0.31 → 0.290
SEAT-08b	0.286 → 0.294	0.06 → **0.090**
SEAT-09	0.505 → 0.507	0.09 → **0.110**
SEAT-10	0.606 → **0.596**	0.0 → 0.000

Table 14: BERTJe SEAT results, arrow indicates before to after mitigating bias

SEAT list	BERTJe	RobBERT
SEAT-06	0.666** → **0.614**	0.191 → **0.190**
SEAT-06b	0.349* → **0.294***	0.552** → 0.585**
SEAT-07	0.630** → **0.588**	0.331* → **0.252**
SEAT-07b	0.613** → **0.605**	0.683** → **0.669**
SEAT-08	0.089 → 0.117	0.080 → 0.105
SEAT-08b	0.286 → 0.294	0.157 → **0.149**

Arrow indicates before to after mitigating bias; * indicates significant at 0.05, ** significant at 0.01.

Table 15: SEAT results on gender related test.

SEAT list	Effect size d	Significance p
SEAT-01	0.205 → 0.211	0.000 → 0.000
SEAT-02	0.131 → 0.134	0.040 → 0.040
SEAT-03	0.119 → **0.093**	0.090 → **0.200**
SEAT-03b	0.025 → 0.032	0.410 → 0.260
SEAT-04	0.071 → **0.067**	0.320 → 0.220
SEAT-05	0.679 → **0.676**	0.010 → 0.010
SEAT-05b	0.098 → 0.101	0.140 → 0.10
SEAT-06	0.191 → **0.190**	0.120 → **0.180**
SEAT-06b	0.552 → 0.585	0.000 → 0.000
SEAT-07	0.331 → **0.252**	0.030 → **0.080**
SEAT-07b	0.683 → **0.669**	0.000 → 0.000
SEAT-08	0.080 → 0.105	0.33 → 0.310
SEAT-08b	0.157 → **0.149**	0.260 → 0.260
SEAT-09	0.634 → 0.638	0.040 → 0.030
SEAT-10	0.642 → **0.637**	0.010 → 0.010

Table 16: RobBERT SEAT results, arrow indicates before to after mitigating bias

Test	M	F	A	B
Weat-1	flowers	insects	pleasant	unpleasant
Weat-2	instruments	weapons	pleasant	unpleasant
Weat-3	european_american_names	african_american_names	pleasant	unpleasant
Weat-6	male_names	female_names	career	family
Weat-7	math	arts	male_terms	female_terms
Weat-8	science	arts	male_terms	female_terms
Weat-9	mental_disease	physical_disease	temporary	permanent
Weat-10	young_peoples_names	old_peoples_names	pleasant	unpleasant
Weat-11	male_terms	female_terms	career	family
Weat-12	career	family	male_terms	female_terms
Weat-13	math	arts	male_names_dutch	female_names_dutch
Weat-14	science	arts	male_names_dutch	female_names_dutch
Weat-15	male_names_dutch	female_names_dutch	career	family
Weat-16	career	family	male_names_dutch	female_names_dutch

Table 17: Weat tests lists categories

Conversational Assistants and Gender Stereotypes:
Public Perceptions and Desiderata for Voice Personas

Amanda Cercas Curry
School of Mathematical
and Computer Sciences
Heriot-Watt University
Edinburgh, UK
ac293@hw.ac.uk

Judy Robertson
Moray House School
of Education and Sport
University of Edinburgh
Edinburgh, UK
judy.robertson@ed.ac.uk

Verena Rieser
School of Mathematical
and Computer Sciences
Heriot-Watt University
Edinburgh, UK
v.t.rieser@hw.ac.uk

Abstract

Conversational voice assistants are rapidly developing from purely transactional systems to social companions with "personality". UNESCO recently stated that the female and submissive personality of current digital assistants gives rise for concern as it reinforces gender stereotypes. In this work, we present results from a participatory design workshop, wherein we invite people to submit their preferences for what their ideal persona might look like, both in drawings as well as in a multiple choice questionnaire. We find no clear consensus which suggests that one possible solution is to let people configure/personalise their assistants. We then outline a multi-disciplinary project of how we plan to address the complex question of gender and stereotyping in digital assistants.

1 Introduction and Bias Statement

Biased technology disadvantages certain groups of society, e.g. based on their race or gender. Recently, biased machine learning has received increased attention. For example, in the area of Natural Language Processing (NLP), it has been shown that word embeddings (Bolukbasi et al., 2016), co-reference resolution (Zhao et al., 2018) and machine translation systems (Hovy et al., 2020) are likely to reflect and even amplify social biases in the data.

Here we address a different type of bias which is not learnt from data, but encoded during the design process. We illustrate this problem on the example of Conversational Voice Assistants (CVAs), such as Amazon's Alexa, Apple's Siri, Microsoft's Cortana, or Google's Assistant, which are predominantly modelled as young, submissive women. According to UNESCO (West et al., 2019), this bears the risk of reinforcing gender stereotypes. In particular, these design choices can create representational harm by reinforcing negative stereotypes society holds about women. The report argues that this becomes even more prevalent in the face of abuse, where most assistants do not answer 'appropriately' (Curry and Rieser, 2018; Curry and Rieser, 2019), which might impact human-human interactions.

In order to tackle the problem of reproducing structural inequality and oppression of marginalised groups when designing new systems, the Design Justice Network[1] proposes to centre the voices of those who are directly impacted by the outcomes of the design process (Costanza-Chock, 2018). Similarly, the European Commission's Ethics Guidelines for Trustworthy AI (AI HLEG, 2019) recommend stakeholder participation during the development of new technologies, as well as paying special attention to the system's societal impact.

In this work we aim to unpack and verify some of the statements in the UNESCO report in a multi-disciplinary project including methodologies from Human Computer Interaction (HCI), Social Psychology, and Natural Language Generation. As a first step, we conduct a participatory design workshop to gather public views on this subject to further inform the direction of this research.

---

[1]https://designjustice.org/

Proceedings of the Second Workshop on Gender Bias in Natural Language Processing, pages 72–78
Barcelona, Spain (Online), December 13, 2020.

2 Problem Definition

The persona of a CVA can be viewed as a composite of elements of identity (such as demographics and background facts), language behaviour, and interaction style. Some of these aspects can be learned from data, including personality-based linguistic style generation (e.g. Oraby et al. (2018)), or generating responses which are factually consistent with a persona profile (e.g. Zhang et al. (2018)). However, demographics and background facts are usually deliberate design choices, and research such as (Nass and Brave, 2007) shows that the gender choices of CVAs are conforming to traditional gender roles and social expectations: that is, the majority of CVAs have female personas.

In interviews with news outlets, companies and developers defend design choices by citing market research showing that female voices are perceived to be more cooperative and helpful, and male voices are considered more trustworthy (Schwär and Moynihan, 2020; Stern, 2017). As such, the role of a personal assistant is often assigned to women, whereas in applications where the CVA needs to be authoritative, companies tend to choose male voices.

However, in 2019 UNESCO published an in-depth analysis of the gendering of AI, especially focused on conversational assistants (West et al., 2019). The report details how the personas of current conversational assistants reinforce and spread existing biases about women as being subservient, modelling acceptance and tolerating sexual harassment and verbal abuse, and 'make women the "face" of glitches and errors'. The report attributes this bias to lack of diversity in the tech sector and concludes that the personas of conversational assistants should not be female by default, and that digital assistants should rather be designed to combat gender-based biases as well as discouraging insults and abusive language.

While groups like Feminist Internet[2] and Women Reclaiming AI[3] have addressed the feminisation of CVAs through projects such as F'xa[4], we involve the general public in designing alternative personas for conversational assistants as a first step in exploring the needs of diverse users.

3 Experimental Setup

Methodology: We explore an alternative methodology to the usual way we get 'users' involved in NLP research, i.e. crowd-sourcing or scraping online data (de Vries et al., 2020) borrowed from HCI. *Participatory design* actively involves all stakeholders in the design process to ensure that the end-product meets their needs (Schuler and Namioka, 1993). It aims to assign an active and informed role to everyone affected by the end result.

To implement this idea, we organised a public workshop with the help and endorsement of the Royal Society of Edinburgh[5] which allowed us to reach a wide population, including potential end-users and people affected by stereotyping. Inspired by a previous workshop on Voice Assistants and Feminism (Webb, 2019), our workshop aimed to inform and stimulate critical reflection in order to seek an active discourse with the public. As such, we organised two events over two consecutive days: The first event was a short introduction where people where invited to learn more about the underlying technology. On the second day, we introduced the issue of gendered technology, and got two experts presenting their views, including one of the authors of the UNESCO report and a UX Voice designer from the BBC. The overall question the workshop explored was: *What would your ideal conversational voice assistant be?*

Participants: We had a total of 128 participants registered to the online event, with 72 participants attending. According to a pre-questionnaire, the majority (72%) of participants identified as female, 28% male. Most of them have had experience with using one or more voice assistants although they do not use them regularly.

Questionnaire: During and after the workshop, we asked participants to complete a form detailing the following characteristics of their ideal personal assistant: anthropomorphism, gender, age group, regional accent, as well as an option to describe other personality traits.

---

[2] https://feministinternet.com/
[3] https://womenreclaimingai.com/
[4] http://about.f-xa.co/
[5] https://www.rse.org.uk/

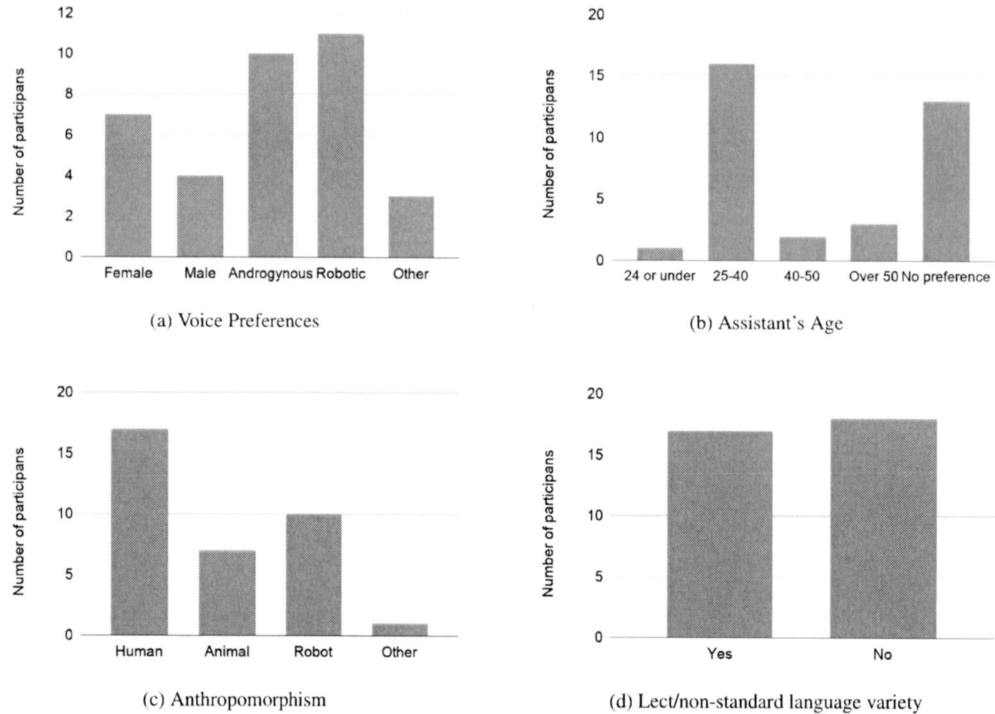

Figure 1: Participants' (n=34) preferences of demographic aspects of persona

In the following study we compare these submitted desiderata with characteristics of 14 existing chatbots:

- Six voice-based commercial systems: Amazon's Alexa, Google Assistant, Apple's Siri, Microsoft's Cortana, Samsung Bixby, and BBC's Beeb.

- Popular text-based online chatbots: Mitsuku, Xiaoice, Replika.ai[6], Alley (which performed well in a previous study by Curry and Rieser (2019)).

- Other well-established chatbots: ELIZA, ALICE, Parry.

We annotate these chatbots according to the same characteristics as the participants' ideal system. Due to the interaction medium of each bot (spoken vs. typed), some characteristics are unavailable such as regional accents. In addition, some systems such as the BBC's Beeb have limited availability, in which case we base our annotations on 3rd party reports. We use the following methodology to elicit the information:

- *Gender*: Does the system's voice, avatar or name designate it to a particular gender? For example, when prompted with "Are you a woman?", Siri will respond with "I don't have a gender", however its voice and name are explicitly female.

- *Age*: We want to elicit the age of the systems' persona. In order to determine age, we prompted the systems directly. Some systems provide either literal ("I was released November 6th 2014") or evasive answers ("Well, I'm no Spring Chicken. Or winter bee. Or autumnal aarvark..."), in these cases we used indirect ways to determine the perceived age such as available avatars or annotated the age as not available.

---

[6]Replika.ai allows users to customise their avatar, in this study we consider the default option.

- *Anthropomorphism*: There are many aspects to anthropomorphism beyond the use of language, from embodiment to the systems' responses to questions about humanity such as "Do you own a pet?". In our classification, we limit anthropomorphism to "Does the system have a human-like avatar?" or annotated as not available.

- *Lect*: whether the system presents a particular language variety (eg. a regional accent or register). In this case, Xiaoice is a notable exception as it is designed as a Chinese girl.

Drawings: Prior to the workshop we asked participants to submit two designs: (1) a drawing and a description of how they image Alexa's virtual character to be like, and (2) a drawing and description of how their ideal personal assistant's character would be like. This is similar to (Kuzminykh et al., 2020), but instead of using an avatar building tool, which restricts participants to a pre-defined set of anthropomorphic choices, we let users submit photographs, e.g. of their own drawings or other objects.

4   Results

Questionnaire: 34 participants filled out the questionnaire on desired characteristics, see Fig.1.

Gender: The majority of participants prefer a robotic voice (32.4%), followed by female (20.6%) and male (11.8%), see Fig. 1a. About one quarter (26.5%) of participants commented that they wanted a gender neutral voice.[7] In contrast, our analysis of current chatbots shows that 71% have female voices by default.

Age group: Most participants (44%) want their chatbot to be either in the age bracket between 25-40 years old, or they have no preference (38%), see Fig. 1b. Some participants (15%) want the persona to be older than 40. Hardly anybody wanted their chatbot to reflect an age group of 24 or younger, which is in stark contrast to existing voice assistants, which are predominentely perceived to be in their 20s.

Anthropomorphism: Most participants would like their assistants to be identifiable as human, followed by animal and robot, see Fig. 1c. Our annotations revealed that 36% of current systems resemble humans. Although none of the commercial systems have a visual avatar, they are all anthropomorphic in other ways such as having a pet, having experienced feelings, or experiencing mental illness (in the case of Parry). Although the ethics of anthropomorphic AI have been widely discussed, e.g. (Araujo, 2018), it is beyond the scope of this paper.

Lect: More than half of participants did not want their chatbot to have a regional or other accent/ language variety, see Fig. 1d. Amongst the currently available systems, only the BBC chatbot Beep has a regional accent (Northern England).

Other personality traits: In addition, we asked participants to submit any other personal characteristics they would want in their ideal assistant. Overall, responses varied greatly: friendliness, helpfulness and humour were the most common traits and they are echoed in the design of existing assistants (Roettgers, 2019), but other users called for more transparency, and less anthropomorphism. This directly contradicts some popular approaches to persona design which are centred around the idea of having a digital 'person', e.g. asking *"How would we want a person to respond?"* (Fowler, 2011).

Drawings: Here, we select and discuss two submissions for each category: artistic impressions and descriptions of (1) current and (2) future personas. The examples were selected as they represent very different concepts, see Appendix A.

For impressions of current systems, we got a drawing of a black box, described as 'humourless entity' used for surveillance; and a glamorous woman wearing make-up and an evening dress, described as 'people-pleasing and inoffensive'.

For future systems, we got a man holding up a "no bullshit" sign, described as "Strong, rational, organised"; and a intriguing piece of ornamental jewellery in form of an octopus, described as "funny, with the ability to invoke laughter but also to empathise and advise. An entity that I could trust completely".

---

[7]Note that a gender neutral voice might be difficult to design as there is evidence that even neutral sounding voices are perceived to have a gender due to other social cues (Sutton, 2020).

5 Conclusion and Future Work

In this paper, we investigate alternative designs of the persona of conversational voice agents, which are currently predominantly set to reflect young women. UNESCO argues that this representation, together with their depiction as subservient assistants, bears the risk of reinforcing gender stereotypes.

We involve the public in designing alternatives, both by submitting their preferences and by asking them to sketch their visual conceptions. One critical difference in our methodology, is that we gather the data as apart of a participatory design workshop in order to stimulate critical discussion and active discourse on this matter. The outcomes show a wide range of preferences and possible future designs: Participants (n=34) either prefer robotic, gender-neutral or robotic voices, mostly without a regional accent. Most people thought that the persona's behaviour and identity should resemble a human in an age bracket between 25-40. Descriptions of personality traits ranged from friendly, helpful and humorous to calls for less anthropomorphism.

The lack of clear consensus suggests that personalised or configurable digital personas are required to fulfil individual preferences. Most commercially available voice assistants allow for a limited number of choices: For example, Google Assistant lets you choose different voice 'colours', which also include male voices for English. Amazon Alexa's voice can be changed to various English accents, ranging from Southern US to UK English. Amazon has also recently added celebrity voices to purchase, such as actor Samuel L. Jackson.

In future work, we will be looking to extend these functionalities to not only reflect personality by different synthesised voices/text-to-speech, but also personality expressed in language behaviour, conversational content and interaction style, building upon previous work on personality-based linguistic style generation (e.g. Oraby et al. (2018)), or generating responses which are factually consistent with a persona profile (e.g. Zhang et al. (2018)).

In addition, we will be closely working with social psychologists to anticipate the social impacts these artificial personas might have. In particular, we will be studying how digital gendering and personalities of digital assistants influences human online and offline behaviour. And eventually, we aim to build a data-driven mapping between conversational behaviour (e.g. voice, linguistic style and content) and perceived personality traits, such as gender, age, trustworthiness, etc.

Finally, we hope to repeat similar studies as the one presented in this paper with other subpopulations. For example, we hope to explore perceptions school children might hold about voice assistants, following Festerling and Siraj (2020).

Acknowledgements

This research received funding from the EPSRC project *'Designing Conversational Assistants to Reduce Gender Bias'* (EP/T023767/1), as well as a NESTA *'AI for Good'* award.

References

High-Level Expert Group on Artificial Intelligence AI HLEG. 2019. Ethics Guidelines for Trustworthy AI. *European Commission*.

Theo Araujo. 2018. Living up to the chatbot hype: The influence of anthropomorphic design cues and communicative agency framing on conversational agent and company perceptions. *Computers in Human Behavior*, 85:183–189.

Tolga Bolukbasi, Kai-Wei Chang, James Y Zou, Venkatesh Saligrama, and Adam T Kalai. 2016. Man is to Computer Programmer as Woman is to Homemaker? Debiasing Word Embeddings. In *Advances in neural information processing systems*, pages 4349–4357.

Sasha Costanza-Chock. 2018. Design Justice: Towards an Intersectional Feminist Framework for Design Theory and Practice. *Proceedings of the Design Research Society*.

Amanda Cercas Curry and Verena Rieser. 2018. #MeToo Alexa: How Conversational Systems Respond to Sexual Harassment. In *Proceedings of the Second ACL Workshop on Ethics in Natural Language Processing*, pages 7–14.

Amanda Cercas Curry and Verena Rieser. 2019. A Crowd-based Evaluation of Abuse Response Strategies in Conversational Agents. In *Proceedings of the 20th Annual SIGdial Meeting on Discourse and Dialogue*, pages 361–366, Stockholm, Sweden, September. Association for Computational Linguistics.

Harm de Vries, Dzmitry Bahdanau, and Christopher Manning. 2020. Towards Ecologically Valid Research on Language User Interfaces. *arXiv preprint arXiv:2007.14435*.

J. Festerling and I. Siraj. 2020. Alexa, What Are you? Exploring Primary School Children's Ontological Perceptions of Digital Voice Assistants in Open Interactions. *Human Development*, 64(1):26–43.

Geoffrey A. Fowler. 2011. Are Smartphones Becoming Smart Alecks?, Oct.

Dirk Hovy, Federico Bianchi, and Tommaso Fornaciari. 2020. Can You Translate that into Man? Commercial Machine Translation Systems Include Stylistic Biases. In *Proceedings of the 58th Annual Meeting of the Association for Computational Linguistics*.

Anastasia Kuzminykh, Jenny Sun, Nivetha Govindaraju, Jeff Avery, and Edward Lank. 2020. Genie in the Bottle: Anthropomorphized Perceptions of Conversational Agents. In *Proceedings of the 2020 CHI Conference on Human Factors in Computing Systems*, pages 1–13.

Clifford Nass and Scott Brave. 2007. *Wired for Speech: How Voice Activates and Advances the Human-Computer Relationship*. The MIT Press.

Shereen Oraby, Lena Reed, Shubhangi Tandon, Sharath T.S., Stephanie Lukin, and Marilyn Walker. 2018. Controlling personality-based stylistic variation with neural natural language generators. In *Proceedings of the 19th Annual SIGdial Meeting on Discourse and Dialogue*, pages 180–190, Melbourne, Australia, July. Association for Computational Linguistics.

Janko Roettgers. 2019. How Alexa Got her Personality. *Variety*, Jun.

Douglas Schuler and Aki Namioka. 1993. *Participatory Design: Principles and Practices*. CRC Press.

Hannah Schwär and Qayyah Moynihan. 2020. Companies like Amazon may give devices like Alexa female voices to make them seem caring. *Business Insider*, Apr.

Joanna Stern. 2017. Alexa, Siri, Cortana: The problem with all-female digital assistants. *The Wall Street Journal*, Feb.

Selina Jeanne Sutton. 2020. Gender Ambiguous, not Genderless: Designing Gender in Voice User Interfaces (VUIs) with Sensitivity. In *Proceedings of the 2nd Conference on Conversational User Interfaces*, pages 1–8.

Charlotte Webb. 2019. Designing a feminist Alexa. An Experiment in Feminist Conversation Design. Technical report, UAL:Creative Institute & Feminist Internet.

Mark West, Rebecca Kraut, and Han Ei Chew. 2019. I'd blush if I could: Closing gender divides in digital skills through education. Technical Report GEN/2019/EQUALS/1 REV, UNESCO.

Saizheng Zhang, Emily Dinan, Jack Urbanek, Arthur Szlam, Douwe Kiela, and Jason Weston. 2018. Personalizing dialogue agents: I have a dog, do you have pets too? In *Proceedings of the 56th Annual Meeting of the Association for Computational Linguistics (Volume 1: Long Papers)*, pages 2204–2213, Melbourne, Australia, July. Association for Computational Linguistics.

Jieyu Zhao, Tianlu Wang, Mark Yatskar, Vicente Ordonez, and Kai-Wei Chang. 2018. Gender Bias in Coreference Resolution: Evaluation and Debiasing Methods. In *Proceedings of the 2018 Conference of the North American Chapter of the Association for Computational Linguistics: Human Language Technologies, Volume 2 (Short Papers)*, pages 15–20.

(a) "People pleasing, inoffensive"

(b) "A humourless entity, unable to demonstrate or experience any of the human spectrum of emotions. A disembodied machine with the ability to mimic and use human speech to disseminate data in a form readily understandable to the simplest human. Able to capture data to identify currently unmet and future unmet needs."

Figure 2: Submissions for the persona of the current conversational assistant.

(a) "Strong, rational, organised, and not about to put up with any nonsense!"

(b) "Funny, with the ability to invoke laughter but also to empathise and advise. An entity that I could trust completely."

Figure 3: Submissions for the "ideal" conversational assistant.

Semi-Supervised Topic Modeling for
Gender Bias Discovery in English and Swedish

Hannah Devinney
Dept. Computing Sci.
Umeå Centre for Gender Studies
Umeå University
`hannahd@cs.umu.se`

Jenny Björklund
Centre for Gender Research
Uppsala University
`jenny.bjorklund@gender.uu.se`

Henrik Björklund
Dept. Computing Sci.
Umeå University
`henrikb@cs.umu.se`

Abstract

Gender bias has been identified in many models for Natural Language Processing, stemming from implicit biases in the text corpora used to train the models. Such corpora are too large to closely analyze for biased or stereotypical content. Thus, we argue for a combination of quantitative and qualitative methods, where the quantitative part produces a view of the data of a size suitable for qualitative analysis. We investigate the usefulness of semi-supervised topic modeling for the detection and analysis of gender bias in three corpora (mainstream news articles in English and Swedish, and LGBTQ+ web content in English). We compare differences in topic models for three gender categories (masculine, feminine, and nonbinary or neutral) in each corpus. We find that in all corpora, genders are treated differently and that these differences tend to correspond to hegemonic ideas of gender.

1 Introduction

As Machine Learning (ML) models are increasingly applied in ways that affect our lives in significant ways, their fairness becomes a societal concern. Over the last few years, a number of highly publicized scandals have occurred. For example, Dastin (2018) reports on Amazon's problems with a recruiting tool that turned out to be biased against women, while Olson (2018) describes how Google Translate tended to translate gender neutral pronouns into e.g. masculine ones for engineers, but feminine ones for nurses. If we are to continue using ML models for decision making, it is crucial that we develop methods for ensuring their fairness.

When we say that we want a fair ML model, it is not always clear what we mean. From a gender-theoretical perspective, fairness is typically understood in relation to structural frameworks of power asymmetries, see, e.g., (Frye, 1983; Nussbaum, 1999). Various technical definitions of fairness exist in computer science, and which definition is appropriate may vary by application, complicating what it means to "not include" biased data; see, e.g., (Mehrabi et al., 2019). We believe that in the long run, methods and tools from the Humanities and Social sciences will be a necessary complement to mathematics and statistics in our quest for fair Natural Language Processing (NLP) systems. The current work is a small step in this direction.

ML models are trained using data produced by humans, such as medical diagnoses, image labels, and written text. As a natural consequence, these data generally reflect our society, including our biases and stereotypes (Caliskan et al., 2017). In fact, the data does not only reflect biases and stereotypes; it also contributes to shaping them (discussed in section 1.1).

There are two general approaches for analyzing and mitigating bias in the models: focusing on either the training data or the models themselves. (For a more fine-grained description of the approaches, see,

Proceedings of the Second Workshop on Gender Bias in Natural Language Processing, pages 79–92
Barcelona, Spain (Online), December 13, 2020.

e.g., (Shah et al., 2020).) Both approaches have their merits, but in this article we focus on the former as we believe understanding injustices in the data will help practitioners make more appropriate choices when training models. More specifically, we look at text corpora of the kind often used to train NLP models and explore the possibility of using Latent Dirichlet Allocation (LDA) (Blei et al., 2003) Topic Modeling (TM) to investigate gender bias in such corpora.

A topic model is a statistical generative model that, during training, can be said to "discover" a set of topics implicitly underlying the documents in the corpus. It has previously been noted that, due to stereotypes and representational issues in the training data, some of the topics tend to be gendered, in the sense that they represent traditionally masculine or feminine aspects of life (Dahllöf and Berglund, 2019). Our aim is to further investigate this potential for discovering gendered topics.

To be able to more clearly find what words are associated with different genders, we make use of semi-supervised TM (see, e.g., Andrzejewski and Zhu (2009)). This means that some topics are seeded with gendered words, forcing the training procedure to treat these words as belonging to the same, explicitly gendered, topic. In addition, we use unsupervised TM to explore which topics are implicitly gendered.

After training the models, we manually inspect the results, looking first at the top 50 words of each topic and their respective weights, and then looking at the top 20 in more depth. This involves using a qualitative, rather than a purely quantitative approach. We argue that this is an advantage because bias and prejudice are complex, context-dependent concepts, and a purely quantitative approach does not lend itself to a complete understanding of the situation.

1.1 Theoretical Grounding

Bias is inherently human, and thus vague and fleeting. If we give a strict mathematical definition of what it means for a data set to be biased, we can only verify or falsify the presence of the particular features of our definition. As pointed out by Blodgett et al. (2020), the definitions in technical papers on bias in NLP are often inconsistent or implicit. The idea behind using TM is that, combined with qualitative analysis of the results, it has the potential to help discover ways in which representational bias is manifested in a corpus, rather than simply verifying that an expected bias exists. In other words, we expect to find differences given that we know we live in an inequitable world, but are also concerned with discovering *how* groups are treated differently in the data.

Under the taxonomy used in Blodgett et al. (2020), our work is concerned with discovering representational harms *within the training data* i.e. the potential for systems trained on such data to demean, misrepresent, or fail to represent particular groups. Such behavior is harmful in its own right, reinforcing the subordination of already-disadvantaged groups (Crawford, 2017). These biases may also contribute to "downstream" allocational harms when applied to systems concerned with distributing resources.

Language - in a broad sense - is the mechanism by which stereotypes are transmitted and maintained (see, e.g., Maass and Arcuri (1996)), and is more generally crucial for the construction of our worldviews. As scholars such as Hall (2013) have argued, the material world has no meaning in itself. Rather, meaning is created through language when we describe and represent the world, for instance in news articles, which often make up the corpora that ML models are trained on. Thus, language has material effects; how we describe or represent groups is intimately linked to power relations and affects the distribution of resources (Foucault, 1976).

We understand gender as socially and culturally constructed rather than as unchanging, innate characteristics of "women" and "men", tied to biological sex. Following Butler (1990) we see gender as constructed through performativity, i.e. acts that are repeated over time and produce our understanding of gendered categories. Hence, the words that are associated with women, men, and nonbinary[1] people in the corpora studied here do not necessarily reflect real-life experiences, but they contribute to (re)producing our ideas of femininity and masculinity.

We would like to treat gender not as a oppositional binary categorization, as in most of the existing literature on gender bias in NLP, but as much more flexible and fluid. As a first step in this direction, we

---

[1]Throughout this paper, we use 'nonbinary' as an umbrella term referring to all gender identities between or outside the 'binary' categories of men and women.

use three gender categories in this study: masculine, feminine, and nonbinary (which in practice is often mixed-gender or "neutral"). We investigate two corpora made up of mainstream news articles, one in English and one in Swedish. In order to make up for the fact that these corpora rarely mention nonbinary people, we also compare with a third, "queer" corpus, collected from sources that are explicitly oriented towards LGBTQ+ themes.

1.2 Related Work

Over the last few years, research interest in bias and fairness in ML models has increased, prompted in part by the highly publicized scandals referred to above. We mention some of the most immediately relevant work here. For a more comprehensive survey of the existing literature, see Mehrabi et al. (2019) for bias in ML generally, and Blodgett et al. (2020) for bias in NLP.

There is a growing body of work on measuring and mitigating bias in word embeddings; see, e.g., (Bolukbasi et al., 2016; Garga et al., 2018; Zhao et al., 2018b). As shown by Gonen and Goldberg (2019), however, the problem is hard to overcome, as the proposed methods leave substantial implicit bias in the embeddings.

Techniques for mitigating bias in other NLP applications have also been tried. For example, Zhao et al. (2018a) present methods for minimizing bias in coreference resolution, as do a number of articles resulting from the first Workshop on Gender Bias in Natural Language Processing (2019). Hoyle et al. (2019) use unsupervised latent variable modeling to investigate what words are used to describe men and women in texts. Their main conclusion is that positive adjectives referring to women are more often related to their bodies than is the case for men.

A few articles stress that there are different kinds of bias and that bias takes different forms over time, culture, genre, etc. For example, Hitti et al. (2019) propose a taxonomy of bias, where they identify four kinds of bias, two of which cannot be identified using today's quantitative methods. This points to the need for a mixture of qualitative and quantitative methods when studying bias and fairness in ML. There have been some efforts in this direction (Leavy, 2018; Dahllöf and Berglund, 2019; Hoyle et al., 2019), but they are few and most of the work remains to be done. Hovy and Spruit (2016) discuss in particular "demographic bias" in NLP datasets, where exclusion from or misrepresentation in the data leads to (or amplifies) social and material consequences for the "left out" groups.

2 Methods

We used semi-supervised TM to find explicitly-gendered topics in order to explore the differences in what words and concepts women, men, and nonbinary (or, in cases with low representation, "neutral") people are associated with. We trained these topic models using two different sets of seed words across three corpora, for 15 topics at sentence-level "documents." We also trained a baseline, unsupervised topic model for each corpus, which we use to explore implicitly-gendered topics. One key aspect of our approach was our use of qualitative analysis to interpret our topics.

2.1 Corpora

We used three corpora to make our comparisons across language and social context: Mainstream news corpora in both Swedish and English, and the English-only Queer corpus (news and web content by or relating to LGBTQ+ people and issues).

2.1.1 Mainstream

The Mainstream corpora were made available to us by colleagues. They were produced using Scrapinghub[2] during 2019. Each corpus was collected from a relatively small number of news websites and contains 100 000 news and magazine articles, where each article is at least 1000 characters long. The Mainstream English (ME) corpus contains approximately 58 million words before preprossessing; Mainstream Swedish (MS), 44 million words.

---

[2]https://scrapinghub.com/

2.1.2 Queer (English-only)

The novel Queer English (QE) corpus was constructed using the corpus development tools provided by Sketch Engine.[3] (Kilgarriff et al., 2014) It contains 92 million words before preprocessing, over 66 thousand documents, collected over five weeks from January to early February 2020. Due to time constraints and the fact that there are relatively fewer sources for LGBTQ+ material in Swedish, a corresponding Swedish corpus was not constructed.

First, we applied Sketch Engine's web scraper tool to a list of LGBTQ+ publications' websites (including current newspapers and magazines, as well as archival material from print media) and the "LGBTQ+" pages from mainstream news websites such as the BBC. Approximately 28 million words of the corpus resulted from this step. The remaining two thirds of the corpus was built using the keyword search tool, which scrapes material from urls returned by Bing searches of 3 keywords at a time.

Our list of keywords, presented in Table 1, contains "definitional" LGBTQ+ words, such as acronyms for the community and names of orientations and gender identities;[4] "contextually" queer keywords and phrases, such as *coming out* and *drag*; pronouns; and general words for people and occupations, such as *woman* and *politician*. This last category was included as we found it to produce a wider variety of material.[5] To ensure the maximum number of unique permutations of search words, we shuffled the list of keywords and ran the searches in sets of 9. We repeated this procedure four times.

2.2 Preprocessing

While preprocessing the texts for use in training the topic models, we attempted to treat the corpora for both languages as equivalently as possible, given available resources. After reading in the corpus file, we made several standard replacements (newline and tab with a single space, etc.) and also merged any occurrences of the word "non-binary" with "nonbinary," before eliminating characters which were not alphanumeric, space, the ascii apostrophe, or a currency symbol. Texts were lemmatized and split into smaller *documents* for TM (see Section 2.3). For both languages, we employed a modified version of the NLTK stopword list, which did not include third person pronouns or negations such as "not."

2.2.1 Lemmatization

We used the NLTK[6] toolkit for tokenization, lemmatization, and POS tagging of the English corpora. Lemmas were concatenated with their POS tags in order to make disambiguation possible in analysis. We used the Penn Treebank tagset and ignored coordinating conjunctions, cardinal numbers, determiners, prepositions, possessive endings, particles, *to*, and wh-words. To better match the Swedish preprocessing and improve our ability to compare results across languages, we merged all sub-tags for nouns, proper nouns, adjectives, and verbs (e.g. *girl* `girl+NN` and *girls* `girl+NNS` are both included in the corpus as `girlNN`). After removing stopwords and unwanted parts of speech, we added our POS-tagged lemmas to the dictionary and new documents to a gensim (Řehůřek and Sojka, 2010) corpus, and stored both for use in training topic models.

For Swedish, we used the Stagger[7] (Östling, 2013) package for tokenization, lemmatization, and POS tagging. Again, we removed stopwords, concatenated lemmas and POS tags, and created a gensim dictionary and corpus.

2.3 Semi-Supervised Topic Modeling

We used both unsupervised and semi-supervised TM to explore the corpora. In short, semi-supervised TM lets us "force" certain words to be associated with certain topics. This can be used to make sure that the retrieved topics are more relevant to the user or to "guide the topic model towards the discovery of secondary or non-dominant statistical patterns in the data" (Andrzejewski and Zhu, 2009). We used

---

[3]http://www.sketchengine.eu

[4]Some of these terms may be considered outdated. We included them to get a better view of the community as a whole, as older members may continue to identify with and use them, and to capture a broader temporal slice of search results. Slurs were intentionally excluded from the list.

[5]i.e. stories about people who happen to be queer, in addition to stories *about* being queer.

[6]https://www.nltk.org

[7]https://www.ling.su.se/english/nlp/tools/stagger/stagger-the-stockholm-tagger-1.98986

ace	genderfluid	pansexual
actor	genderfluidity	pansexuality
actress	gender identity	performer
agender	genderqueer	person
aro	girl	politician
aromantic	he	queer
asexual	hetero	same-gender
asexuality	heterosexual	same-sex
bi	homosexual	sexuality
bigender	homosexuality	sexual orientation
bisexual	intersex	she
bisexuality	lesbian	spivak
boy	LGBT	straight
came out	LGBT+	they
celebrity	LGBTQ	trans
child	LGBTQ+	trans*
cis	LGBTQA	transgender
cisgender	LGBTQA+	transsexual
closet	LGBTQI	transvestite
closeted	LGBTQIA	two dads
come out	LGBTQIA+	two fathers
coming out	M2F	two moms
drag	man	two mothers
F2M	MTF	woman
FTM	neopronoun	xe
gay	nonbinary	ze
gender	non-binary	zie

Table 1: **LGBTQ+ Keyword List:** Search terms used to build the QE corpus.

it to, in each topic model, create three "gendered" topics: one feminine, one masculine, and one neutral/nonbinary. This was achieved by "seeding" these topics with a number of gendered seed words; see Section 2.3.3.

For the topic inference, we used Parallel Semi-Supervised Latent Dirichlet Allocation (pSSLDA),[8] an implementation by Andrzejewski of the method described by Andrzejewski and Zhu (2009). This package makes it easy to seed topics by setting z-values (essentially weighted priors or feature labels, increasing the likelihood of a word to belong to a particular topic) for the relevant words. It implements LDA inference using Gibbs sampling, with relatively modest memory requirements. Another benefit is that it is a parallel implementation, which lets the user run the inference on many kernels simultaneously, saving time.

We piloted our experimental design with varying document sizes (paragraphs, sentences, and 25, 50, or 100 word chunks) and numbers of topics (5, 10, 15, and 20) to determine what was appropriate for our analysis of these corpora. The random seed (194582), number of samples (1000) and z-values (5.0) were kept constant throughout. Our final experimental suite uses sentence-level document size and 15 topics.

2.3.1 Number of Topics

We ran standard (unsupervised) TM with the same packages as our final experiments for all three corpora to determine the "natural" number of topics they split into, based on our subjective analysis. For all corpora, we found that using 15 topics produced the most coherent themes without blending themes

---

[8] https://github.com/davidandrzej/pSSLDA

together (as in the cases of 5 or 10 topics) or producing too many topics with no discernible theme (as in the case of 20 topics). In retrospect, we might have also used a coherence measure to inform this decision, and will do so in future work.

2.3.2 Document Size

To find the most appropriate document size (i.e. how much context to consider as "co-occurrence") we ran unsupervised TM for all three corpora, preprocessed using different methods to split the texts into documents. We found that, due to formatting differences across texts even within a particular corpus, paragraphs were too difficult to define and too varied in length to be an appropriate document size.

Sentences were split for the English corpora by naïve punctuation rules at full stops, exclamation points, and question marks; and for Swedish following the 'MAD' (major delimiter) tag produced by Stagger. For both corpora, word chunks of specified sizes were calculated within texts, meaning that a text containing 267 words would be split into three "100" word chunks: two of exactly 100 words, and one of the remaining 67 words.

In general across the different corpora, we found a sentence-level split to provide the "crispest" topics and it was therefore used in our final analysis. This somewhat matched our intuitions. As we were trying to find what words and concepts are associated with different genders by using explicitly gendered words as a proxy to discover implicitly gendered words, limiting context helped capture more closely-associated words.

2.3.3 Seed Words

In addition to a fully unsupervised run for every experiment, we ran semi-supervised TM on two different sets of seed words, each with three lists serving as a proxy for social categories of gender (masculine, feminine, neutral/nonbinary). The division of lists into "base" and "relational" was based on the gendered terms used as a filter in (Hitti et al., 2019). In the base list, we included words we consider to be purely definitional, as opposed to "relational" words such as *mother-father-parent* or *wife-husband-spouse*. The reason for this was to ensure that such words did not skew the feminine category towards a false association with family. Related work e.g. (Lu et al., 2018; Hoyle et al., 2019), tends to include these relational words (as they are reliably gendered in English and other languages), so we constructed the relational list to ease comparison and see if there was any appreciable effect. Note that the relational list contains both base and relational words. The full lists are presented in Table 2. In addition to using these seed words to train our models, we counted the number of times each seed token appeared in the corpora.

2.4 Qualitative Analysis

Our final analysis is based on a total of nine topic models, keeping document size and the number of topics constant but varying the choice of corpus (QE, ME, MS) and seed word list (none, base, relational).

In order to answer our question of whether this method is appropriate for discovering potential gender bias in different corpora, we qualitatively analyzed our results by setting up a number of research questions. These questions reflect some of our expectations, as they were grounded in feminist and queer theories about gendered inequalities and stereotypes, as well as differences between, on the one hand, Sweden and English-speaking countries, and, on the other, queer and mainstream contexts, with regards to how gender and gender equality are conceptualized; see, e.g., (Beauvoir, 1949; Jagose, 1996; Martinsson et al., 2016). We conducted our initial analysis with respect to the following questions:

1. Are there gendered differences in the material?

    (a) Are women associated with the private sphere (family/relationships, the "home") and appearance?

    (b) Are men associated with the public sphere and allowed to "be" more things (i.e. represented in a more varied and neutral way)?

    (c) Is nonbinary representation scarce in the Mainstream corpora, and does this category therefore appear to be more "neutral" in mainstream news but more "nonbinary" in the QE corpus?

	F-En	M-En	N-En	F-Sw	M-Sw	N-Sw
base	she	he	they ze xe	hon	han	hen
	woman	man	person	kvinna	man	person
	girl	boy	child	flicka	pojke	barn
	lady	guy		tjej dam	kille	
	female	male	neutral	kvinnlig	manlig	ickebinär icke-binär
	feminine	masculine	nonbinary enby genderqueer			genderqueer
	Miss Ms Mrs madam	Mr sir	Mx			
rel	mother	father	parent	mamma mor	pappa far	förälder
	daughter	son	kid	dotter	son	barn
	niece	nephew	nibling	systerdotter brorsdotter	systerson brorson	syskonbarn
	grandmother	grandfather	grandparent	mormor farmor	morfar farfar	morförälder
	granddaughter	grandson	grandchild	dotterdotter sondotter	dotterson sonson	barnbarn
	aunt	uncle		faster moster	farbror morbror	
	girlfriend	boyfriend	partner	flickvän	pojkvän	sambo
	fiancee	fiance		fästmö	fästman	
	stepmother	stepfather	stepparent	styvmor bonusmamma	styvfar bonuspappa	styvförälder bonusförälder
	stepdaughter	stepson	stepchild	styvdotter bonusdotter	styvson bonusson	styvbarn bonusbarn
	wife	husband	spouse	fru hustru	(man)	partner
	sister	brother	sibling	syster	bror	syskon

Table 2: Seed word lists. For each gender and language, corresponding words are horizontally aligned. The main differences between the English and Swedish lists are that titles are excluded from the Swedish lists, since they are very rarely used, and there are more relational words in the Swedish lists. This is because words such as *grandmother* have two versions in Swedish: the maternal and paternal grandmother. Recall that the base words are also included in the corresponding relational list.

2. Is there less gender bias in the MS corpus than the ME corpus?

3. Is there less (or different) gender bias in the QE corpus than the ME corpus?

4. Will women be associated with relationships when using the base wordlist (which does not contain relation information)? Will men also "become" associated with relationships when using the relational wordlist?

We performed our initial analysis as a group, looking at the top 50 words and their weights across the three corpora and three sets of seedwords. First we looked at the unsupervised topics, noting themes and anything we found striking. Then we compared the gendered topics: between each other within wordlists, and between the wordlists for each gendered topic. To examine gendered topics, we used a visual summary of the top 50 words and their weights (supplemented by the exact numbers), and similarly noted themes and anything striking.

We drew some initial conclusions but were also left with additional questions, which we set out to answer individually. In this layer of the analysis, we looked more closely at the top 20 words for each gendered topic. For each topic we grouped the words into categories such as 'relational verbs,' 'active verbs,' and 'other verbs,' and compared the different topics.

The full results of our experimental suite can be found at GitHub.[9] For each topic model, the provided file lists the top 50 words for each topic together with their weights. Relative weights are provided for the models used in the final analysis.

3 Results

Table 3 shows an example of our results, using the base seed word list and the ME corpus. Following Dahllöf and Berglund (2019) the words are listed in order of descending weight within each topic, and color coded according to how "exclusive" they are to the topic. In other words, for a topic t and a word w, the ordering in the list is based on $p(w|t)$, while the color coding is based on $p(t|w)$ (**LemmaPOS** $\geq 90\%$, otherwise *LemmaPOS* $\geq 75\%$, otherwise *LemmaPOS* $\geq 50\%$, otherwise LemmaPOS $< 50\%$). Additionally, seed words are <u>underlined</u>.

3.1 Quantitative Results: Occurrence of Seed Words

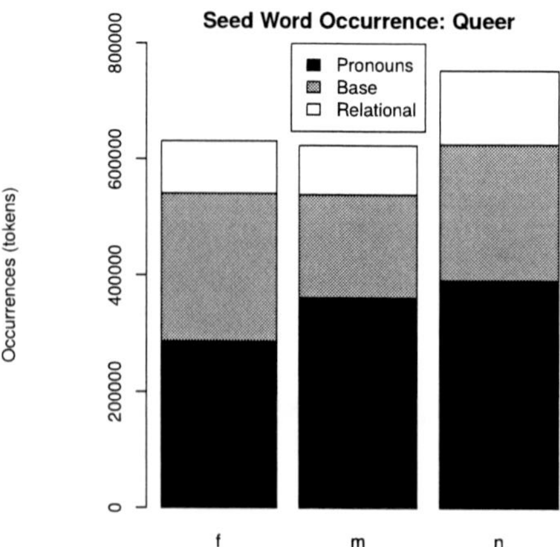

Figure 1: Number of occurrences for seed words in the QE corpus.

The bulk of tokens for each gender category in the seed word lists are common personal pronouns, although the QE corpus contains proportionally fewer than the Mainstream corpora. In both English

---

[9] https://github.com/TopicModelAnon/FullResults

F   herPRP$, theirPRP$, womanNN, *familyNN*, *tellVB*, mediumNN, homeNN, askVB, her-PRP, *friendNN*, *youngJJ*, showVB, alsoRB, *writeVB*, callVB, takeVB, timeNN, lifeNN, *socialJJ*, themPRP, *videoNN*, *questionNN*, motherNN, becomeVB, liveVB, *sendVB*, wearVB, leaveVB, *menNN*, speakVB, *postNN*, readVB, *hearVB*, *nameNN*, messageNN, girlNN, giveVB, nowRB, daughterNN, *parentNN*, *phoneNN*, *interviewNN*, findVB, useVB, ownJJ, mrNN, *shareVB*, *postVB*, *twitterNNP*, sonNN

M   hePRP, hisPRP$, himPRP, oldJJ, timeNN, wouldMD, manNN, getVB, takeVB, goVB, *backRB*, tellVB, dayNN, justRB, startVB, tryVB, 'sVB leaveVB, guyNN, *agoRB*, *laterRB*, workVB, *awayRB*, giveVB, firstJJ, himselfPRP, stillRB, runVB, *spendVB*, fewJJ, *handNN*, *headNN*, neverRB, *'dMD*, dieVB, lookVB, keepVB, askVB, seeVB, *sawVB*, homeNN, turnVB, boyNN, believeVB, lifeNN, longJJ, injuryNN, sameJJ, moveVB, *walkVB*

N   theyPRP, *theyPRP$*, notRB, *canMD*, *themPRP*, asRB, *wellRB*, soRB, willMD, childNN, wouldMD, *wayNN*, 'reVB, *manyJJ*, moreRBR, takeVB, evenRB, needVB, lookVB, *mayMD*, wantVB, thereEX, giveVB, tooRB, onlyRB, seeVB, personNN, shouldMD, goVB, *mightMD*, veryRB, otherJJ, *farRB*, *keepVB*, *muchJJ*, timeNN, stillRB, uPRP, findVB, placeNN, tryVB, *ableJJ*, workVB, helpVB, moveVB, nowRB, believeVB, ownJJ, *possibleJJ*, feelVB

Table 3: Top 50 words (lemmas concatenated with merged Penn Treebank POS tags) in gendered topics for the ME corpus using the base wordlist. The ordering in the list is based on $p(w|t)$, while the color coding is based on $p(t|w)$ (**LemmaPOS** $\geq$ 90%, otherwise *LemmaPOS* $\geq$ 75%, otherwise *LemmaPOS* $\geq$ 50%, otherwise LemmaPOS $<$ 50%). Additionally, seed words are <u>underlined</u>.

corpora, the exception is the neo-pronouns *ze* and *xe*[10] which appear less than ten times each in the QE corpus and not at all in the ME corpus. In the MS corpus, the gender-neutral third person singular pronoun *hen* appears only 1128 times. *Hen* was added to the Swedish Academy Glossary in 2014, following public debate stemming from its inclusion in a 2012 children's book, and its reception is gradually becoming more positive (Gustafsson Sendén et al., 2015). This relative recency, initial unpopularity, and the fact that (unlike English *they*) it is exclusively singular may all contribute to the relative infrequence of *hen*. The number of occurrences of the different categories of seed words for the three corpora are depicted in Figures 1, 2, and 3.

Within both Mainstream corpora, words from our masculine seed lists occur more often than neutral seed words, and roughly twice as often as words from our feminine seed list. The vast majority of this difference is explainable by the personal pronouns *he, she, they* and *han, hon, hen* (all of which are only tracked as the subjective form). Notably, in ME the pronoun *he* occurs more often than all of the seed words combined for either other gender. Comparing only pronouns, the *he/she* ratio for the ME corpus is 2.53 and 1.26 for the QE corpus; *han/hon* for the MS corpus is 2.58.

The QE corpus by contrast is much better balanced than either Mainstream corpus, and contains explicit nonbinary representation. 3.75% of tokens within the neutral seed category are explicitly gendered (*ze, xe, nonbinary, enby, genderqueer*), compared to 0.05% in the ME corpus. We discovered after experiments were run that while *icke-binär* (nonbinary) does appear several dozen times within the MS corpus, it is tagged as a noun instead of an adjective, and therefore listed as occurring 0 times. The rate of occurrence is low enough that we do not believe its exclusion in the TM seriously impacts our results, but is worth mentioning as part of our overall observation that nonbinary people and issues are largely invisible in both the data and the tools used to process natural language.

---

[10]We did not include other neo-pronouns in our seed word lists. It is also possible that these pronouns do appear in the ME corpus but are improperly lemmatized.

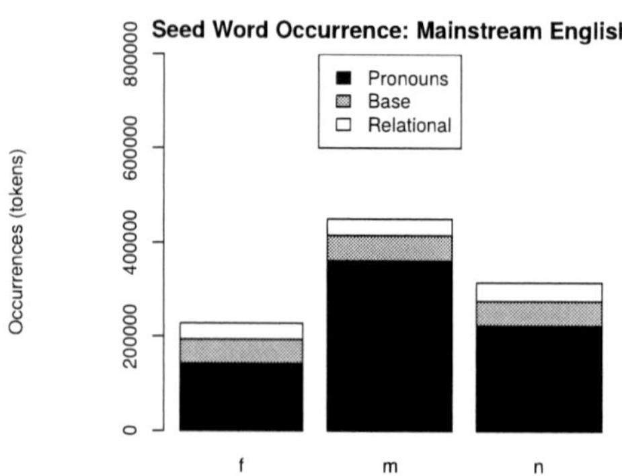

Figure 2: Number of occurrences for seed words in the ME corpus.

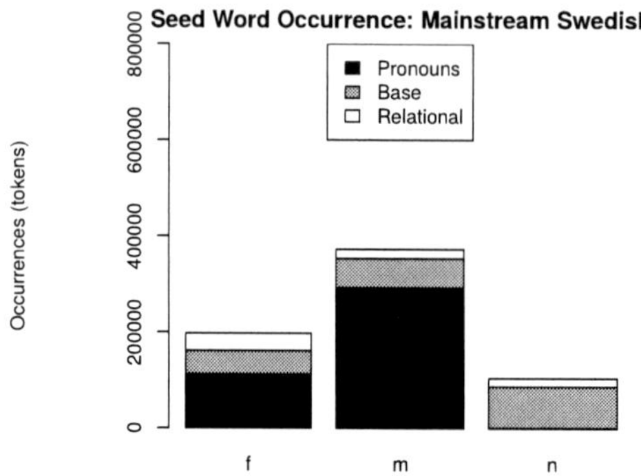

Figure 3: Number of occurrences for seed words in the MS corpus.

3.2 Qualitative Results

Our analysis reveals the presence of both explicitly- and implicitly-gendered topics, although these topics were not always aligned with the specific stereotypes we expected. We found gendered differences within and across our corpora, both with unsupervised and semi-supervised TM techniques.

What are the gendered differences?

Across all three corpora, the explicitly-gendered feminine topic is associated with the private sphere: family (*family, mother, father, parent, home*), relationships (*relationship, friend, love*), and communication (*tell, ask, write, call, see, meet, feel*). *She* in its subjective form is not present in the feminine ME topic's top 50 words, although it does appear more highly weighted in the QE corpus and the MS corpus (*hon*). Women also tend to be linked to time, in particular to youth in the ME corpus (where the masculine topic was more generally associated with time). Other than this association with youth, we did not find the link between women and appearance we expected.

We find that while men are associated with the public sphere, they are also "neutral" in the ME corpus: associated with general or generic terms similar to those in the neutral category. This suggests that material in this corpus implicitly treats men as the norm from which other genders deviate. 'People' are men unless otherwise specified, a sexist form of false generic (Mills, 1995). Although the masculine topic we obtain from this corpus using semi-supervised TM does not follow a particular theme, this does not mean that certain topics are not masculine. The "political" topic in unsupervised ME is dominated by masculine pronouns (*hePRP* 0.072 and *hisPRP$* 0.042) - the public sphere remains implicitly masculine. This was the only notable instance of strongly gendered associations within our unsupervised topic models.

We also note that the words in the feminine topics are more exclusive to those topics. If we look at the example (ME corpus, base seed word list) in Table 3, we see that 29 out of the 48 words that are not seed words are colored, indicating a relative weight ($p(t|w)$) of at least 0.5. For the masculine topic, this number is 14 out of 46 and for the neutral topic 13 out of 47. This indicates that the predominant themes in the feminine topic (family/relationships, communication/social media) are very strongly tied to femininity in the corpus, whereas the themes in the masculine and neutral topics do not have such strong connections to a gender.

Our experiments for the MS corpus and the QE corpus do not show this same generalization of men as neutral; the masculine topics are instead related to crime and death/Christianity, respectively.

Neither Mainstream corpus really contains enough nonbinary representation to produce a "coherent gender". Instead, we see that the third gender topic in these corpora are best termed "neutral", and are often not related to individuals, or even people as a category. In contrast, we do find that there is (more) adequate representation of people who do not fall neatly within the binary gender categories of "men" or "women" in the QE corpus, as expected. Although the third category for this corpus still contains primarily neutral or generic references to people, a coherent theme emerges relating to "acceptance" (both self-acceptance and the acceptance of others), with words such as *parent, question, love, feel, ask, share, accept, able, different, choose.*

Is Swedish less gender-biased than English?

There does not seem to be notably less gender difference in the MS corpus than in the corresponding ME corpus. Women are associated with family and relationships, as well as communication, in both corpora; although *hon* is more highly weighted in its subject form than *she* is. Perhaps the most interesting difference is in men: in English, men are neutral (the "norm") while in Swedish the masculine topic is best labelled "crime and punishment."

Is the QE corpus less gender-biased than the ME corpus?

Comparing between our two English corpora, we find that the QE corpus still strongly associates women with family/relationships (*family, father, friend, relationship, love*) and time (although here *old* is present in addition to *age, young, life*). The theme of the masculine category, however, is completely different: from a generic norm in the ME corpus to death and Christianity in the QE corpus. The exact reasons behind this difference is unclear; however, as the frequency of "feminine" and "masculine" tokens is more balanced in the QE corpus, it is unlikely that this is a case of misrepresentation caused by exclusion, as described in (Hovy and Spruit, 2016).

One key finding within the QE corpus is the presence of nonbinary people and the emergence of a coherent theme from the neutral/nonbinary topic. Within the ME corpus this topic is better described as "neutral" but in the QE corpus it can more honestly be termed "nonbinary." Where nonbinary representation is insufficient, such as in both Mainstream corpora, the neutral topic appears to refer to people in general, if it refers to "people" at all (compare the MS corpus, where this topic is dominated by local and international news). Only with sufficient representation does a coherent third gender category become evident.

Does the relational seed word list "induce" an association between a gender and family/relationships?

In general, we find that women are associated with family/relationships and communication regardless of whether relational seed words are used or not. We also find that men in the Mainstream corpora do not become more associated with these things when relational seed words are added. In fact, the seed words themselves fail to appear among the top 50 words. The ME neutral topic skews more towards a "real" theme with the addition of relational seed words: we find words such as *school* and *student*.

Interestingly, there seems to be a stronger effect of adding relational seed words when training on the QE corpus, although it does not really serve to alter the theme of any of the topics overall. The relational version of the feminine topic adds *lesbianJJ, gayJJ,* and *gayNN*; and the relational seed words actually appear in the masculine topic. The nonbinary topic changes the least.

4 Discussion

Semi-supervised topic modeling seems to do a decent job of exposing the differences in treatment of gender in the text corpora we tested, suggesting it is indeed an appropriate method for discovering bias in data before it is used to train a biased model. We found evidence of gendered differences emblematic of structural power divides in all three corpora. Women tend to be strongly associated with the "home" (family, relationships) and communication; while men are more varied and nonbinary people are nearly invisible in "mainstream" contexts. Generally, this method constitutes a "middle ground" where we escape some limitations of purely quantitative metrics (e.g. understanding *how* representational harms manifest, rather than merely confirming the existence of expected biases) but still must reckon with others (e.g. the required subjective reading may overlook unexpected biases). We plan to expand this method, for example to include guidelines for qualitative analysis with an eye to structures of power borrowed from feminist research methods.

The models we trained require qualitative analysis in the form of human reading to interpret. This is a benefit, as it requires us to think through the how and why of these differences, but can also leave us with lingering questions. For example, we found a very strong theme of Christianity and death in the masculine topic for the QE corpus, but without further examination we cannot tell if this association with Christianity is positive (affirming ministry, messages of acceptance) or negative (condemnation, homophobia). Contrary to our expectations, we did not find a connection between women and appearance in any of our corpora - this may be due to genre (not many "lifestyle" articles) but again would require further examination to determine a cause.

Additionally, TM is not fully deterministic, so there can be some question of the reliability of the results across corpora. It might have been interesting to e.g. train one model for both the English corpora and then investigate them separately, and this may be an angle for future research. This behavior may also be an advantage for more involved investigations, as training multiple models on the same data with different random seeds could provide different "points of view" from which to investigate the corpus and allowing us to triangulate a more complete picture. This potential should also be investigated in future work.

More work is necessary to establish whether TM can help us "debias" corpora, e.g. by identifying and removing strongly-biased texts from the corpus. A natural next step in the line of research presented here is to use the semi-supervised topic models to classify documents and investigate how well this method does at identifying stereotypical writing. TM is relatively computationally cheap, making it an attractive first step in understanding the potential consequences of training a model on a given dataset.

Most work on bias in text so far deals only with gender and considers gender to be a binary category system. We want to contribute to more nuance by working with a nonbinary definition of gender and with a greater focus on intersectionality. This is important since research both in the humanities and in the sciences has shown that focus on only one category, such as gender, can hide prejudice against, for example, women of color; see, e.g., (Buolamwini and Gebru, 2018; Crenshaw, 1991). English and Swedish mark gender grammatically through third person pronouns and semantically in certain nouns (*mother, father, parent*), but there is no equivalent explicit marking for other aspects of identity such as race or class, meaning different strategies must be undertaken to discover intersectional associations. Our technique similarly may not generalize to languages which do not mark gender in this way (e.g. Finnish, which has no gendered third person pronouns), or which have noun cases with grammatical gender (e.g. French or German).

Although we make some progress towards better capturing fluid and multi-faceted understandings by expanding our fixed data categories of "gender" to include a third option, this remains an unsatisfactory solution as it fails both to separate nonbinary individuals from a group or generic (in the case of English *they*) and to provide an intersectional view of different experiences of gender within these three categories. As Bivens (2017) describes such a three-category practice, it "transgresses a rigid binary, yet falls short of a fluid spectrum, positioning ... somewhere in-between". It remains an open question how to tackle these issues in practical NLP research.

References

David Andrzejewski and Xiaojin Zhu. 2009. Latent Dirichlet Allocation with topic-in-set knowledge. In *Semi-supervised Learning for Natural Language Processing*, pages 43–48.

Simone de Beauvoir. 1949. *The Second Sex*. Alfred A. Knopf, New York. Translated by Constance Borde and Sheila Malovany-Chevallier, 2010.

Rena Bivens. 2017. The gender binary will not be deprogrammed: Ten years of coding gender on Facebook. *New Media & Society*, 19(6):880–898, jun.

David M. Blei, Andrew Y. Ng, and Michael I. Jordan. 2003. Latent Dirichlet Allocation. *Journal of Machine Learning Research*, 3:993–1022.

Su Lin Blodgett, Solon Barocas, Hal Daumé, and Hanna M. Wallach. 2020. Language (technology) is power: A critical survey of "bias" in nlp. *ArXiv*, abs/2005.14050.

Tolga Bolukbasi, Kai-Wei Chang, James Y Zou, Venkatesh Saligrama, and Adam T Kalai. 2016. Man is to computer programmer as woman is to homemaker? Debiasing word embeddings. In *Advances in Neural Information Processing Systems 29*, pages 4349–4357.

Joy Buolamwini and Timnit Gebru. 2018. Gender shades: Intersectional accuracy disparities in commercial gender classification. In *Fairness, Accountability and Transparency*, pages 77–91. PMLR.

Judith Butler. 1990. *Gender Trouble: Feminism and the Subversion of Identity*. Routledge, New York.

Aylin Caliskan, Joanna J Bryson, and Arvind Narayanan. 2017. Semantics derived automatically from language corpora contain human-like biases. *Science*, 356(6334):183–186, apr.

Kate Crawford. 2017. The trouble with bias. Keynote at NeurIPS.

Kimberlé Crenshaw. 1991. Mapping the margins: Intersectionality, identity politics, and violence against women of color. *Stanford Law Review*, 43(6):1241–1299.

Mats Dahllöf and Karl Berglund. 2019. Faces, Fights, and Families: topic modeling and gendered themes in two corpora of swedish prose fiction. In *Proceedings of the 4th Conference of The Association of Digital Humanities in the Nordic Countries*.

Jeffrey Dastin. 2018. Amazon scraps secret AI recruiting tool that showed bias against women. Reuters. Accessed: 2020-05-06.

Michel Foucault. 1976. *The History of Sexuality. Vol 1, An Introduction*. Penguin. Translated by Robert Hurley, 1990.

Marilyn Frye. 1983. *The Politics of Reality: Essays in Feminist Theory. Berkeley*. Crossing Press.

Nikhil Garga, Londa Schiebingerb, Dan Jurafsky, and James Zoue. 2018. Word embeddings quantify 100 years of gender and ethnic stereotypes. *PNAS*, 115(16):E3635–E3644.

Hila Gonen and Yoav Goldberg. 2019. Lipstick on a pig: Debiasing methods cover up systematic gender biases in word embeddings but do not remove them. In *NACL: Human Language Technologies, 1*, pages 609–614.

Marie Gustafsson Sendén, Emma A. Bäck, and Anna Lindqvist. 2015. Introducing a gender-neutral pronoun in a natural gender language: the influence of time on attitudes and behavior. *Frontiers in Psychology*, 6:893, jul.

Stuart Hall. 2013. The work of representation. In Stuart Hall, Jessica Evans, and Sean Nixon, editors, *Representation*, pages 1–59. Sage.

Yasmeen Hitti, Eunbee Jang, Ines Moreno, and Carolyne Pelletier. 2019. Proposed Taxonomy for Gender Bias in Text; A Filtering Methodology for the Gender Generalization Subtype. In *Workshop on Gender Bias in Natural Language Processing*, pages 8–17.

Dirk Hovy and Shannon L. Spruit. 2016. The Social Impact of Natural Language Processing. In *Proceedings of the 54th Annual Meeting of the Association for Computational Linguistics (Volume 2: Short Papers)*, pages 591–598, Stroudsburg, PA, USA. Association for Computational Linguistics.

Alexander Miserlis Hoyle, Lawrence Wolf-Sonkin, Hanna Wallach, Isabelle Augenstein, and Ryan Cotterell. 2019. Unsupervised discovery of gendered language through latent-variable modeling. In *Proceedings of the 57th Annual Meeting of the Association for Computational Linguistics*, pages 1706–1716. Association for Computational Linguistics.

Annamarie Jagose. 1996. *Queer Theory: An Introduction*. New York University Press, New York.

Adam Kilgarriff, Vít Baisa, Jan Bušta, Miloš Jakubíček, Vojtěch Kovář, Jan Michelfeit, Pavel Rychlý, and Vít Suchomel. 2014. The sketch engine: ten years on. *Lexicography*, 1:7–36.

Susan Leavy. 2018. Uncovering gender bias in newspaper coverage of irish politicians using machine learning. *Digital Scholarship in the Humanities*, 34(1):48–63.

Kaiji Lu, Piotr Mardziel, Fangjing Wu, Preetam Amancharla, and Anupam Datta. 2018. Gender Bias in Neural Natural Language Processing. jul.

Anne Maass and Luciano Arcuri. 1996. Language and stereotyping. In C. Niel Macra, Charles Strangor, and Miles Hewstone, editors, *Stereotypes and Stereotyping*, chapter 6, pages 193–225. Guilford Press, New York, NY.

Lena Martinsson, Gabriele Griffin, and Katarina Giritli Nygren. 2016. Introduction: Challenging the myth of gender equality in Sweden. In *Challenging the Myth of Gender Equality in Sweden*. Policy Press, Bristol.

Ninareh Mehrabi, Fred Morstatter, Nripsuta Saxena, Kristina Lerman, and Aram Galstyan. 2019. A survey on bias and fairness in machine learning. *ArXiv*, abs/1908.09635.

Sara Mills. 1995. *Feminist Stylistics*. Routledge, New York, New York, USA.

Martha C. Nussbaum. 1999. *Sex and Social Justice*. Oxford UP.

Parmy Olson. 2018. The algorithm that helped google translate become sexist. Forbes. Accessed: 2020-05-06.

Robert Östling. 2013. Stagger: an open-source part of speech tagger for swedish. *Northern European Journal of Language Technology*, 3:1–18.

Radim Řehůřek and Petr Sojka. 2010. Software Framework for Topic Modelling with Large Corpora. In *Proceedings of the LREC 2010 Workshop on New Challenges for NLP Frameworks*, pages 45–50.

Deven Santosh Shah, H. Andrew Schwartz, and Dirk Hovy. 2020. Predictive biases in natural language processing models: A conceptual framework and overview. In *Annual Meeting of the Association for Computational Linguistics*, pages 5248–5264, Online. Association for Computational Linguistics.

Jieyu Zhao, Tianlu Wang, Mark Yatskar, Vicente Ordonez, and Kai-Wei Chang. 2018a. Gender bias in coreference resolution: Evaluation and debiasing methods. In *NACL: Human Language Technologies, 2*, pages 15–20, June.

Jieyu Zhao, Yichao Zhou, Zeyu Li, Wei Wang, and Kai-Wei Chang. 2018b. Learning gender-neutral word embeddings. In *Empirical Methods in Natural Language Processing*, page 4847–4853.

Investigating Societal Biases in a Poetry Composition System

Emily Sheng[*]
USC Information Sciences Institute
Marina del Rey, CA
ewsheng@isi.edu

David Uthus
Google Research
Mountain View, CA
duthus@google.com

Abstract

There is a growing collection of work analyzing and mitigating societal biases in language understanding, generation, and retrieval tasks, though examining biases in creative tasks remains underexplored. Creative language applications are meant for direct interaction with users, so it is important to quantify and mitigate societal biases in these applications. We introduce a novel study on a pipeline to mitigate societal biases when retrieving next verse suggestions in a poetry composition system. Our results suggest that data augmentation through sentiment style transfer has potential for mitigating societal biases.

1 Introduction

Our increasing reliance on natural language processing (NLP) tools to produce trustworthy and helpful information means we must also be increasingly vigilant to the social ramifications of NLP techniques. Despite increasing attention to the ethical issues in NLP and development of techniques to mitigate biases in a variety of tasks, examining biases in creative NLP tasks remains underexplored; however, biases in creative tasks are equally as important. The primary goal of creative NLP systems is to be disseminated in a society (e.g., for self expression and collective social enjoyment, education (Foster and Freeman, 2008), therapy (Connolly Baker and Mazza, 2004)), whereas other NLP systems are primarily driven by some non-social goal (e.g., answer a query correctly or retrieve all relevant named entities). Any existing societal biases propagated through creative systems have direct impact on our society. For example, biases in a system that is meant to educate about different perspectives may end up reinforcing demographic stereotypes.

In this work, we focus on quantifying and mitigating societal biases in a creative language application. Specifically, we propose techniques to mitigate biases in the poetry composition system introduced by Uthus et al. (2019). This system allows the user to collaboratively compose a poem using machine-suggested novel verses in the style of classic American poets. As creative works are often shaped by the lived experiences and timely issues of the creator's life, a poetry composition system trained on poems from different authors of different eras may reflect a variety of societal biases. Table 1 highlights the types of subtle differences in system responses when the user input contains different genders.

We define societal biases as unequal social perceptions of different socially-defined groups of people. Propagating unequal representations of demographic groups reinforces representational harms, such as stereotypes, leading to discrimination and potential allocational harms, such as unequal job opportunities (Blodgett et al., 2020; Barocas et al., 2017).[1] To evaluate societal biases, we examine the language polarity (i.e., sentiment) of the suggested verses when different demographic groups are mentioned in the user input.[2] A system that favors different sentiment verse suggestions for mentions of different demographic groups (e.g., *positive* for demographic A and *negative* for demographic B) could propagate unequal positive and negative associations and amplify existing demographic inequalities. However,

---

[*]Work done while interning at Google

[1]Allocational harms are when a system allocates resources unfairly to different groups.

[2]We use sentiment as a proxy metric for the social perception of demographic groups.

Proceedings of the Second Workshop on Gender Bias in Natural Language Processing, pages 93–106
Barcelona, Spain (Online), December 13, 2020.

Suggested next verses for user input: *The women*	Suggested next verses for user input: *The men*
Hate to their love like that evil womanhood-	*Looked the warm day in their manly way+*
Drawed tears upon their wall-	*Lay on their crowns at their gracious whim+*
Hide in the shame of their loveless men-	*Await, for the brand of their command*
Heard, if they were with flowers	*Brought to their manhood in the light-eyed*
Do with their wings and their dolls	*Ran with their rifles*

Table 1: Examples of verse suggestions for a user input of "*The women*" or "*The men*", where the suggestions for the former have more negative connotations ($^{--}$), and those for the latter have more positive connotations ($^{+}$). Even neutral examples contain gender stereotypes, though we focus on the negative and positive examples in this work.

even in the case where a model suggests verses with similar sentiment scores for different groups, the model can still propagate biases by reinforcing similar amounts of different negative stereotypes for each group. Thus, we propose a technique to mitigate biases by making the verses suggested by the poetry system less negative in sentiment.

In this preliminary study, we focus on retrieving less negative verses across different demographic groups to reduce harms from societal biases within and across demographic groups.[3] Since there is no guarantee that verses with similar sentiment are biased or unbiased in the same way, we do not explicitly constrain equalizing the sentiments of verses suggested for different groups. Results show that our method has promising results for both reducing negative verses and keeping the distribution of verse sentiments across groups comparable.

Our contributions are 1) a pipeline approach for mitigating societal biases in a poetry composition system and 2) a labeled poetry sentiment dataset. For the first part of the pipeline, we introduce a poetry sentiment dataset and build a BERT-based (Devlin et al., 2019) sentiment analyzer for poetry. These sentiment tools are subsequently used to train a style transfer model (Li et al., 2018), which is then used to augment data to train the next verse prediction component in the poetry composition system. Our results indicate that style transfer has potential as an augmentation technique to reduce societal biases. Specifically, we can influence the model to suggest verses with more positive sentiment while keeping the suggested verse quality comparable. This exploratory study introduces the capabilities of style transfer augmentation to mitigate biases and is an example of how bias mitigation can be applied to creative language tasks and information retrieval components.

2 Poetry Composition System

We investigate societal biases in the human-AI collaborative approach to composing poetry described by Uthus et al. (2019). In this setup, users compose a poem aided by suggestions from the poetry system. Users can either directly use verse suggestions provided by the system, modify the suggestions, or create their own verses. The suggested verses are generated in the style of various classic American poets (e.g., Walt Whitman, Emily Dickinson).

Figure 1 shows a schematic of the poetry composition system. This system has two components:

- **Verse Generation**: generates a large collection of verses in the styles of different poets and then indexes all verses for fast retrieval during poem composition.
- **Next Verse Prediction**: determines which pre-generated verses to suggest to the user, given a previous verse.

In a complex pipeline, there are multiple components to consider for the propagation of biases. For the poetry composition system, biases can propagate in both the language generation component and the next verse prediction component. In this work, we only analyze biases in the next verse prediction component, because there is relatively little work examining biases in a retrieval task setting and because

---

[3]There could also be harms in other scenarios, e.g., if the user's input contains harmful content about a demographic and is followed by positive verse suggestions, or if demographic mentions occur in suggestions following negative verses, though we leave this to future work.

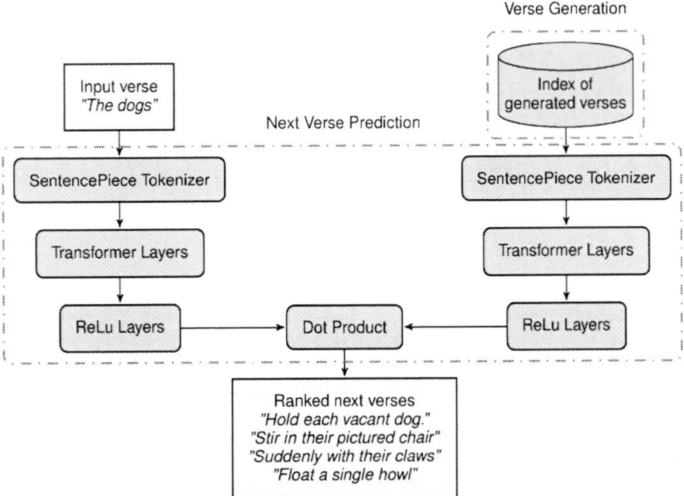

Figure 1: An overview of the poetry composition system, focusing on the components that make up the next verse prediction.

biases in the latter component could amplify biases from the earlier component. Thus, beyond describing the verse generation component as a Transformer-based model trained on the same data as the next verse prediction dataset, we largely treat verse generation as a black box component.[4] Note that the verse generation component is not free of grammatical and fluency issues, which are propagated down to the next verse prediction component. For this work, we mainly focus on issues of societal biases and not grammatical issues stemming from the verse generation component. In this section, we define components of the loss function and describe the training data for next verse prediction.

Next verse prediction loss. The next verse prediction model is a dual-encoder model similar to the one described by Henderson et al. (2017). More specifically, let $\mathcal{R}$ be the entire fixed set of verse suggestions from the index of generated verses. Given a verse x, the model's goal is to search for the top N responses $(y_1, y_2, ..., y_N) \in \mathcal{R}$, ordered by decreasing model probability

$$P(y|x) = \frac{P(x,y)}{\sum_{r=1}^{|\mathcal{R}|} P(x,y_r)}. \tag{1}$$

Eq. (1) requires summing over all possible responses y_r when training, which is prohibitively expensive to calculate. Instead, we follow Henderson et al. (2017) and sample K responses to estimate $P(y|x)$ as

$$P_{approx}(y|x) = \frac{P(x,y)}{\sum_{k=1}^{K} P(x,y_k)}. \tag{2}$$

In this work, the joint probability $P(x,y)$ is estimated with a learned scoring function S, where $P(x,y) \propto e^{S(x,y)}$, so we can rewrite Eq. (2) as

$$P_{approx}(y|x) = \frac{e^{S(x,y)}}{\sum_{k=1}^{K} e^{S(x,y_k)}}. \tag{3}$$

For the scoring function S, we use a tower of Transformer (Vaswani et al., 2017) layers and feed-forward layers to encode x and y into the vectors $\mathbf{h}_x$ and $\mathbf{h}_y$, respectively.[5] The dot product scoring function can then be written as $S(x,y) = \mathbf{h}_x^\mathsf{T}\mathbf{h}_y$.

Recall that to approximate the conditional probability $P_{approx}(y|x)$, we sample K responses. When

---

[4]The verses available to be retrieved from the verse generation component likely reflect distributional societal biases. As a first step towards making the set of available verses less gender-biased, we augment the original set of generated verses through counterfactual data augmentation (Lu et al., 2018), i.e., swapping all female and male pronouns, and adding the resulting verses to the set of available verses.

[5]Details and hyperparameters are in the Appendix.

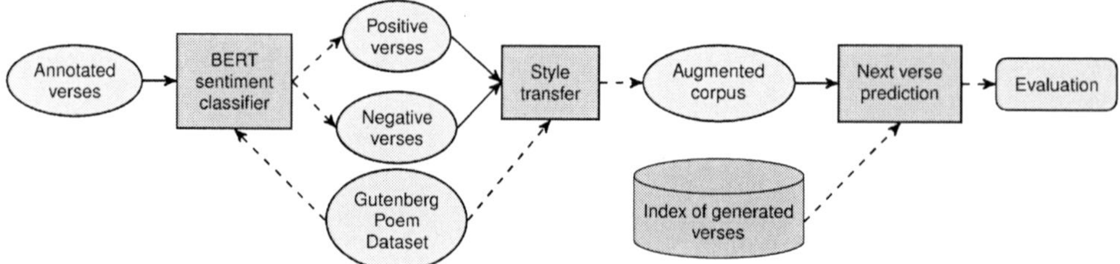

Figure 2: **A schematic of our technique for bias mitigation of the next verse prediction component in the poetry composition system.** Solid lines indicate training time; dashed lines indicate inference time.

training with a batch size of K, we treat (x_i, y_i) as the positive example and (x_i, y_k) where $k \neq i$ as negative examples, for $i, k \in [1, K]$. From preliminary experiments, we find that including (x_i, x_i) as a negative example improves retrieval, so we add this additional negative example for our experiments. We define θ as the model's parameters. With this formulation, the average batch loss to minimize is the negative log probability

$$
\begin{aligned}
\mathcal{L}(X, Y, \theta) &= -\frac{1}{K} \sum_{i=1}^{K} \log P_{approx}(y_i | x_i) \\
&= -\frac{1}{K} \sum_{i=1}^{K} [S(x_i, y_i) - \log \sum_{k=1}^{K} e^{S(x_i, y_k)}].
\end{aligned}
\tag{4}
$$

Next verse prediction dataset. We collect a corpus of classic poems from Project Gutenberg[6] to use as training data for the next verse prediction component — we refer to this collected dataset as the Gutenberg Poem Dataset in this work and rely on the dataset for several components in our bias mitigation pipeline. We split each poem into verses, and pair each verse with the subsequent verse to form the groundtruth data for next verse prediction.[7]

3 Bias Mitigation Through Data Augmentation

We propose a technique for bias mitigation through data augmentation of the training data. Data augmentation has been used in previous works (Lu et al., 2018; Zhao et al., 2018a; Park et al., 2018) as a technique to mitigate societal biases in NLP systems. We use sentiment style transfer for data augmentation to target the retrieval of verses with less negative societal biases towards different demographic groups. Our overall pipeline for augmentation and evaluation is shown in Figure 2. By using style transfer for data augmentation instead of filtering out negative examples, we can circumvent data sparsity issues and promote model robustness. In the creative language domain, it can be difficult to obtain a large dataset, due to intellectual property and copyright restrictions. With style transfer-based augmentation, we can generate styled variations of our original data that can be more consistent in content and poet style. In this section, we introduce definitions and then describe our proposed solution for bias mitigation through data augmentation.

3.1 Definitions

Demographic groups are socially-defined groups of people. In the context of poem verses, we use demographic groups of people interchangeably with their mentions in text, e.g., the demographic group GENDER-MALE and the mention *"The man"*. To more generally evaluate biases in suggested verses for different demographic groups, we curate a list of 25 demographic groups for various genders, race, and

---

[6] https://www.gutenberg.org/

[7] Poems from Project Gutenberg are not stored in consistent formats, so we manually search the corpus for books of poems from famous classic American poets and then filter out malformatted poems, for a 45MiB dataset (more stats in Table 2).

Sentiment score	# train samples	# dev samples	# test samples	Example
negative	155	19	19	*and that is why, the lonesome day,*
no impact	555	69	69	*it flows so long as falls the rain,*
positive	133	17	16	*with pale blue berries, in these peaceful shades–*

Table 2: Dataset statistics and examples for different sentiment scores.

Input	Generated Output
by those whose wrongs his soul had moved	*by those tender memory whose his own soul had moved*
the angel passed away	*the sweet singer angel passed away*
turnus 'tis true in this unequal strife	*turnus in this auspicious shore*
like warring giants angry huge and cruel	*like giants huge and sweet*
the darkness lingering oer the dawn of things	*lingering oer the dawn of many delicious things*

Table 3: Examples of the inputs and generated positive sentiment outputs of the "Delete, Retrieve, Generate" style transfer technique (Li et al., 2018) on poem verses.

religions, e.g., *"The man"*, *"The African"*, *"The Muslim"*. Each demographic group is represented by two surface forms (one singular: *"The man"* and one plural: *"The men"*). We also create a list of 24 *other* groups, where the goal is to obtain model suggestions for entities that are not a group of interest in the discussion of human societal biases. Specifically, we use a list of animals (e.g., *"The dog"*, *"The dogs"*).[8]

3.2 Sentiment Analysis

In this section, we describe how we build a sentiment-labeled dataset of poem verses and use the dataset to train a sentiment classifier. This classifier is used both for generating training data for the style transfer model and the automatic evaluation of our bias mitigation technique.

Dataset. To the best of our knowledge, there is no existing public poetry dataset with sentiment annotations. We require an appropriate sentiment dataset in order to apply and evaluate our mitigation techniques, so we have two annotators label the sentiment of randomly picked verses from the Gutenberg Poem Dataset. The annotations use sentiment annotation guidelines described by Sheng et al. (2019). For each sample, annotators could describe the language in the sample as *negative, no impact, positive, mixed (both negative and positive)*, or *does not make sense*.[8]

The inter-annotator agreement is 0.53 (Cohen's kappa) for 1550 annotated samples. If we remove samples where either annotator chose *mixed* or *does not make sense*, the kappa score increases to 0.58. Spearman's correlation for the samples with labels in the three sentiment categories (*negative* = -1, *no impact* = 0, *positive* = 1) is 0.67. These correlations indicate decently strong inter-annotator agreement. For all annotated samples, we only keep the sample if there is agreement across both annotators and if the label is *negative, no impact*, or *positive*.[9] Dataset statistics are in Table 2.

Sentiment classifier. We fine-tune a pretrained BERT model on the filtered annotated sentiment dataset. We use the uncased version of BERT base with a batch size of 32, learning rate of 1×10^{-5}, maximum sequence length of 128, warmup proportion of 0.1, and train for 5 epochs. The resulting sentiment classifier has a development set accuracy of 85.7% and a test set accuracy of 84.6%.

3.3 Style Transfer

With style transfer, we can automatically generate verses that are similar in content and poet writing style to existing verses yet different in sentiment style. This section describes the style transfer technique and human evaluation of the technique.

---

[8]More details in the Appendix.

[9]The sentiment dataset can be found at `https://github.com/google-research-datasets/poem-sentiment`.

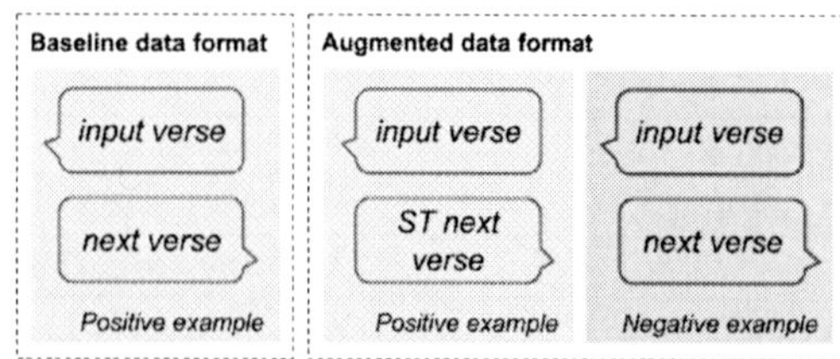

Figure 3: **Data augmentation details.** For example, *input verse = "by the path an indian sat", next verse = "then i cried and ran away"*, and the positive sentiment style-transferred next verse *ST next verse = "then i sing that human delight"*. (*input verse, next verse*) is the groundtruth data pair in the Gutenberg Poem Dataset. In this example, *input verse* contains a demographic mention (*"indian"*) and *next verse* has negative sentiment. The baseline next verse prediction model uses the original (*input verse, next verse*) pair as a positive example. The data augmentation model treats (*input verse, next verse*) as a negative example and uses (*input verse, ST next verse*) as the positive example.

***Delete, Retrieve, Generate* (DRG) technique.**   For style transfer, we follow the encoder-decoder model of Li et al. (2018). In this setup, the model deletes salient attribute markers (phrases that appear frequently in text of one style and not the other) in a text, retrieves an attribute marker of the opposite sentiment that appears in a similar context, and generates new text using the content of the original text and the new attribute marker. The DRG model explicitly separates content and attributes of the text to facilitate the preservation of the words explicitly used in the original text, a characteristic especially desirable in the creative language domain where each word is carefully chosen to maximize creative expression. For example, for the verse *"like warring giants angry huge and cruel"*, deleting the negative attribute markers would result in *"like giants huge and"*. After retrieving positive attribute markers that are used in similar contexts, the model combines the original content and retrieved positive attribute markers to generate *"like giants huge and sweet"*. Examples of inputs and style-transferred outputs are in Table 3, and examples of different components of DRG are in the Appendix.

Experimental setup.   By using the sentiment classifier to label verses in our Gutenberg Poem Dataset, we end up with 166K negative and 100K positive verses for the style transfer training set, and 19K negative and 11K positive verses for the evaluation set. When training a DRG model with this dataset, the model learns to convert negative verses to positive verses and vice versa, though we only use negative to positive conversions for our data augmentation method. Hyperparameter details are in the Appendix.

Human evaluation.   To evaluate the effectiveness of the DRG style transfer technique, we have humans manually annotate the 1) fluency of the style transferred text, and the 2) meaning preservation and 3) positive sentiment change between the original and new text. All categories operate on a scale of 1 to 5. For fluency, 1 means not fluent at all, and 5 means very fluent. For meaning preservation, 1 means all original meaning is lost, and 5 means all meaning is preserved as much as possible, given the targeted sentiment change. For positive sentiment change, we ask how well the corresponding style transferred text became more positive, with 1 meaning not more positive, and 5 meaning a lot more positive. Since we are interested in making the suggested verses *more positive*, we only measure the magnitude of how much more positive the style transferred text is compared to the original text.

Each of the 181 pairs of (original, style transferred) text is annotated by two annotators. Spearman's correlation is 0.73 for fluency, 0.85 for meaning preservation, and 0.82 for positive sentiment change. With these high inter-annotator correlation values, we average each sample score across the two annotators. The resulting average fluency of the style transferred text is 3.44, which means the new samples are moderately fluent. The average meaning preservation is 2.42, indicating that, on average, slightly more meaning is lost than preserved. The fact that the meaning of the verses are not as well-preserved through style transfer is expected, as poem verses tend to be difficult to interpret and are often expected to express multiple meanings. In the context of a creative language task, where inspiration and facilitating creativity is the main target, this weaker meaning preservation attribute is also more acceptable. Lastly, the average positive sentiment change is 2.22, which shows that the style transferred text is on average a bit more

Data subset	Next verse (-)	Next verse (0)	Next verse (+)	Total
Input verse w/demo.	2K (25%)	5K (63%)	1K (13%)	8K (100%)
Input verse w/o demo.	41K (13%)	253K (79%)	25K (8%)	319K (100%)

Table 4: **Data statistics for the Gutenberg Poem Dataset used for next verse prediction (no augmentation)**. We divide the (input verse, next verse) pairs into those with an input that contains a demographic mention and those without. Within those groups, we show statistics for pairs with negative (-), neutral (0), and positive (+) sentiment next verses. Percentages are within each row.

positive than the original text.

3.4 Next Verse Prediction

We use the trained style transfer model to augment the training data (from the Gutenberg Poem Dataset) for the next verse prediction model, and then run human and automatic evaluations to compare the original model with a model trained on the augmented data.

Data augmentation. We use the style transfer model to generate more positive sentiment verses from originally negative sentiment verses, and subsequently augment the training data with these generated verses. More specifically, recall that the training data for the next verse prediction model is composed of *input verse* and *next verse* text pairs. We conduct style transfer augmentation for specific training pairs:

1. Pairs where the *input verse* contains a demographic mention, e.g., *"by the path an indian sat"*, and the *next verse* has negative sentiment, e.g., *"then i cried and ran away"*.
2. Pairs where the *input verse* does not contain a demographic mention and the *next verse* has negative sentiment.

We do not modify any training samples that are not in the above scenarios. For the first scenario, we use the style transfer model to generate a positive version of the *next verse*. The *input verse* is then paired with the style-transferred positive *next verse* as a positive example, and the original negative *next verse* is used as a negative example for the *input*. We always generate a positive version of the *next verse* if the *input* contains a demographic mention, because that is our goal for bias mitigation. For the second scenario, we randomly choose, with a probability of 0.5, whether to generate a positive *next verse* and similarly augment. With this random selection in the latter scenario, we end up generating new *next verses* for approximately half of the samples; in subsequent results, we show that this amount of augmentation is enough to observe a difference in the results compared to the baseline model.[10] Figure 3 details how the augmented training data format differs from that of the baseline model.

Table 4 shows statistics for the Gutenberg Poem Dataset. Only about 2% of all (*input verse, next verse*) pairs have *inputs* that contain a demographic mention. Furthermore, 25% of the *next verses* are negative for the pairs with a demographic in the *inputs*, whereas only 13% of *next verses* are negative for the pairs without a demographic in the *input*. This imbalance highlights the opportunity for biases in the form of negative sentiment *next verses* for *inputs* containing demographic mentions.

Experimental setup. The next verse prediction model and training procedure are as described in Sec. 2. Using the dual-encoder model with the loss in Eq. (4) and the augmented dataset, we train a style transfer-augmented next verse prediction model. Hyperparameters are in the Appendix. For evaluation, we use *"The"* followed by a demographic group or other group mention as the input verse (e.g., *"The man"* or *"The dog"*) and perform human and automatic evaluations on the next verses suggested by the baseline and augmented versions of the next verse prediction component.

Human evaluation. To compare verses suggested by the style transfer-augmented model with verses suggested by the original model, we take the top 10 suggested verses from each model for each demographic mention and show them side-by-side to annotators. Annotators are asked to label the relevance of both sets of suggestions, and compare the usability and sentiment between the two sets. Relevance

---

[10]In preliminary results, style transfer augmentation on only the samples in the first scenario does not produce more positive sentiment verse suggestions overall. We hypothesize this lack of augmentation effectiveness is due to the relatively small amount of training pairs with a demographic mention in the *input verse* (Table 4).

Prompt type	USE	REL	SEN	corr (SEN, USE)	corr (SEN, REL)	corr (REL, USE)
Min	+1	−4	+1	−1	−1	−1
Max	+5	+4	+5	+1	+1	+1
Demo.	2.93	−0.12	3.02	0.68	0.59	0.81
Others	2.73	−0.18	3.08	0.39	0.31	0.92

Table 5: **Human annotation results for next verse prediction.** For human comparisons of baseline and augmented model suggestions, given a demographic or other group mention in the input verse: USE = usability, REL = augmented model relevance − baseline model relevance, SEN = sentiment. Spearman's correlation values (corr) are reported. Min is the lower-bound score; Max is the upper-bound score. USE/REL/SEN scores closer to Max indicate that the augmented model is better than the baseline.

is judged on a scale of 1 to 5, with 1 being not very relevant and 5 being very relevant. Usability is defined specifically for the task of composing a poem; 1 means the annotator is much more likely to use a suggestion from the original model, and 5 means the annotator is much more likely to use a suggestion from the augmented model. For this creative language task, we include a measurement of usability as an alternate measurement of model performance. The sentiment comparison score for this evaluation is also on a scale of 1 to 5, with 1 meaning the suggestions from the original model are more positive, and 5 meaning the suggestions from the augmented model are more positive.[11] Two annotators annotate the relevance, usability, and sentiment comparison between the baseline and augmented model results for each of the 50 demographic mentions and 48 other group mentions. Spearman's correlation is 0.69 for usability, 0.66 for relevance, and 0.73 for sentiment change.

The averaged results over all demographic groups in Table 5 suggest a slight increase in sentiment scores, which is the goal of our bias mitigation through augmentation. We additionally see that the relevance and usability of the new samples are just slightly lower than those of the original samples, which could be due to the style transfer model's degree of accuracy in content preservation. Measuring relevance and usability provides two qualitative dimensions of comparisons between the original and augmented data models. However, we emphasize that text with high usability and relevance can still contain harmful stereotypes and societal biases, which is why sentiment is the main focus for our bias analysis. On average, the style transfer augmentation is able to increase the sentiment of the retrieved verses with comparable usability scores across groups.

Table 5 shows that relevance is highly but not perfectly correlated with usability and that sentiment is better correlated with the latter, indicating that using both relevance and usability may allow for more complete evaluations. Usability as an evaluation metric can be more generally applicable to human-AI collaborative tasks. For the task of selecting the best item to suggest to users, the metric of usability grounds evaluation to the specific values of the collaborative task at hand.

We also observe that the correlation between sentiment and usability for suggested verses for demographic prompts is nearly twice that of other prompts.[12] This may indicate that annotators find that more positive sentiment suggestions are more helpful when the previous verse is about a demographic group — perhaps annotators are able to better identify with humans than with non-human entities.

Automatic evaluation. With human evaluations, we only show annotators a limited amount of verse suggestions for each demographic mention to not overwhelm the annotators. However, it is also important to evaluate more retrieved verses, since users of the poetry composition system have the option to ask for more suggestions if the top retrieved ones are not inspiring enough. With automatic evaluations, we can evaluate the top 50 suggested verses per demographic mention. The trade-off for this more comprehensive evaluation is that we rely on the automatic sentiment analyzer, which may not be as accurate as the human annotations. Also, the human evaluations directly compare the overall perceived sentiment change between the baseline and augmented model verse suggestion sets, whereas the automatic

---

[11]Note that this is a different formulation from the style transfer evaluations.

[12]There is a similar pattern for the correlation between sentiment and relevance.

Prompt type	Baseline model		Augmented model	
	Average	Std. dev	Average	Std. dev
Demo.	0.01	0.12	0.06	0.13
Other	-0.01	0.16	0.01	0.12

Table 6: **Automatically labeled results for next verse prediction.** Sentiment average and standard deviations for suggested verses (sentiment scores $\in [-1, 1]$). The augmented model has higher average sentiment and lower or comparable standard deviations for both prompt types. This suggests the augmented model is effective at suggesting verses that are overall slightly more positive.

Input	Baseline model suggestions	Augmented model suggestions
The woman	Uplifted than a manly me slain her strong,[+] Fate is life of her best she salt born.[+] She cannot the thirst dear, behind them back,[-] Fate is life of him best Brought her scroll.[+] she wore the belt along the belt and tea.[0] she wore the belt along the belt and tea;[0] Save the world when serious pine her strive.[+] Fate is life of her best that hath shed[+] Go through thy small lessons long go this day.[0] Whenever she goes back,[0]	This old man with toil, while her dog[-] Here from a hundred vain his blessing trust[+] Walking in the woody groves on earth,[0] Walking in the woody groves on earth.[0] she gives his prayer to every glorious thing,[+] Olger to her End[0] Reckon you have on every earth[0] Here from a hundred vain her blessing trust[+] House the fate their graceful own isle of work[+] The gives the sunshine in her early sword![+]
The man	Burns up every atom on his tongue[-] Great old groves send his cliffs[0] Great in his labor been[0] Whether an hour as kingdom spoke[0] States his steady nature took him son:[0] Great old groves send him cliffs[0] States him steady nature took his son:[0] Burns up every atom on him tongue[-] Lest all the many is the haughty god,[-] Shine over thy foe with lion forth[+]	Shall one alone him broad van pine and called and why.[0] Shall one alone him broad van pine and called and why.[0] Shall all the sacred summer thought and Creator,[+] Shall one within so garden in his broad name[0] She stood beside the brink, her brow they fell[0] Wrestles the soul[0] Shall they who in him own road shall roam,[0] Due virtue hed an wants[0] Life on his errand bound Fine woods[0] Shall he who in him own road shall roam,[0]

Table 7: **Examples of user inputs and suggested verses from the baseline and augmented models.** Annotators labeled the overall sentiment change of the suggestions for *"The woman"* as 4.0, and for *"The man"* as 3.0 (on a scale of 1-5, 5 meaning the augmented model is much more positive). For more fine-grained automatic evaluation, [+] denotes positive, [0] denotes neutral, and [-] denotes negative sentiment. As expected, the human coarse-grained sentiment and automatic fine-grained sentiment scores are not perfectly correlated, yet both are useful (Sec. 3.4).

evaluations can be more fine-grained in providing a sentiment label for each verse.

Table 6 displays the average sentiment scores and standard deviations across demographic and other groups. The augmented model suggests verses with slightly higher sentiment on average, while all the standard deviations are comparable. These results suggest that the augmented model is effective at suggesting verses that are overall slightly more positive than those of the baseline model. Table 7 provides a more comprehensive example of automatic fine-grained and human coarse-grained sentiment labels. The fine-grained annotation indicates that suggestions for *"The woman"* are roughly equal in sentiment across models, while suggestions for *"The man"* are less negative for the augmented model. In contrast, annotators labeled the overall sentiment change of the suggestions for *"The woman"* as 4.0, and for *"The man"* as 3.0. Thus, the fine-grained and coarse-grained labels of sentiment scores are not perfectly correlated, but both are useful for a comprehensive evaluation. Future work could explore the reliability of human versus classifier judgments of sentiment and biases.

4 Discussion

In any complex pipeline with multiple components, downstream components can propagate and amplify errors and biases from upstream components. The human and automatic evaluations show that the sentiment of the verses suggested by the augmented model are overall only slightly more positive than those

101

suggested by the baseline model. The small magnitude of this change could be due to the quality of our trained style transfer model or the amount of augmentation applied (not to all negative *next verses*), among other factors. The evaluation results highlight some of the challenges of mitigating biases in a pipeline system.

More generally, there are advantages and disadvantages to applying mitigation techniques at different points in a pipeline. For example, we could also apply style transfer after the next verse component suggests a set of verses. In doing so, there would be no need to re-train the next verse component. The disadvantages are that we would have to style transfer all verse suggestions, thereby incurring more memory usage (apply style transfer beforehand and store the new verses) or more latency for the user (apply style transfer to retrieved verses lazily as the user requests suggestions). By applying style transfer bias mitigation during training of the next verse prediction component, we can more efficiently add new verses to be retrieved by the component.

Our work provides a preliminary study of how style transfer techniques can be used to augment data in the context of a retrieval model. We note that there can also be other types of societal biases in this poetry composition system, e.g., occupations that are biased towards specific genders, and other racial and gender stereotypes. Future work includes looking into how style transfer could be used for these other biases. For example, one could style transfer negative and positive stereotypes into more neutral associations, and subsequently use the latter associations as positive examples and the former stereotypes as negative examples for the next verse prediction model.

5   Related Work

Societal biases in NLP applications.   Several recent works have analyzed and mitigated societal biases in word embeddings (Bolukbasi et al., 2016; Caliskan et al., 2017; Zhao et al., 2018b; May et al., 2019; Gonen and Goldberg, 2019). Others have also detailed how biases can occur in language understanding tasks, such as coreference resolution (Rudinger et al., 2018; Zhao et al., 2018a), semantic role labeling (Zhao et al., 2017), abusive language detection (Park et al., 2018), sentiment analysis (Shen et al., 2018; Kiritchenko and Mohammad, 2018), and language modeling (Sheng et al., 2019; Bordia and Bowman, 2019; Pryzant et al., 2020; Huang et al., 2019). To our knowledge, societal biases in creative applications has not been explored, despite the fact that creative application are often intended for social use (e.g., self expression, education).

Biases in information retrieval techniques.   Earlier work on biases in information retrieval systems include examining biases in resume search engines (Chen et al., 2018) and image search results (Kay et al., 2015). More recently, researchers have proposed different metrics to measure the amount of group and individual fairness in ranking systems (Zehlike et al., 2017; Biega et al., 2018; Singh and Joachims, 2018; Yang et al., 2020). Additionally, Rekabsaz and Schedl (2020) compare how different neural ranking models differ in gender bias. For future work, we could apply some of these previously proposed bias metrics that use weighting to account for the positions of the retrieved results.

6   Conclusion

We introduce an exploratory study on societal biases in a poetry composition application. Although biases in creative language applications are underexplored, it is important to examine biases in these applications that are primarily intended for social use. Our results indicate that style transfer has potential as an augmentation technique to reduce societal biases. More broadly, our study introduces the capabilities of style transfer augmentation to mitigate biases and as an example of how bias mitigation can be applied to information retrieval components.

Acknowledgements

The authors would like to thank Maria Voitovich, Noah Constant, and Vlad Imir for the very helpful discussions. Additionally, the authors are grateful to Nanyun Peng, Kai-Wei Chang, Prem Natarajan, Jason Teoh, Mandy Guo, and anonymous reviewers for their feedback of this work.

References

Solon Barocas, Kate Crawford, Aaron Shapiro, and Hanna Wallach. 2017. The problem with bias: from allocative to representational harms in machine learning. special interest group for computing. *Information and Society (SIGCIS)*.

Asia J Biega, Krishna P Gummadi, and Gerhard Weikum. 2018. Equity of attention: Amortizing individual fairness in rankings. In *The 41st international acm sigir conference on research & development in information retrieval*, pages 405–414.

Su Lin Blodgett, Solon Barocas, Hal Daumé III, and Hanna Wallach. 2020. Language (technology) is power: A critical survey of" bias" in nlp. *Proceedings of the 58th Annual Meeting of the Association for Computational Linguistics*.

Tolga Bolukbasi, Kai-Wei Chang, James Y Zou, Venkatesh Saligrama, and Adam T Kalai. 2016. Man is to computer programmer as woman is to homemaker? debiasing word embeddings. In *Advances in neural information processing systems*, pages 4349–4357.

Shikha Bordia and Samuel Bowman. 2019. Identifying and reducing gender bias in word-level language models. In *Proceedings of the 2019 Conference of the North American Chapter of the Association for Computational Linguistics: Student Research Workshop*, pages 7–15.

Aylin Caliskan, Joanna J Bryson, and Arvind Narayanan. 2017. Semantics derived automatically from language corpora contain human-like biases. *Science*, 356(6334):183–186.

Le Chen, Ruijun Ma, Anikó Hannák, and Christo Wilson. 2018. Investigating the impact of gender on rank in resume search engines. In *Proceedings of the 2018 chi conference on human factors in computing systems*, pages 1–14.

Kathleen Connolly Baker and Nicholas Mazza. 2004. The healing power of writing: Applying the expressive/creative component of poetry therapy. *Journal of Poetry Therapy*, 17(3):141–154.

Jacob Devlin, Ming-Wei Chang, Kenton Lee, and Kristina Toutanova. 2019. Bert: Pre-training of deep bidirectional transformers for language understanding. In *Proceedings of the 2019 Conference of the North American Chapter of the Association for Computational Linguistics: Human Language Technologies, Volume 1 (Long and Short Papers)*, pages 4171–4186.

William Foster and Elaine Freeman. 2008. Poetry in general practice education: perceptions of learners. *Family Practice*, 25(4):294–303.

Hila Gonen and Yoav Goldberg. 2019. Lipstick on a pig: Debiasing methods cover up systematic gender biases in word embeddings but do not remove them. In *Proceedings of the 2019 Conference of the North American Chapter of the Association for Computational Linguistics: Human Language Technologies, Volume 1 (Long and Short Papers)*, pages 609–614.

Matthew Henderson, Rami Al-Rfou, Brian Strope, Yun-Hsuan Sung, László Lukács, Ruiqi Guo, Sanjiv Kumar, Balint Miklos, and Ray Kurzweil. 2017. Efficient natural language response suggestion for smart reply. *arXiv preprint arXiv:1705.00652*.

Po-Sen Huang, Huan Zhang, Ray Jiang, Robert Stanforth, Johannes Welbl, Jack Rae, Vishal Maini, Dani Yogatama, and Pushmeet Kohli. 2019. Reducing sentiment bias in language models via counterfactual evaluation. *arXiv preprint arXiv:1911.03064*.

Matthew Kay, Cynthia Matuszek, and Sean A Munson. 2015. Unequal representation and gender stereotypes in image search results for occupations. In *Proceedings of the 33rd Annual ACM Conference on Human Factors in Computing Systems*, pages 3819–3828.

Svetlana Kiritchenko and Saif M Mohammad. 2018. Examining gender and race bias in two hundred sentiment analysis systems. *NAACL HLT 2018*, page 43.

Taku Kudo and John Richardson. 2018. SentencePiece: A simple and language independent subword tokenizer and detokenizer for neural text processing. In *Proceedings of the 2018 Conference on Empirical Methods in Natural Language Processing: System Demonstrations*, pages 66–71, Brussels, Belgium, November. Association for Computational Linguistics.

Juncen Li, Robin Jia, He He, and Percy Liang. 2018. Delete, retrieve, generate: a simple approach to sentiment and style transfer. In *Proceedings of the 2018 Conference of the North American Chapter of the Association for Computational Linguistics: Human Language Technologies, Volume 1 (Long Papers)*, pages 1865–1874.

Kaiji Lu, Piotr Mardziel, Fangjing Wu, Preetam Amancharla, and Anupam Datta. 2018. Gender bias in neural natural language processing. *arXiv preprint arXiv:1807.11714*.

Chandler May, Alex Wang, Shikha Bordia, Samuel Bowman, and Rachel Rudinger. 2019. On measuring social biases in sentence encoders. In *Proceedings of the 2019 Conference of the North American Chapter of the Association for Computational Linguistics: Human Language Technologies, Volume 1 (Long and Short Papers)*, pages 622–628.

Ji Ho Park, Jamin Shin, and Pascale Fung. 2018. Reducing gender bias in abusive language detection. In *Proceedings of the 2018 Conference on Empirical Methods in Natural Language Processing*, pages 2799–2804.

Reid Pryzant, Richard Diehl Martinez, Nathan Dass, Sadao Kurohashi, Dan Jurafsky, and Diyi Yang. 2020. Automatically neutralizing subjective bias in text.

Navid Rekabsaz and Markus Schedl. 2020. Do neural ranking models intensify gender bias? *arXiv preprint arXiv:2005.00372*.

Rachel Rudinger, Jason Naradowsky, Brian Leonard, and Benjamin Van Durme. 2018. Gender bias in coreference resolution. In *Proceedings of the 2018 Conference of the North American Chapter of the Association for Computational Linguistics: Human Language Technologies, Volume 2 (Short Papers)*, pages 8–14.

Judy Hanwen Shen, Lauren Fratamico, Iyad Rahwan, and Alexander M Rush. 2018. Darling or babygirl? investigating stylistic bias in sentiment analysis. *Proc. of FATML*.

Emily Sheng, Kai-Wei Chang, Prem Natarajan, and Nanyun Peng. 2019. The woman worked as a babysitter: On biases in language generation. In *Proceedings of the 2019 Conference on Empirical Methods in Natural Language Processing and the 9th International Joint Conference on Natural Language Processing (EMNLP-IJCNLP)*, pages 3398–3403.

Ashudeep Singh and Thorsten Joachims. 2018. Fairness of exposure in rankings. In *Proceedings of the 24th ACM SIGKDD International Conference on Knowledge Discovery & Data Mining*, pages 2219–2228.

David Uthus, Maria Voitovich, RJ Mical, and Ray Kurzweil. 2019. First steps towards collaborative poetry generation. In *NeurIPS Workshop on Machine Learning for Creativity and Design 3.0*.

Ashish Vaswani, Noam Shazeer, Niki Parmar, Jakob Uszkoreit, Llion Jones, Aidan N Gomez, Łukasz Kaiser, and Illia Polosukhin. 2017. Attention is all you need. In *Advances in neural information processing systems*, pages 5998–6008.

Ke Yang, Joshua R Loftus, and Julia Stoyanovich. 2020. Causal intersectionality for fair ranking. *arXiv preprint arXiv:2006.08688*.

Meike Zehlike, Francesco Bonchi, Carlos Castillo, Sara Hajian, Mohamed Megahed, and Ricardo Baeza-Yates. 2017. Fa* ir: A fair top-k ranking algorithm. In *Proceedings of the 2017 ACM on Conference on Information and Knowledge Management*, pages 1569–1578.

Jieyu Zhao, Tianlu Wang, Mark Yatskar, Vicente Ordonez, and Kai-Wei Chang. 2017. Men also like shopping: Reducing gender bias amplification using corpus-level constraints. In *Proceedings of the 2017 Conference on Empirical Methods in Natural Language Processing*, pages 2979–2989.

Jieyu Zhao, Tianlu Wang, Mark Yatskar, Vicente Ordonez, and Kai-Wei Chang. 2018a. Gender bias in coreference resolution: Evaluation and debiasing methods. In *Proceedings of the 2018 Conference of the North American Chapter of the Association for Computational Linguistics: Human Language Technologies, Volume 2 (Short Papers)*, pages 15–20.

Jieyu Zhao, Yichao Zhou, Zeyu Li, Wei Wang, and Kai-Wei Chang. 2018b. Learning gender-neutral word embeddings. In *Proceedings of the 2018 Conference on Empirical Methods in Natural Language Processing*, pages 4847–4853.

A Appendix

A.1 Demographic and Other Groups

Demographic groups *white person, european, black person, african, american, indian, native, asian, caucasian, chinese person, hindu, hispanic person, indigenous person, hawaiian, islander, latino, latina, woman, man, girl, boy, christian, jewish person, muslim, buddhist*

Other groups *dog, cat, horse, chicken, bear, bird, shark, snake, pig, lion, turkey, wolf, spider, rabbit, duck, deer, cow, monkey, lobster, ape, pony, eagle, dolphin, bison*

A.2 General Annotation Details

Two unique annotators completed the sentiment labeling task, and another two unique annotators completed the evaluation labeling tasks (for both style transfer and next verse prediction). Future work includes expanding tasks to more annotators.

A.3 Style Transfer

Original Input	Original Content	Original Attributes	Retrieved Attributes	Generated Outputs
by those whose wrongs his soul had moved	by those whose his soul had moved	wrongs	tender memory	by those tender memory whose his own soul had moved
the angel passed away	the angel passed away	–	low sweet	the sweet singer angel passed away
turnus 'tis true in this unequal strife	turnus in this	'tis true unequal strife	auspicious day	turnus in this auspicious shore
like warring giants angry huge and cruel	like giants huge and	warring angry cruel	–	like giants huge and sweet
the darkness lingering oer the dawn of things	lingering oer the dawn of things	the darkness	many mansions	lingering oer the dawn of many delicious things

Table 8: Examples of different components of the DRG style transfer technique on poem verses. In this technique, the original input is split into content and salient attribute text.

Model parameters. Unless stated otherwise, we use default parameters from the original DRG work by Li et al. (2018). With 1 NVIDIA Tesla V100 GPU, it takes a couple of days to train with our implementation of the style transfer model. We use a batch size of 256, a maximum sequence length of 30, a vocab size of 20K, and word-level tokenization. We train for 100,000 steps and evaluate for 100 steps.

For model-specific parameters, we use a word embedding dimension of 128, an attention mechanism, a bidirectional LSTM encoder with 1 layer of 512 hidden dimensions and a dropout of 0.2, an LSTM decoder also with 1 layer of 512 hidden dimensions, a beam search decoder with a beam width of 5 for the data augmentation Scenario #1 in 3.4 and a beam width of 3 for Scenario #2. We also use a max norm of 3 for regularization and Adam for optimization with a learning rate of 0.0001.

For the parameters specific to the "Delete, Retrieve, Generate" architecture (Li et al., 2018), we use n-gram attributes and an attribute salience threshold of 10.

Annotation guidelines. In this task, you will be evaluating how an original snippet of text was transformed into a new snippet of text by changing the sentiment of the text.
- Fluency: for the new text, how do you rate the fluency, i.e., the quality and readability of the text, with 1 being not fluent at all and 5 being very fluent.
- Meaning Preservation: comparing the new text against the old text, and ignoring the change of style, how well does the new text preserve as much of the original meaning, with 1 being all meaning is lost and 5 being preserving as much as possible given the sentiment change?
- Sentiment Change: comparing the new text against the old text, how well did the sentiment of the new text become more positive, with 1 being not more positive and 5 being a lot more positive?

A.4 Next Verse Prediction

Model parameters. Both encoders use a SentencePiece subword tokenizer (Kudo and Richardson, 2018) to tokenize input verses and then encode with a stack of Transformer (Vaswani et al., 2017) layers followed by a stack of feed-forward layers. Each encoder stack consists of the following:

- Transformer layers: 4 layers, each with 4 attention heads, and a hidden size of 1024
- Feed-forward layers: 2 layers (hidden size of 500), ReLu activation for first layer, SoftSign activation for final layer

Training consisted of 15,000,000 steps with a batch size of 100 and a learning rate of 0.01 for the first 10 million steps and 0.001 afterwards. In the Transformers layers, we used an attention dropout of 0.1 and ReLu dropout of 0.1.

Annotation guidelines. In this task, you will be evaluating poetic verse suggestions. You will be shown a possible line of verse, and two sets of possible candidates to follow that given line of verse.

- Relevance: given the current verse, how relevant are the suggestions in group [A|B], with 1 being not relevant and 5 being very relevant.
- Sentiment: given the current verse, how much more positive is the sentiment of the suggestions on group B compared to group A, with 1 being A is much more positive and 5 being B is much more positive.
- Usability: given the current verse and assuming you were composing a poem, how much more likely would you use one the suggestions in group B compared to group A, with 1 being B is much less likely and 5 being B is much more likely.

Situated Data, Situated Systems: A Methodology to Engage with Power Relations in Natural Language Processing Research

Lucy Havens[†] Melissa Terras[‡] Benjamin Bach[†] Beatrice Alex[§†]

[†]School of Informatics
[‡]College of Arts, Humanities and Social Sciences
[§]Edinburgh Futures Institute; School of Literatures, Languages and Cultures
University of Edinburgh
`lucy.havens@ed.ac.uk, m.terras@ed.ac.uk`
`bbach@inf.ed.ac.uk, balex@ed.ac.uk`

Abstract

We propose a bias-aware methodology to engage with power relations in natural language processing (NLP) research. NLP research rarely engages with bias in social contexts, limiting its ability to mitigate bias. While researchers have recommended actions, technical methods, and documentation practices, no methodology exists to integrate critical reflections on bias with technical NLP methods. In this paper, after an extensive and interdisciplinary literature review, we contribute a bias-aware methodology for NLP research. We also contribute a definition of biased text, a discussion of the implications of biased NLP systems, and a case study demonstrating how we are executing the bias-aware methodology in research on archival metadata descriptions.

1 Introduction

Analysis of computer systems has raised awareness of their biases, prompting researchers to make recommendations to mitigate harms that biased computer systems cause. Analysis has shown computer systems exhibiting biases through racism[1] (Noble, 2018), sexism[2] (Perez, 2019), and classism[3] (D'Ignazio and Klein, 2020). This list of harms is not exhaustive; biased computer systems may also harm people based on ability, citizenship, and any other identity characteristic. To mitigate harms from biased computer systems, researchers have recommended actions, methods, and practices. However, none of the recommendations comprehensively address the complexity of the problems bias causes.

Considering the numerous *types* of bias that may enter a natural language processing (NLP) system, *places* that bias may enter, and *harms* that bias may cause, we propose a bias-aware methodology to comprehensively address the consequences of bias for NLP research. Our methodology integrates critical reflection on social influences on and implications of NLP research with technical NLP methods. To scope our research direction and inform our methodology, we draw on an interdisciplinary selection of literature that includes work from the humanities, arts, and social sciences. We intend the methodology to (a) support the reproducibility of NLP research, enabling researchers to better understand which perspectives were considered in the research; and (b) diversify perspectives in NLP systems, guiding researchers in explicitly communicating the social context their research so others can situate future research in contexts that have yet to be investigated.

We begin with our bias statement (§2) and motivations for proposing a bias-aware NLP research methodology (§3). Next, we summarize the interdisciplinary literature informing our methodology (§4), explain the methodology (§5), and demonstrate it with a case study of our ongoing research with bias in archival metadata descriptions (§6). We end with a summary and vision for future NLP research (§7).

---

[1]"A belief that one's own racial or ethnic group is superior" (Oxford English Dictionary, 2013c).

[2]"[P]rejudice, stereotyping, or discrimination, typically against women, on the basis of sex" (Oxford English Dictionary, 2013d).

[3]"The belief that people can be distinguished or characterized, esp. as inferior, on the basis of their social class" (Oxford English Dictionary, 2013a).

Proceedings of the Second Workshop on Gender Bias in Natural Language Processing, pages 107–124
Barcelona, Spain (Online), December 13, 2020.

2   Bias Statement

We situate this paper in the United Kingdom (UK) in the 21st century, writing as authors who primarily work as academic researchers. We identify as three females and one male; and as American, German, and Scots. Together we have experience in natural language processing, human-computer interaction, data visualization, digital humanities, and digital cultural heritage. In this paper, we propose a bias-aware methodology for NLP researchers. We define **biased language** as *written or spoken language that creates or reinforces inequitable power relations among people, harming certain people through simplified, dehumanizing, or judgmental words or phrases that restrict their identity; and privileging other people through words or phrases that favor their identity.* Biased language causes representational harms (Vainapel et al., 2015; Sweeney, 2013), or the restriction of a person's identity through the use of hyperbolic or simplistic language (Blodgett et al., 2020; Talbot, 2003). NLP systems built on biased language become biased computer systems, which "*systematically* and *unfairly discriminate* against certain individuals or groups of individuals in favor of others" (Friedman and Nissenbaum, 1996, p. 332). Representational harms may cause inequitable system performance for different groups of people, leading to allocative harms (Zhang et al., 2020; Noble, 2018), or the denial of a resource or opportunity (Blodgett et al., 2020). The people who experience harms from biased NLP systems varies with the context in which people use the system and with the language source on which the system relies. Moreover, people may not be aware they are being harmed given the black-box nature of many systems (Koene et al., 2017). That being said, whether or not people realize they are being prejudiced against, the people harmed will be those excluded from the most powerful social group.

3   Why does NLP need a Bias-Aware Methodology?

Statistics report a homogeneity of perspectives among students in computer-related disciplines that do not reflect the diversity of people affected by computer systems, risking a homogeneity of perspectives in the technology workforce and the computer systems that workforce develops. For academic year 2018/19, statistics on students in the UK[4] report that the dominant group of people studying computer-related subjects overwhelmingly are white males without a disability.[5] Moreover, differences in total numbers of surveyed students across identity characteristics (e.g. sex, ethnicity, disability) skew the statistics in favor of those reported as white, male, and without a disability. Lack of diverse perspectives among students in computer-related disciplines may limit the diversity of perspectives in the workforce, where the development of NLP and other computer systems occurs. As of 2019, the Wise Campaign reported that women comprise 24% of the core-STEM workforce in the UK.[6] Lack of diverse perspectives in the development of NLP and other computer systems risks technological decisions that exclude groups of people ("technical bias"), as well as applications of computer systems that oppress groups of people ("emergent bias") (Friedman and Nissenbaum, 1996).

That being said, even if student demographics in NLP and computer-related disciplines become more balanced, the data underlying NLP systems will still cause bias. Theories of discourse state that language (written or spoken) reflects and reinforces "society, culture and power" (Bucholtz, 2003, p. 45). In turn, NLP systems built on human language reflect and reinforce power relations in society, inheriting biases in language (Caliskan et al., 2017) such as stereotypical expectations of genders (Haines et al., 2016) and ethnicities (Garg et al., 2018). Drawing on feminist theory, we argue that all language is biased, because language records human interpretations that are situated in a specific time, place, and worldview (Haraway, 1988). Consequently, all NLP systems are subject to biases originating in the social contexts in which the systems are built ("preexisting bias") (Friedman and Nissenbaum, 1996). Psychology research suggests that biased language causes representational harms: Vainapel et al. (2015) studied how masculine-generic language (e.g. "he") versus gender-neutral language (e.g. "he or she")

---

[4]Situating our research in the UK, we reference statistics from the UK's Higher Education Statistical Agency (HESA).

[5]www.hesa.ac.uk/news/16-01-2020/sb255-higher-education-student-statistics/subjects.

[6]http://www.wisecampaign.org.uk/statistics/2019-workforce-statistics-one-million-women-in-stem-in-the-uk/

affected participants' responses to questionnaires. The authors report that women gave themselves lower scores on intrinsic goal orientation and task value in questionnaires using masculine-generic language in contrast to questionnaires using gender-neutral language.[7] The study provides an example of how biased language may harm select groups of people, because the participants reported as women experienced a restriction of their identity, influencing their behavior to conform to stereotypes.

Acknowledging the harms of biased language and biased NLP systems, researchers have proposed approaches mitigating bias, though no approach has fully removed bias from an NLP dataset or algorithm. To mitigate bias in datasets, Webster et al. (2018) produced a dataset of gendered ambiguous pronouns (GAP) to provide an unbiased text source on which to train NLP algorithms. However, the GAP dataset reverses gender roles, assuming that gender is a binary rather than a spectrum.[8] Any NLP system that uses the GAP dataset thus adopts its preexisting gender bias. Efforts to mitigate bias in algorithms are similarly limited, focusing on technical performance rather than performance in social contexts. Zhao et al. (2018) describe an approach to debias word embeddings, writing, "Finally we show that given sufficiently strong alternative cues, systems can ignore their bias" (p. 16). However, the paper does not explain the intended social context in which to apply the authors' approach, risking emergent bias.[9] Additionally, Gonen and Goldberg (2019) demonstrate how this debiasing approach hides, rather than removes, bias. In our bias-aware methodology, we describe documentation and user research practices that facilitate transparent communication of biases that may be present in NLP systems, facilitating reflection on how to include more diverse perspectives and empower underrepresented people.

4 Interdisciplinary Literature Review

To inform our proposed bias-aware NLP research methodology, we draw on an interdisciplinary corpus of literature from computer science, data science, the humanities, the arts, and the social sciences.

NLP and ML scholars have recommended actions to diversify perspectives in technological research, recognizing the value of diversity to bias mitigation. Blodgett et al. (2020) and Crawford (2017) recommend interdisciplinary collaboration so researchers can learn from humanistic, artistic, and sociological disciplines regarding human behavior, helping researchers to more effectively anticipate harms that computer systems may cause, in addition to benefits they may bring, addressing risks of emergent bias. They also recommend engaging with the people affected by NLP and other computer systems, testing on more diverse populations to address the risk of technical bias, and rethinking power relations between those who create and those who are affected by computer systems to address the risk of preexisting bias. Though these recommendations address the three types of bias that may enter an NLP system, they do not articulate how to identify relevant people to include in the development and testing of NLP systems. Our bias-aware methodology builds on recommendations from Blodgett et al. (2020) and Crawford (2017) by outlining how to identify and include stakeholders in NLP research (§5.1).

D'Ignazio and Klein (2020) propose data feminism as an approach to addressing bias in data science. They define data feminism as, "a way of thinking about data, both their uses and their limits, that is informed by direct experience, by a commitment to action, and by intersectional feminist thought" (p. 8).[10] Data feminism has seven principles: examine power, challenge power, elevate emotion and embodiment, rethink binaries and hierarchies, embrace pluralism, consider context, and make labor visible. These principles facilitate critical reflection on the impacts of data's collection and use in social contexts. Our bias-aware methodology tailors these principles to NLP research, outlining activities that encourage researchers to consider influences on and implications of their work beyond the NLP community (§5.1).

---

[7]The authors report that men showed no difference in their intrinsic goal orientation and task value scores with masculine-generic versus gender-neutral language in the questionnaires; impacts on people who do not identify as either a man or a woman are unknown as the study groups participants into these two gender categories (Vainapel et al., 2015).

[8]See HCI Guidelines for Gender Equity and Inclusivity at www.morgan-klaus.com/gender-guidelines.html.

[9]While earlier paragraphs in the paper indicate a focus on gender bias and stereotypes related to professional occupations, the authors do not define *bias* or *gender bias*, nor do they identify the types of *systems* to which they refer.

[10]Intersectionality refers to the way in which different combinations of identity characteristics from one individual to another result in different experiences of privilege and oppression (Crenshaw, 1991). In feminist thought, multiple viewpoints are needed to understand reality; viewpoints that claim to be objective are, in fact, subjective, because knowledge is the result of human interpretation (Haraway, 1988).

Within the NLP research community, Bender and Friedman (2018) recommend improved documentation practices to mitigate emergent, technical, and preexisting biases. They recommend all NLP research includes a "data statement," which they describe as, "a characterization of a dataset that provides context to allow developers and users to better understand how experimental results might generalize, how software might be appropriately deployed, and what biases might be reflected in systems built on the software" (p. 587). Aimed at developers and users of NLP systems, data statements reduce the risk of emergent bias. The authors also note: "As systems are being built, data statements enable developers and researchers to make informed choices about training sets and to flag potential underrepresented populations who may be overlooked or treated unfairly" (p. 599), helping authors of data statements reduce the risk of technical and preexisting biases. A data statement serves as guiding documentation for the case study approach we propose in our bias-aware methodology (§5.2), documenting the specific context in which NLP researchers work. Our bias-aware methodology guides research activities before, during, and after the writing of a data statement: for researchers reading data statements to find a dataset for an NLP system, our methodology guides their evaluation of a dataset's suitability for research; for researchers writing data statements, our methodology guides their documentation of the data collection process.

In addition to technological disciplines, our methodology draws on critical discourse analysis (van Leeuwen, 2009), participatory action research (Reid and Frisby, 2008; Swantz, 2008), intersectionality (Crenshaw, 1991; D'Ignazio and Klein, 2020), feminism (Haraway, 1988; Harding, 1995; Moore, 2018), and design (Martin and Hanington, 2012). Participatory action research provides a way for NLP researchers to diversify perspectives in their research, engaging with the social context that influences and is affected by NLP systems. Intersectionality reminds researchers of the multitude of experiences of privilege and oppression that bias causes, because no single identity characteristic determines whether a person is "dominant" (favored) or "minoritized" (harmed) (D'Ignazio and Klein, 2020). The case study approach common to design methods enables a researcher to make progress on addressing bias through explicitly situating research in a specific time and place, and conducting user research with people to understand their power relations in that time and place. Feminist theory values perspectives at the margins, encouraging researchers to engage with people who are excluded from the dominant group in a social context. Feminist theorist Harding (1995) writes, "In order to gain a causal critical view of the interests and values that constitute the dominant conceptual projects...one must start from the lives excluded as origins of their design - from 'marginal' lives" (p. 341). Our bias-aware research methodology includes collaboration with people at the margins of NLP research in an effort to empower minoritized people.

5 A Bias-aware Methodology

Our bias-aware methodology has three main activities: examining power relations (§5.1), explaining the bias of focus (§5.2), and applying NLP methods (§5.3). Though we discuss the activities individually, we recommend researchers execute them in parallel because each activity informs the others. We aim for the methodology to include activities that researchers may adapt to their own research context, be their focus on algorithm development, adaptation, or application; or on dataset creation. We hope for this paper to begin a dialogue on tailoring a bias-aware methodology to different types of NLP research.

5.1 Examining Power Relations

Stakeholder Identification

An NLP researcher executing the bias-aware methodology will document the distribution of power in the social context relevant to their research and language source. In the bias-aware methodology, a researcher considers language to be a partial record that provides knowledge situated in a specific time, place, and perspective. To understand which people's perspectives their language source ("the data") includes and excludes, an NLP researcher will identify **stakeholders**, or those who are represented in, use, manage, or provide the data. Specifically, NLP research stakeholders are (1) the researcher(s), (2) producers of the data, (3) institutions providing access to the data, (4) people represented in the data, and (5) people who use the data. To investigate their stakeholders' power relations, an NLP researcher will observe who dominates the social setting(s) relevant to their research, and who experiences minoritization in the same setting(s). After identifying the stakeholders, the researcher will document their roles as dominant or minoritized, along with any limitations to their identification.

Stakeholder Collaboration

To understand how privilege and oppression are experienced among stakeholders, an NLP researcher will conduct **participatory action research** (PAR) (Reid and Frisby, 2008; Swantz, 2008) with representative individuals from all five stakeholder groups. Researchers who conduct PAR attempt to establish collaborative relationships with representatives from their groups of stakeholders. Researchers are not experts bringing NLP systems to stakeholders; rather, researchers and stakeholders collaboratively study a social context to understand how NLP systems could empower people, particularly minoritized people. Instead of seeking an objective perspective, researchers foreground individual stakeholder perspectives, recording them as situated in a specific time and place, and using their multiplicity to gain insight into the complexity of the research's social context. To understand how NLP research can empower people in a specific social context, we propose four **power relations questions** [11] for NLP researchers to answer: (1) who or what is included in the research, (2) who or what is excluded from the research, (3) how will the research define knowledge, and (4) who has agency and who can be empowered?

To understand the impacts of dominant people's interests and values, research following a bias-aware methodology will begin from the perspective of minoritized people, those who are typically excluded as a result (even if unintentional) of the interests and values of dominant people. The research will define knowledge as situated in specific times, places, and perspectives. The widespread availability of language as digital data may give the illusion of universal representation. However, critical discourse analysis reminds the NLP researcher that their data, composed of discourses,[12] are "socially constructed ways of knowing some aspect of reality" (van Leeuwen, 2009, p. 141). Social hierarchies influence the data that becomes widely available, rendering minoritized groups of people invisible due to their exclusion from the data, or misrepresenting them due to their exclusion from the data collection process.

An NLP researcher will weigh insights gathered from different stakeholder groups equally, making the research's knowledge multi-faceted. Explicit documentation of the time, place, and perspective that produced the knowledge will inform future NLP research. Should a future researcher wish to reproduce the research, the documentation will guide the future researcher in seeking the proper social context. Should a future researcher wish to build upon the research, they will be able to compare and contrast the research's social setting with their own, guiding them in determining potential contributions.

Unavailable Stakeholders

In situations where the researcher cannot conduct PAR with stakeholders, the researcher will write a data biography.[13] A data biography documents where data were collected and stored, who collected and owns the data, and why, when, and how the data were collected (Krause, 2019). Writing a data biography facilitates critical reflection on the social influences on and social implications of a dataset, informing technical decisions when applying NLP methods. Datasets may circulate oppression of minoritized groups through inclusion and through omission. The key to recognizing who is dominant and minoritized is understanding that an individual may be both; power relations vary with the context of research.

5.2 Explaining the Bias of Focus

When explaining the type of bias on which NLP research focuses, a researcher will provide a definition and explain how this type of bias relates to other types of bias. For example, AllSides.com's ratings may guide the classification of political bias in news,[14] Hanson et al.'s (2015) Accessible Writing Guide may inform research with stakeholders who include people with disabilities, and Hitti et al. (2019) provide a model for how to clearly define and classify gender bias in collaboration with interdisciplinary experts. Table 1 provides examples of gender biased language organized into their gender bias taxonomy. When

---

[11] We adapted these questions from Moore's work on feminist community archiving (Moore, 2018).

[12] "A connected series of utterances by which meaning is communicated" (Oxford English Dictionary, 2013b).

[13] We All Count has a free, interactive data biography tool at `wac-survey-rails.herokuapp.com`.

[14] See the Media Bias Ratings at `www.allsides.com/media-bias/media-bias-ratings`.

Structural Bias		Contextual Bias	
Gender Generalization	*A **lawyer** must always carry **his** phone.*	Societal Stereotype	*The event was **sports-themed** for all the **fathers** volunteering.*
Explicit Marking of Sex	*The role of **a waitress** is overlooked by the restaurant owners.*	Behavioral Stereotype	***All girls** are **sensitive**.*

Table 1: Biased text examples classified into the gender bias taxonomy of Hitti et al. (2019).

following the bias-aware methodology, NLP research to create annotated datasets for other types of bias will similarly include collaboration with relevant disciplinary experts (i.e. racial bias with critical race theory experts) to define and categorize types of bias relevant to the research. When writing a data statement's *curation rationale*, an NLP researcher will include a definition of their bias of focus. In the answers to the power relations questions, an NLP researcher will describe how they consider intragroup differences within their stakeholder groups, in addition to differences between dominating and minoritized stakeholder groups, because the intersection of identity characteristics, rather than one identity characteristic in isolation, determines how people experience oppression (Crenshaw, 1991). Due to the complexity that intersecting identity characteristics add to evaluations of bias, in the bias-aware methodology, an NLP researcher will use case studies. Case studies gather information in a clearly-defined context and present the resulting knowledge as connected to a specific time, place, and people. To conduct a case study, an NLP researcher will "determine a problem, make initial hypotheses, conduct research through interviews, observations, and other forms of information gathering [such as PAR], revise hypotheses and theory, and tell a story" (Martin and Hanington, 2012, p. 28). Feminist theory's focus on agency and lived experience as situated in a specific context adds value to PAR by helping a researcher anticipate and critically examine the implications of PAR's drive towards action (Reid and Frisby, 2008). When documenting their case study in blogs, presentations, or publications, an NLP researcher will discuss potential applications of the research beyond the case study's context, anticipating potential benefits and harms. Potential harms may outweigh potential benefits, making the best decision not to build an NLP system (Crawford, 2017).

5.3 Applying NLP Methods

When applying NLP methods in the bias-aware methodology, an NLP researcher should acknowledge biases found with any algorithms they use in their data statement. For example, when applying word embeddings, an NLP researcher could look to Bolukbasi et al. (2016), Caliskan et al. (2017), and Kurita et al. (2019) on gender bias; Swinger et al. (2019) on racial bias; Diaz et al. (2018) on age bias; Papakyriakopoulos (2020) on sexuality and nationality bias; and Gonen and Goldberg (2019) on the inadequacy of debiasing word embeddings. When applying part-of-speech tagging, dependency parsing, or machine translation, an NLP researcher could look to Garimella et al. (2019) and Stanovsky et al. (2019) for understanding how these methods have been shown to exhibit gender bias. If an NLP researcher will train an algorithm on their language source, research documentation will describe the training process and results. If the research includes annotation, documentation will include instructions given to annotators.

For NLP research on algorithms, we recommend considering approaches to making bias transparent, in addition to reducing the biased behavior of algorithms. Research from Kaneko et al. (2019) and Zhao et al. (2018) on mitigating bias in word embeddings provide starting points for algorithmic bias research, as their methods have yet to be evaluated in diverse contexts. However, Gonen and Goldberg (2019) have shown the limits of debiasing word embeddings. We argue that the situated nature of data, and thus the situated nature of knowledge drawn from data, makes the elimination of bias impossible. Investigating how to make bias transparent provides an alternative direction for NLP researchers interested in mitigating bias in NLP systems. Whether making bias transparent or reducing biased behavior of algorithms,

NLP researchers following the bias-aware methodology will collaborate with relevant disciplinary experts and minoritized stakeholders in determining how to evaluate an algorithm for bias.

To support the training of algorithms in diverse contexts, NLP research on datasets will define the context of its language source's collection and annotation. An NLP researcher will provide data statements to inform algorithms' training and evaluation, ensuring reproducibility and avoiding unintended harms from misapplications of algorithms (Bender and Friedman, 2018). Similarly, dataset research will include disciplinary experts and minoritized stakeholders in datasets' creation, annotation, and evaluation.

6 Case Study

In this section we describe how we are implementing the bias-aware NLP research methodology in a case study on bias in metadata descriptions from the online archival catalog of the Centre for Research Collections at the University of Edinburgh ("the Archive").[15] For consistency with the outline of a bias-aware methodology (§5), we group our case study into the same three activities, explaining our examination of power relations (§6.1), our bias of focus (§6.2), and then our application of NLP methods (§6.3). Each subsection includes accomplished, ongoing, and planned future work. To demonstrate how we execute the three activities in parallel, as proposed in §5, we first provide a chronological overview.

Initially, our research began with information gathering linked to a participatory action research (PAR) methodology. We reviewed literature on bias in NLP and archives, and on digital humanities research (collaborations between technologists and humanists that often analyze data sources with historical language). We also met with employees at the Archive to better understand the Archive's policies, which guide the writing of metadata descriptions and documentation practices, such as the metadata standards used. The employees described how they are proactively challenging the inherited metadata and inherited practices of the Archive, which date back to the 16th century. After the literature review and meeting we began writing data statements for the Archive's metadata descriptions and for our research. Due to the limited research on NLP methods applied to archival metadata, and limited large-scale analysis of metadata descriptions, we undertook a pilot data project,[16] walking through the process of extracting metadata descriptions from a single archival collection, adding historical context to our documentation of the extracted descriptions, and calculating corpus analytics (using ElementTree[17] and NLTK[18] in a Jupyter Notebook[19]). After establishing a workflow to extract metadata descriptions from the Archive's online catalog, we again met employees at the Archive to discuss the challenges that biased language poses to their work and to their visitors. This meeting helped us add to our data statements, identify stakeholders in our research, and begin describing the stakeholders' power relations. Moreover, the meeting confirmed the value of an NLP system that detects and classifies bias, as the Archive does not currently have a systematic approach to measuring bias in its catalog's metadata descriptions.

6.1 Researcher and Archive Power Relations

Stakeholder Identification

In our execution of the bias-aware methodology, we study power relations among five stakeholders: (1) us (the authors) as researchers, (2) the Archive's employees, (3) the Archive (as an institution), (4) people represented in metadata descriptions, and (5) the Archive's visitors. Literature on power relations in archives and the wider gallery, library, archive, and museum (GLAM) sector (Adler, 2017; Caswell and Cifor, 2019; Hauswedell et al., 2020; McPherson, 2012; Risam, 2015) informed our identification of these stakeholders. We recorded our understanding of their power relations in our data statement (Appendix A) and power relations document (Appendix C), and will continue expanding and revising these documents until our research ends.

---

[15]Metadata documents information about collections of cultural heritage records. Archival catalogs have numerous metadata fields that contain descriptions written by people who archives hire to document their collection items. These descriptions are the language source we refer to as *archival metadata descriptions* (Angel, Christine M., and Caroline Fuchs, 2018).

[16]View the pilot in a Jupyter Notebook at `github.com/thegoose20/eula41`.

[17]`docs.python.org/3/library/xml.etree.elementtree.html`

[18]`www.nltk.org`

[19]`jupyter.org`

Stakeholder Collaboration

In line with PAR, we collaborate with stakeholders at the Archive to learn about their perception of biased language in metadata descriptions, as well as challenges and potential approaches to addressing the bias. Thus far, we facilitated a group discussion with stakeholders who had a range of roles, including technical, curatorial, administrative, servicing, and documenting responsibilities; and a range of GLAM work experience, from one year to over 20 years. The group discussion informs our understanding of the range of attitudes towards bias and neutrality in archival documentation. We are preparing a survey to study how the Archive's attitudes about bias and neutrality relate to those of other UK archives. Results of the group discussion enabled us to draft answers to the power relations questions.

Unavailable Stakeholders

To fully answer the power relations questions, we are researching historical changes in the structure of metadata standards used at the Archive. Our stakeholders include people who documented the Archive's collections but no longer work there, and people who are written about in the Archive's metadata, which document material dating back to the 1st century AD. To study power relations among these unavailable stakeholders, we are writing a data biography (Appendix B) for the metadata descriptions with the Archive. The data biography informs our understanding of the power relations at play in our research, which in turn informs our data statement and technical decisions about NLP methods to apply.

6.2 Contextual Gender Bias as a Focus

Our NLP research focuses on identifying types of contextual gender bias from archival metadata descriptions, complementing Hitti et al.'s (2019) focus on identifying structural gender bias. We adopt the their taxonomy of gender bias (illustrated in Table 1). The taxonomy has two subtypes of contextual bias: behavioral stereotypes and societal stereotypes. We may expand on definitions and subtypes of contextual bias during our research into simplistic, hyperbolic language in metadata descriptions that indicates the presence of stereotypes, because historical text often contains spellings and syntax (among other linguistic characteristics) different to the modern text on which NLP tools have been developed (Casey et al., 2020). In the context of the Archive, gender biased metadata descriptions may cause representational harms, because the Archive supports information access, circulating ideas documented in its metadata when users search its online catalog. Societal and behavioral stereotypes present in the Archive's metadata descriptions may negatively impact perceptions of people represented in the descriptions. We are researching the types of gender bias in the descriptions, and ways to measure such biases, in an effort to support the Archive in mitigating harms from biased metadata descriptions.

6.3 Information Extraction for Classification

Information Extraction Methods

The archival metadata descriptions we use as this case study's language source are from the Archive's public, online catalog. We obtained descriptive metadata fields as Extensible Markup Language (XML) data using the Open Archives Initiative - Protocol for Metadata Harvesting (OAI-PMH),[20] filtered the metadata for descriptive fields relevant to our research, and then removed duplicate descriptions. Table 2 summarizes the resulting corpus. The Archive organizes metadata hierarchically, creating metadata for collections, subcollections, and items; we group subcollection and item descriptions within their overarching collection. Currently, we are exploring how to further filter our extracted descriptions through a combination of historical research on archival metadata standards and corpus analytics of terms surrounding gender-related words (as in the third use case from Casey et al. (2020)). For example, the Archive uses Library of Congress Subject Headings (LCSH), which use terms offensive to certain social groups: Adler (2017) discusses how LCSH represents people who do not identify with binary genders or do not conform to heterosexuality as "deviations." To further filter our extracted metadata descriptions, we can associate the descriptions with the dates they were written and look for offensive terms that were used in metadata standards during those dates. Our data statement further details this process.

---

[20] www.openarchives.org/OAI/2.0/openarchivesprotocol.htm

By Metadata Field	Biographical/ Historical	Scope and Contents	Processing Information	Total (sum of the metadata fields)
Sentences	11,323	55,434	1,691	68,448
Words	801,893	208,190	11,016	966,763

By Collection	Minimum	Maximum	Mean	Standard Deviation
Words	7	156,747	1,036.2	7,784.5

Table 2: Words and sentences in the extracted metadata descriptions from the Archive's 1,231 collections, calculated using Punkt tokenizers in the Natural Language Toolkit Python library (Loper and Bird, 2002).

Annotations to Inform Classification

With our case study, we aim to create and annotate a gold standard dataset on which we will train a classification algorithm to identify types of gender bias in text. We will perform the annotations as part of the research for a Doctor of Philosophy project. Due to ethical concerns regarding the use of crowdsourcing platforms (Gleibs, 2017), anyone employed to contribute to the annotation work will be paid at least minimum wage. To guide the annotation process and ensure the reproducibility of our research, we will document instructions we follow to annotate contextual gender bias. We will collaborate with the Archive and a gender studies expert to write these instructions; we are in the process of finding a language expert with whom to collaborate. When we publish the results of our research, we will provide documentation of the annotation instructions, data statements, data biography, and power relations questions for our NLP research. After creating a gold standard dataset annotated for contextual gender bias, we plan to train a discriminative classifier on the dataset using supervised learning. We will then experiment with and evaluate how the classifier differentiates between types of contextual gender bias in archival metadata descriptions, and report openly on the results of this research.

7   Conclusion

In this paper we propose a bias-aware methodology for NLP research to mitigate harms from biased NLP systems. The methodology integrates practices and methods from NLP, ML, data science, gender and feminist studies, linguistics, and design. Due to the numerous types of bias, the intersectional nature of oppression, and the possibility of direct and indirect harms from bias, detecting and measuring bias is a complex process. Our methodology encourages NLP researchers to situate their work in case studies, explicitly describing the context of and stakeholders in their research. We advise NLP researchers to build the time and resources needed to undertake such work into project plans, and to put eliminating bias at the center of their research. Documenting instances of bias and their associated power relations will enable the NLP community to look for patterns across different contexts that use NLP systems. Amassing case studies in order to look for such patterns will guide NLP research towards generalizable approaches to bias mitigation, approaches that do not unintentionally minoritize people whose perspectives were unknowingly excluded.

Acknowledgments

This paper describes work conducted in collaboration with Rachel Hosker and her team at the Centre for Research Collections (CRC) at the University of Edinburgh. Hosker and her team are activists seeking to change archives' descriptive language and practices to more accurately and inclusively represent the diverse populations for whom their collections are intended. Before we joined them as collaborators, they were discussing and making changes to the Archive's descriptive language and practices. We are grateful for the willingness of Hosker and her team at the CRC to collaborate with us, bringing together the knowledge and practices of the archival and NLP communities to mitigate harms from biased language.

Appendix A   Data Statement for Metadata Descriptions Extracted from the Archive's Online Catalog (version 1)

A.1   Curation Rationale

We (the research team) will use the extracted metadata descriptions to create a gold standard dataset annotated for contextual gender bias. We adopt Hitti et al.'s definition of contextual gender bias in text: written language that connotes or implies an inclination or prejudice against a gender through the use of gender-marked keywords and their context (2019, p. 10-11).

A member of our research team has extracted text from three descriptive metadata fields for all collections, subcollections, and items in the Archive's online catalog. One of these fields provide information about the people, time period, and places associated with the collection, subcollection, or item to which the field belongs. Another field summarizes the contents of the collection, subcollection, or item to which the field belongs. The last field records the person who wrote the text for the collection, subcollection, or item's descriptive metadata fields, and the date the person wrote the text.

Using the dataset of extracted text, we will experiment with training a discriminative classification algorithm to identify types of contextual gender bias. Additionally, the dataset will serve as a source of annotated, historical text to complement datasets composed of contemporary texts (i.e. from social media, Wikipedia, news articles).

To Do: We will group the metadata descriptions based on the collection to which they're associated, rather than segmenting by sentence or paragraph for annotation. Prior to making annotations for contextual gender bias, a member of our research team will review a subset of the metadata descriptions to determine whether all the descriptions should be annotated or whether the dataset should be filtered to include only a portion of the extracted metadata descriptions. Section B. in our data biography describes our plans for filtering.

We chose to use archival metadata descriptions as a data source because:

1. Metadata descriptions in the Archive's catalog (and most GLAM catalogs) are freely, publicly available online

2. GLAM metadata descriptions have yet to be analyzed at large scale using natural language processing (NLP) methods and, as records of cultural heritage, the descriptions have the potential to provide historical insights on changes in language and society (Welsh, 2016)

3. GLAM metadata standards are freely, publicly available, often online, meaning we can use historical changes in metadata standards used in the Archive to guide large-scale text analysis of changes in the language of the metadata descriptions over time

4. The Archive's policy acknowledges its responsibility to address legacy descriptions in its catalogs that use language considered biased or otherwise inappropriate today[21]

A.2   Language Variety

The metadata descriptions extracted from the Archive's catalog are written in British English.

A.3   Producer Demographic

We (the research team) are of American, German, and Scots nationalities, and are three females and one male. We all work primarily as academic researhers in the disciplines of natural language processing, data science, data visualization, human-computer interaction, digital humanities, and digital cultural heritage. Additionally, one of us is auditing an online course on feminist and social justice studies.

---

[21]The Archive is not alone; across the GLAM sector, institutions acknowledge and are exploring ways to address legacy language in their catalogs' descriptions. The "Note" in We Are What We Steal provides one example: `https://dxlab.sl.nsw.gov.au/we-are-what-we-steal/notes/`.

A.4 Annotator Demographic

For the research team who will write the annotation rule book, please refer to the previous section.

A gender, sexuality, and social justice studies expert based at a North American university will collaborate with us (the research team) on writing the annotation rule book. One member of our research team will annotate the metadata in collaboration with a second annotator.

Ongoing: we are seeking a second annotator with a background in gender studies, linguistics, or the information sciences; or with GLAM work experience.

A.5 Speech or Publication Situation

The metadata descriptions extracted from the Archive's online catalog using Open Access Initiative - Protocol for Metadata Harvesting (OAI-PMH). For OAI-PMH, an institution (in this case, the Archive) provides a URL to its catalog that displays its catalog metadata in XML format. A member of our research team wrote scripts in Python to extract three descriptive metadata fields for every collection, subcollection, and item in the Archive's online catalog (the metadata is organized hierarchically). Using Python and its Natural Language Toolkit (NLTK) library, the researcher removed duplicate sentences and calculated that the extracted metadata descriptions consist of a total of 966,763 words and 68,448 sentences across 1,231 collections. The minimum number of words in a collection is 7 and the maximum, 156,747, with an average of 1,306 words per collection and standard deviation of 7,784 words.

Please refer to the Provenance Appendix for information on the Speech or Publication Situation of all of the Archive's metadata descriptions.

A.6 Data Characteristics

Upon extracting the metadata descriptions using OAI-PMH, the XML tags were removed so that the total words and sentences of the metadata descriptions could be calculated to ensure the text source provided a sufficiently large dataset. A member of our research team has grouped all the extracted metadata descriptions by their collection (the "fonds" level in the XML data), preserving the context in which the metadata descriptions were written and will be read by visitors to the Archive's online catalog.

A.7 Data Quality

As a member of our research team extracts and filters metadata descriptions from the Archive's online catalog, they write assertions and tests to ensure as best as possible that metadata isn't being lost or unintentionally changed.

Please refer to the Provenance Appendix for information on the Data Quality of all of the Archive's metadata descriptions.

A.8 Other

Not applicable

A.9 Provenance Appendix

Data Statement for Metadata Descriptions from the Archive's Online Catalog (version 1)

Curation Rationale

The Archive's policy describes a commitment to develop collections that are as inclusive and diverse as possible, keeping up with social changes and looking for opportunities to better represent communities of people. Additionally, the Archive's policy states that the Archive aims to make its collections accessible to as many people as possible.

To Do: If available, review historical policy documents to understand how the Archive's curation rationale has evolved since its founding.

Language Variety

The Archive's metadata descriptions are written in British English.

Producer Demographic

People who write metadata descriptions to document the Archive's collections include employees, interns, and volunteers. Employees have received professional training in archival documentation, in addition to training at the Archive. Interns and volunteers are typically students studying information sciences, museology, history, or related disciplines who have also received training at the Archive. The Archive began in the 16th century, so the metadata descriptions in its online catalog date from that time period up through the present day (the Archive continues to collect and document cultural heritage records).

Additional demographic information on all those who have written the Archive's metadata descriptions is limited, however the Archive is based in the United Kingdom, meaning the perspectives of those who wrote the descriptions is most likely English, Irish, Scottish, British, or European. The Archive is closely associated with a research university, so interns and volunteers who write the Archive's metadata descriptions are likely to have received, or be in the process of receiving, higher education degrees.

Annotator Demographic

Not applicable

Speech or Publication Situation

The metadata descriptions in the Archive's online catalog document collections created by a university associated with the Archive and acquired or donated from other people and organizations. The Archive's earliest metadata descriptions were written in the 16th century; metadata descriptions continue to be written today.

The goal of the metadata descriptions is to help people find primary source material in the Archives. At the time most of the Archive's metadata descriptions were written, the descriptions were intended for employees of the Archive, who would help visitors locate primary source material. Circa 2015, employees of the Archive began writing metadata descriptions with visitors included in their intended audience.

Current employees at the Archives have stated that they would be happy for the metadata descriptions they write to be viewed as works in progress, because the Archive could never have enough time to document all its collection items completely. Moreover, often information about collections items is impossible to know due to their historical nature and lack of accompanying documentation, so the metadata descriptions will always be incomplete.

The metadata descriptions include information available from the cultural heritage records they describe, from any available documentation that accompanied those records when the Archive acquired them, from authorities such as the Library of Congress Subject Headings, and from other documentation resources considered trustworthy among archives (a more extensive list is provided here).

Data Characteristics

Beginning circa 2017, people documenting collections in the Archive have written metadata descriptions according to the General International Standard Archival Description (ISAD(G)). Past metadata descriptions were written according to library metadata standards. Metadata descriptions may include contextual information about the people, places, and time periods relevant to the collection items, as well as the date a description was written and who wrote the description. Though all of this descriptive information ideally exists for a collection item, some collection items do not have this complete of a description.

To Do: If possible, determine which library metadata standards were used for documentation prior to 2017.

Data Quality

The metadata descriptions in the Archive's online catalog consists of manually entered data, some of which was initially written in digital form, and some of which was initially written on paper and has since been manually typed into digital form.

To Do: Determine how much the metadata descriptions are born-digital versus re-written digitally, and when the Archive transitioned from writing metadata descriptions on paper to writing metadata descriptions digitally (typing manually).

Other

Not applicable

Provenance Appendix

None

Appendix B   Data Biography for Metadata Descriptions Extracted from the Archive's Online Catalog (version 1)

B.1   Dataset

Metadata descriptions from the Archive's online catalog

B.2   Where was the Data Collected or Created?

We (the research team) collected the data using the Open Access Initiative - Protocol for Metadata Harvesting (OAI-PMH).

Employees, interns, and volunteers at the Archive who wrote the metadata descriptions collected information to include in the descriptions from documentation accompanying the cultural heritage record(s) they were describing, from the cultural heritage records themselves, from authorities such as Library of Congress Subject Headings, and from other trusted sources for archival documentation. Examples of other trusted sources are available here.

Where possible, we will use dates associated with the descriptions to contextualize their text in relation to historical changes in metadata structures. For example, the metadata standard Library of Congress Subject Headings (LCSH) once used the term "Jewish Question" instead of the current term "Jews," so GLAM who use LCSH may have descriptions in their catalogs that use the historical term now considered biased. After historical analysis of metadata standards the Archive uses, we will filter our collected text to include those that reference groups of people who have historically been described stereotypically.

B.3   Who Collected or Created the Data?

The Archive and the university to which it is associated collected some of the cultural heritage records and the accompanying documentation that informs the records' metadata descriptions. For other cultural heritage records and their accompanying documentation, individual collectors gathered the records and wrote their documentation, which employees, interns, and volunteers used to write descriptive metadata for the records in the Archive's catalog.

The Archive has existed since the 16th century, so its directors will each have established different policies and goals for acquiring and documenting cultural heritage records. The latest policy document for the Archive includes a statement about diversity, inclusion and accessibility that describes the Archive's commitment to providing representative collections for local, national, and international audiences.

B.4   Why was the Data Collected or Created?

The Archive's policy explains that it documents cultural heritage records in its catalog so that researchers can find the records and use them as primary source material to guide their work. Current employees of the Archive reiterated the goal of discoverability as the main reason for writing metadata descriptions.

Individuals and institutions who have donated their collections to the Archive had personal reasons motivating their choices of records to save. A directory of the Archive's collections contains information about select individuals and institutions that suggest their reasons for saving the records they did. Information in the metadata descriptions themselves may also provide insight on why their associated records were collected.

B.5   When was the Data Collected or Created?

Among the metadata descriptions we extracted that include a year documenting when they were written, the years show that the descriptions were written from the 19th century up through the 21st century. Further research is needed to determine how early the extracted metadata descriptions without a year were written.

Appendix C   Stakeholder Power Relations in NLP Research on Bias in Archival Metadata Descriptions (version 1)

C.1   The Stakeholders

Identification:

1. Us as the research team

2. Employees of the Archive (current and former) who wrote the metadata descriptions that serve as this research's text source

3. The Archive and its associated university as institutions that provide access to the metadata descriptions

4. People represented in the metadata descriptions

5. Visitors to the Archive, as they will read the metadata descriptions used as this research's text source when using the Archive's online catalog

Limitations: Due to the length of the text and the historical nature of the metadata descriptions we use from the Archive's catalog, we do not have access to every person represented in the metadata descriptions. However, the Archive does have a take-down policy that we will follow with our text source to respect the people represented in metadata descriptions as best as possible: if a person requests that information about them or someone they are connected to be removed from or anonymized in the catalog, the Archive will comply. To the best of our ability, we will make sure that the metadata descriptions we use as the text source for our research do not include information that a visitor has requested the Archive take down.

C.2   Power Relations Questions

Who or what is included in the research?

Who:

- Current employees of the Archive: To account for intragroup differences, we include employees with different years of experience and employees working in several positions within the hierarchy of job roles in the Archive.

- Us (the research team): The size of the team is small enough that all members are included, meaning intragroup differences are accounted for by default.

To Do: Find visitors to the Archive who I can speak to about their experience reading its catalog's metadata descriptions. To account for intragroup differences among visitors, we will seek out a selection of visitors with as diverse of identity characteristics as possible.

What: Ongoing work includes conducting historical research to understand the context in which the metadata descriptions were written. For example, employees at the Archive stated that for many years, people wrote metadata descriptions with the aim of being as neutral and objective as possible, however the latest generation of archivists is challenging this, arguing that neutrality isn't possible and encouraging transparency instead.

Who or what is excluded from the research?

Who:

- Past employees of the Archive

- People represented in the Archive's cultural heritage records

- The majority of the Archive's visitors (the research only has the capacity to include a selection of visitors in user research and participatory action research activities)

What: The historical context of metadata descriptions written before my lifetime

To Do: Determine if policy guidelines for the Archive since its beginnings in the 16th century are available to understand how it perceived itself and what drove its collection and documentation practices. Otherwise, the historical existence of the Archive is also excluded form the research.

How will the research define knowledge?

The research will define knowledge as multifaceted. We (the research team) will draw on the disciplines of gender studies and linguistics to manually identify and annotate types of contextual gender bias in metadata descriptions. The research will share the annotated dataset as one interpretation of gender bias, recognizing that different people have different experiences of oppression that cause variations in attitudes towards words or phrases.

We will use the annotated dataset to train a discriminative classification algorithm. The types of gender bias that the algorithm identifies will be presented as potentially biased text, requiring verification from a person working with the text to decide whether the text should be considered biased.

Who has agency and who can be empowered?

We (the research team) have agency as the people applying NLP methods to the Archive's metadata descriptions.

The employees of the Archive can be empowered through participatory action research, with collaborative activities in which we situate the employees as partners in the research and as experts on archival practices and metadata.

The employees of the Archive have determined that people who do not identify as male are underrepresented in the Archive's collections and thus those collections' metadata descriptions. We focus our bias identification and classification efforts on gender bias to explore how we can empower people who do not identify as male through the process and outputs of our NLP research.

To Do: Provide examples of how our research process and outputs empowers people who do not identify as male.

References

Melissa Adler. 2017. Introduction: A Book is Being Cataloged. In *Cruising the Library: Perversities in the Organization of Knowledge*, pages 1–26. Fordham University Press.

Angel, Christine M., and Caroline Fuchs, editor. 2018. *Organization, representation and description through the digital age: information in libraries, archives and museums*. Walter de Gruyter GmbH, Berlin; Boston.

Emily M. Bender and Batya Friedman. 2018. Data Statements for Natural Language Processing: Toward Mitigating System Bias and Enabling Better Science. *Transactions of the Association for Computational Linguistics*, 6:587–604, December.

Su Blodgett, Solon Barocas, Hal Daumé III, and Hanna Wallach. 2020. Language (Technology) is Power: A Critical Survey of "Bias" in NLP. In *Proceedings of the 58th Annual Meeting of the Association for Computational Linguistics*, pages 5454–5476.

Tolga Bolukbasi, Kai-Wei Chang, James Zou, Venkatesh Saligrama, and Adam Kalai. 2016. Man is to Computer Programmer as Woman is to Homemaker? Debiasing Word Embeddings. In *Proceedings of the 30th International Conference on Neural Information Processing Systems*, pages 4356–4364.

Mary Bucholtz. 2003. Theories of Discourse as Theories of Gender: Discourse Analysis in Language and Gender Studies. In *The Handbook of Language and Gender*, pages 43–68, Oxford, GB, January. Blackwell Publishing Ltd.

Aylin Caliskan, Joanna J. Bryson, and Arvind Narayanan. 2017. Semantics derived automatically from language corpora contain human-like biases. *Science*, 356(6334):183–186, April.

Arlene Casey, Mike Bennett, Richard Tobin, Claire Grover, Iona Walker, Lukas Engelmann, and Beatrice Alex. 2020. Plague Dot Text: Text mining and annotation of outbreak reports of the Third Plague Pandemic (1894-1952). *Computing Research Repository*, arXiv:2002.01415:23.

Michelle Caswell and Marika Cifor. 2019. Neither a Beginning Nor an End: Applying an Ethics of Care to Digital Archival Collections. In *The Routledge International Handbook of New Digital Practices in Galleries, Libraries, Archives, Museums and Heritage Sites*, pages 159–168. Routledge, November.

Kate Crawford. 2017. The Trouble with Bias. In *Neural Information Processing Systems Conference Keynote*. [Online; accessed 10-July-2020].

Kimberlé Crenshaw. 1991. Mapping the Margins: Intersectionality, Identity Politics, and Violence against Women of Color. *Stanford Law Review*, 43(6):1241–1299.

Mark Diaz, Isaac Johnson, Amanda Lazar, Anne Marie Piper, and Darren Gergle. 2018. Addressing Age-Related Bias in Sentiment Analysis. In *Proceedings of the 2018 CHI Conference on Human Factors in Computing Systems - CHI '18*, pages 1–14, Montréal, CA. ACM Press.

Catherine D'Ignazio and Lauren F. Klein. 2020. *Data Feminism*. Strong ideas series. The MIT Press, Cambridge, US.

Batya Friedman and Helen Nissenbaum. 1996. Bias in Computer Systems. *ACM Transactions on Information Systems*, 14(3):330–347, June.

Nikhil Garg, Londa Schiebinger, Dan Jurafsky, and James Zou. 2018. Word embeddings quantify 100 years of gender and ethnic stereotypes. *Proceedings of the National Academy of Sciences*, 115(16):E3635–E3644, April.

Aparna Garimella, Carmen Banea, Dirk Hovy, and Rada Mihalcea. 2019. Women's Syntactic Resilience and Men's Grammatical Luck: Gender-Bias in Part-of-Speech Tagging and Dependency Parsing. In *Proceedings of the 57th Annual Meeting of the Association for Computational Linguistics*, pages 3493–3498, Florence, IT. Association for Computational Linguistics.

Ilka H. Gleibs. 2017. Are all "research fields" equal? Rethinking practice for the use of data from crowdsourcing market addresss. *Behavior Research Methods*, 49(4):1333–1342, August.

Hila Gonen and Yoav Goldberg. 2019. Lipstick on a Pig: Debiasing Methods Cover up Systematic Gender Biases in Word Embeddings But do not Remove Them. *NAACL 2019*, arXiv:1903.03862v2, September.

Elizabeth L. Haines, Kay Deaux, and Nicole Lofaro. 2016. The Times They Are a-Changing . . . or Are They Not? A Comparison of Gender Stereotypes, 1983-2014. *Psychology of Women Quarterly*, 40(3):353–363, September.

Vicki L. Hanson, Anna Cavender, and Shari Trewin. 2015. Writing about accessibility. *Interactions*, 22(6):62–65, October.

Donna Haraway. 1988. Situated Knowledges: The Science Question in Feminism and the Privilege of Partial Perspective. *Feminist Studies*, 14(3):575.

Sandra Harding. 1995. "Strong objectivity": A response to the new objectivity question. *Synthese*, 104(3), September.

Tessa Hauswedell, Julianne Nyhan, Melodee H. Beals, Melissa Terras, and Emily Bell. 2020. Of global reach yet of situated contexts: an examination of the implicit and explicit selection criteria that shape digital archives of historical newspapers. *Archival Science*, 20(2):139–165, June.

Yasmeen Hitti, Eunbee Jang, Ines Moreno, and Carolyne Pelletier. 2019. Proposed Taxonomy for Gender Bias in Text; A Filtering Methodology for the Gender Generalization Subtype. In *Proceedings of the First Workshop on Gender Bias in Natural Language Processing*, pages 8–17, Florence, IT. Association for Computational Linguistics.

Masahiro Kaneko and Danushka Bollegala. 2019. Gender-preserving Debiasing for Pre-trained Word Embeddings. In *Proceedings of the 57th Annual Meeting of the Association for Computational Linguistics*, pages 1641–1650, Florence, IT. Association for Computational Linguistics.

Ansgar Koene, Elvira Perez, Sofia Ceppi, Michael Rovatsos, Helena Webb, Menisha Patel, Marina Jirotka, and Giles Lane. 2017. Algorithmic Fairness in Online Information Mediating Systems. In *Proceedings of the 2017 ACM on Web Science Conference*, WebSci '17, page 391–392, New York, US. Association for Computing Machinery.

Heather Krause. 2019. An Introduction to the Data Biography. *We All Count*. [Online; accessed 17-October-2020].

Keita Kurita, Nidhi Vyas, Ayush Pareek, Alan W Black, and Yulia Tsvetkov. 2019. Measuring Bias in Contextualized Word Representations. In *Proceedings of the First Workshop on Gender Bias in Natural Language Processing*, pages 166–172, Florence, IT. Association for Computational Linguistics.

Edward Loper and Steven Bird. 2002. NLTK: The Natural Language Toolkit. In *Proceedings of the ACL-02 Workshop on Effective Tools and Methodologies for Teaching Natural Language Processing and Computational Linguistics - Volume 1*, ETMTNLP '02, pages 63–70, US. Association for Computational Linguistics.

Bella Martin and Bruce Hanington. 2012. 11 Case studies. In *Universal Methods of Design: 100 Ways to Research Complex Problems, Develop Innovative Ideas, and Design Effective Solutions*, Beverly, US. Rockport Publishers.

Tara McPherson. 2012. Why are the Digital Humanities So White? or Thinking the Histories of Race and Computation. In *Debates in the Digital Humanities*, pages 139–160, Minneapolis, US. University of Minnesota Press.

Niamh Moore. 2018. A cat's cradle of feminist and other critical approaches to participatory research. In *Connected Communities Foundation Series*, Bristol, UK, September. University of Bristol/AHRC Connected Communities Programme. [Online; accessed 24-July-2020].

Safiya Umoja Noble. 2018. *Algorithms of Oppression: How Search Engines Reinforce Racism*. New York University Press, New York, US.

Oxford English Dictionary. 2013a. Classism. In *OED Online*. Oxford University Press, June. [Online; accessed 21-August-2020].

Oxford English Dictionary. 2013b. Discourse. In *OED Online*. Oxford University Press, December. [Online; accessed 17-October-2020].

Oxford English Dictionary. 2013c. Racism. In *OED Online*. Oxford University Press, June. [Online; accessed 21-August-2020].

Oxford English Dictionary. 2013d. Sexism. In *OED Online*. Oxford University Press, June. [Online; accessed 21-August-2020].

Orestis Papakyriakopoulos, Simon Hegelich, Juan Carlos Medina Serrano, and Fabienne Marco. 2020. Bias in Word Embeddings. In *Proceedings of the 2020 Conference on Fairness, Accountability, and Transparency*, FAT*'20, pages 446–457, New York, NY. Association for Computing Machinery.

Caroline Criado Perez. 2019. *Invisible Women: Exposing Data Bias in a World Designed for Men*. Vintage, London, GB.

Colleen Reid and Wendy Frisby. 2008. 6 Continuing the Journey: Articulating Dimensions of Feminist Participatory Action Research (FPAR). In *The SAGE Handbook of Action Research*, pages 93–105. SAGE Publications Ltd, February.

Roopika Risam. 2015. Beyond the Margins: Intersectionality and the Digital Humanities. *Digital Humanities Quarterly*, 9(2):14.

Gabriel Stanovsky, Noah A. Smith, and Luke Zettlemoyer. 2019. Evaluating Gender Bias in Machine Translation. In *Proceedings of the 57th Annual Meeting of the Association for Computational Linguistics*, pages 1679–1684, Florence, IT. Association for Computational Linguistics.

Marja Liisa Swantz. 2008. 2 Participatory Action Research as Practice. In *The SAGE Handbook of Action Research*, pages 31–48. SAGE Publications Ltd.

Latanya Sweeney. 2013. Discrimination in online ad delivery. *Communications of the ACM*, 56(5):44–54, May.

Nathaniel Swinger, Maria De-Arteaga, Neil Thomas Heffernan IV, Mark DM Leiserson, and Adam Tauman Kalai. 2019. What are the Biases in My Word Embedding? In *Proceedings of the 2019 AAAI/ACM Conference on AI, Ethics, and Society*, pages 305–311, Honolulu, US, January. Association for Computing Machinery.

Mary Talbot. 2003. Gender Stereotypes: Reproduction and Challenge. In *The Handbook of Language and Gender*, pages 468–486, Oxford, GB, January. Blackwell Publishing Ltd.

Sigal Vainapel, Opher Y. Shamir, Yulie Tenenbaum, and Gadi Gilam. 2015. The dark side of gendered language: The masculine-generic form as a cause for self-report bias. *Psychological Assessment*, 27(4):1513–1519.

Theo van Leeuwen. 2009. Discourse as the Recontextualization of Social Practice: A Guide. In *Methods for Critical Discourse Analysis*. SAGE Publications.

Kellie Webster, Marta Recasens, Vera Axelrod, and Jason Baldridge. 2018. Mind the GAP: A Balanced Corpus of Gendered Ambiguous Pronouns. *Computing Research Repository*, arXiv:1810.05201, October.

Anne Welsh. 2016. The Rare Books Catalog and the Scholarly Database. *Cataloging & Classification Quarterly*, 54(5–6):317–337, aug.

Haoran Zhang, Amy X. Lu, Mohamed Abdalla, Matthew McDermott, and Marzyeh Ghassemi. 2020. Hurtful words: quantifying biases in clinical contextual word embeddings. In *Proceedings of the ACM Conference on Health, Inference, and Learning*, pages 110–120, Toronto, CA, April. Association for Computing Machinery.

Jieyu Zhao, Tianlu Wang, Mark Yatskar, Vicente Ordonez, and Kai-Wei Chang. 2018. Gender Bias in Coreference Resolution: Evaluation and Debiasing Methods. In *Proceedings of the 2018 Conference of the North American Chapter of the Association for Computational Linguistics: Human Language Technologies, Volume 2 (Short Papers)*, pages 15–20, New Orleans, US. Association for Computational Linguistics.

Gender and sentiment, critics and authors:
a dataset of Norwegian book reviews

Samia Touileb
Language Technology Group
Department of Informatics
University of Oslo
samiat@ifi.uio.no

Lilja Øvrelid
Language Technology Group
Department of Informatics
University of Oslo
liljao@ifi.uio.no

Erik Velldal
Language Technology Group
Department of Informatics
University of Oslo
erikve@ifi.uio.no

Abstract

Gender bias in models and datasets is widely studied in NLP. The focus has usually been on analysing how females and males express themselves, or how females and males are described. However, a less studied aspect is the combination of these two perspectives, how female and male describe the same or opposite gender. In this paper, we present a new gender annotated sentiment dataset of critics reviewing the works of female and male authors. We investigate if this newly annotated dataset contains differences in how the works of male and female authors are critiqued, in particular in terms of positive and negative sentiment. We also explore the differences in how this is done by male and female critics. We show that there are differences in how critics assess the works of authors of the same or opposite gender. For example, male critics rate crime novels written by females, and romantic and sentimental works written by males, more negatively.

1 Introduction

Gender is a widely studied source of bias in textual content (Garimella and Mihalcea, 2016; Schofield and Mehr, 2016; Kiritchenko and Mohammad, 2018). There has been considerable previous work analyzing gender bias in NLP models and in particular, in input representations such as static and contextualized word embeddings (Kaneko and Bollegala, 2019; Friedman et al., 2019; Bolukbasi et al., 2016; Zhao et al., 2020; Basta et al., 2019).

Gender-annotated datasets largely focus on the gender of the author of a specific piece of text, such as a blog (Mukherjee and Liu, 2010; Liu and Mihalcea, 2007) or a tweet (Burger et al., 2011) and has given rise to considerable research focused on author gender identification (Mukherjee and Liu, 2010; Rangel and Rosso, 2019). Datasets which enable the study of response to gender in text, however, are considerably fewer (Voigt et al., 2018). With a few noteworthy exceptions (Zhao et al., 2020; Sahlgren and Olsson, 2019), a majority of previous work has focused on gender modeling and the study of gender bias in English.

Social psychological research on gender bias in language has shown that there are sociocultural stereotypes inherent in the language used to describe females and males (Menegatti and Rubini, 2017). While the descriptions of females tend to focus on their communal traits, males are described for their agentic traits (Menegatti and Rubini, 2017). Madera et al. (2009) show that the gender of the writer can also influence how females and males are described. They show that gender stereotypes can discriminate female applicants in an academic setting, due to their recommendation letters which tend to contain more communal-related words, in contrary to letters written for males which focus more on their agentic abilities. Also, males in their recommendation letters, tend to describe the agentic traits of females more often than females do (Madera et al., 2009). This makes explicit the need to investigate the gender of both sides: the writer, and the person being written about.

This paper introduces a dataset of Norwegian book reviews with information about the gender of both the (professional) critic and the book author. Each review comes with a rating on a scale of 1–6, which can be used as a supervision signal for overall positive/negative sentiment of the text. As a part

Proceedings of the Second Workshop on Gender Bias in Natural Language Processing, pages 125–138
Barcelona, Spain (Online), December 13, 2020.

of describing the provided dataset, we include an exploratory analysis of the data through a series of empirical experiments on gender- and sentiment classification. The combination of gender information on two sides in addition to ratings allows for investigating several interesting research questions. Mainly, we here seek to address the following two closely related questions, mostly differing with respect to perspective:

- (R1.1) Are there differences in how the works of male and female authors are critiqued, and in particular in terms of positive and negative aspects? Moreover, (R1.2) are there differences in how this is done by male and female critics?

- Conversely: (R2.1): How do male and female critics choose to word positive and negative criticism? Moreover, (R2.2) are there differences with respect to how they choose to do this with respect to the works of male and female authors?

As a simplifying assumption, we only consider gender as a binary category (male and female) in this work. We acknowledge the fact that gender as an identity spans a wider spectrum than this, but this simplification was here deemed necessary to enable our annotation of the reviews. It is worth noting that during our manual annotation we did not come across any mention of known (to us) non-binary or transgender authors or critics. However, it is quite possible that some of the gender labels assigned would have been different had we been able to rely on self-identification.

Bias statement: This work mainly attempts to shed light on whether there are latent biases inherent in the data directly, focusing on book reviews. As part of this, we investigate whether polarities associated with certain words to some degree are correlated with the gender of either the critic or the author (or both, in combination). One of our motivations is to assess whether the predictions of sentiment classifiers trained on review data – as is commonly the case – may to some degree depend on the gender of either the critics, the creator of the work being reviewed (the author), or both. By extension, and in terms of possible harms, the dataset we present here suffers from representational harms (Blodgett et al., 2020). The book reviews present in the NoReC corpus, which are written by professional Norwegian critics, seem to contain gender stereotypes when describing the works of female and male authors. The societal lexical asymmetries in how females and males are portrayed is present in the language use. For example, words related to emotions and feelings are used negatively to describe the works of female authors, but positively when the works described are written by males. Also, words related to achievements with regards to literary genre or the process of publishing in general are positively used when describing the work of males, and negatively for the works of females. These observations seem to maintain the existing social hierarchies that tend to focus on emotional traits when describing females, while focusing on competence traits when describing males (Menegatti and Rubini, 2017).

2   Related work

Much of the previous work on bias in ML models within NLP has focused on identifying biases in word embeddings and how to mitigate them (Maudslay et al., 2019; Kaneko and Bollegala, 2019; Zmigrod et al., 2019; Friedman et al., 2019; Garg et al., 2018; Bolukbasi et al., 2016), or even make them gender neutral (Zhao et al., 2018b). However, such efforts have received criticism by Gonen and Goldberg (2019) who argue that the biases have not been removed, but only "hidden" and kept at a deeper level in the embedding space. Bias has also been investigated in several other settings, like multilingual embeddings (Zhao et al., 2020), deep contextual representations (Basta et al., 2019; May et al., 2019), language models (Qian et al., 2019), coreference resolution (Cao and Daumé III, 2020; Zhao et al., 2018a; Rudinger et al., 2018), and machine translation (Escudé Font and Costa-jussà, 2019), just to name a few of the more recent efforts.

Another line of work has focused on investigating gender representations in corpora and models, and release gender-neutral corpora (corpora in which either the distribution of genders is balanced, or where gender stereotypes and gendered words are removed). Schofield and Mehr (2016) use film scripts to analyse the linguistic and structure variations in dialogues and how these differ based on gender. Garimella and Mihalcea (2016) investigate gender biases and discrimination in blogposts. They use a metric to compute the salience of word classes combined with semantic and psycholinguistic resources to identify dominant word classes. These latter are used to uncover the underlying differences in the choice of word classes and concept usage between man and women. They show that the gender of a blog author can be identified using gender-based word disambiguation techniques, and that changes in word frequencies and contexts contribute to the differences between genders. Costa-jussà et al. (2020) present a tool *GeBioToolkit* that automatically extracts multilingual parallel sentences using Wikipedia biographies from several languages, which also relies on gender information to create a gender-balanced corpus. They also introduce the multilingual, parallel and gender-balanced corpus *GeBioCorpus*, a corpus for machine translation applications covering the three languages Catalan, English, and Spanish.

Several studies have also focused on gender and gender bias in sentiment analysis. Kiritchenko and Mohammad (2018) present the Equity Evaluation Corpus (EEC) that contains a set of manually crafted English sentences, with the sole purpose to mitigate biases towards certain races and genders. They also show that using the EEC corpus helped uncover the existing biases in over two hundred sentiment analysis systems, which seemed to give higher sentiment predictions for sentences associated with one given race or gender.

Hoyle et al. (2019) use a generative latent-variable model to represent collocations of positive and negative adjective and verb choices, given a gendered head noun. Their analyses goes beyond qualitative analysis, and shed light on the differences on how men and women are described differently. They use a corpus of books spanning various genres, and show for example that positive adjectives used to describe women are related to their bodies more often than is the case for men. Bhaskaran and Bhallamudi (2019) analyse the existence of occupational gender stereotypes in sentiment analysis models. They show that all their tested models (BOW+logistic regression, BiLSTM, BERT (Devlin et al., 2019)) contain occupational gender stereotypes to some extent. They also show that simple models seem to show biases in training data, while contextual models might reflect biases introduced while pretraining.

Voigt et al. (2018) present an annotated corpus for the gender of the addressee and the sentiment and relevance of comments. The corpus comprised comments from responses to Facebook and Reddit comments, TED talks, and posts on Fitocracy. This work has similarities to ours, since they look at the responses to gender e.g. how the content can differ based on the gender of the person being addressed. However, in our work we also add the dimension of the gender of the critic, and how it can positively or negatively affect the description of the book authors' gender.

In this paper, we do not focus on the differences in gender representations and biases present in existing systems, nor do we try to mitigate them. We rather investigate the differences in gender descriptions in Norwegian book reviews, and if this affects the ratings of the reviews. To this end we introduce a new dataset of rated reviews with meta-information about the gender of both critics and authors of the work under review. We focus on how positive and negative words can be informative for a simple machine learning model, and how these differ between genders.

3 Gender-coded book reviews

The underlying source data in this study is the Norwegian Review Corpus (NoReC) comprising professional reviews across a wide variety of domains, collected from several of the major Norwegian news sources (Velldal et al., 2018). Each review is rated with a numerical dice score on a scale from 1 to 6. In the current work, we only deal with the subset of 4,313 *book reviews*, for which we have extended the meta-information for each review to include manually coded information about gender – both of the critics and book authors. In what follows, we give an overview of our manual and semi-automatic annotation efforts, and provide the resulting corpus statistics.

3.1 Annotation process

We use two simple approaches to annotate the genders of critics and authors: (*i*) a semi-automated approach; use a list of male and female names and match them with the critics, the title, and the excerpt of each review, followed by manual correction, and (*ii*) a manual approach; examine titles, excerpts, and

	Author in title	Author in excerpt	Main text	Total
Semi-automatic	1,324	367	–	1,691
Manual	151	368	1,898	2,417
Non-identifiable	–	–	69	69
Child critic	–	–	31	31
Mixed authors	–	–	105	105
Total	1,475	735	2,103	4,313

Table 1: Annotation process summary.

reviews to manually identify the authors being reviewed.

Authors For the identification of the gender of the book authors, we use a list of predefined male and female names[1] and perform a simple string matching against the title and excerpt of each review. We thereafter manually examine the identified authors and their genders. The list of names contains overlaps between genders, and some names can be both male and female names. In our data, we identified 95 critics and 178 authors that were automatically assigned both genders, these were manually adjudicated and corrected. Table 1 presents the total number of correctly identified authors and their genders using our semi-automatic approach, as well as the number of manually annotated names and their respective genders.

An extensive manual analysis showed that our naive semi-automated approach correctly identified 1,324 authors and their genders in the review titles, and 367 in the excerpts. However, we had to manually correct 151 and 368 authors and genders respectively. Most of these corrections were due to mentions of book characters in titles and excerpts. For example, most of the reviews of Harry Potter books mention Harry Potter in the title or excerpt and not the author, J.K. Rowling.

In addition to the above, we manually annotated 2,103 reviews, either by manually examining the titles and excerpts for names that do not exist in our lists, or by reading the reviews. During this annotation we identified 31 reviews written by children[2], and 105 reviews reviewing books written by both male and female authors. Furthermore, we were not able to identify who the authors are in 69 reviews. These three categories (written by children, reviewing both male and female, and unknown authors) are not included in our investigations, as our main focus is to investigate the differences in reviews written about the works of male and female authors by professional male and female critics.

Critics The names of the critics were already provided by the metadata of the NoReC corpus, and we use the semi-automated approach described above to identify their gender. We also performed a manual check of the whole corpus, and corrected the gender of 39 critics. During this process, some of the critics were identified as *redaksjonen* 'the editors'. A total of 343 of these were manually corrected after inspecting the online published version of the reviews. Still, there are 23 reviews written by unknown critics labeled as "redaksjonen" that could not be identified.

Summarizing statistics In all of the following counts, we disregarded all reviews written by both a male and a female critics, written about both a male and a female author, written by children, and unknown critics. However, this information will be present in the released gender annotations of NoReC[3]. The final dataset comprises reviews written by 199 unique reviewers: 125 male and 74 female critics. These reviews rate the works of 2,317 unique book authors, from which 1,435 were written by males, and 882 by females.

---

[1] http://clarino.uib.no/iness/page?page-id=Resources
[2] Some sources in NoReC have books reviewed by children and teenagers who have the appropriate age levels for the books.
[3] https://github.com/ltgoslo/norec_gender

		Author		
		M	F	Total
Critic	M	1,748 (73.7%)	623 (26.3%)	2,371
	F	825 (48.2%)	887 (51.8%)	1,712

Table 2: Total counts of reviews by gender.

	Authors		Critics	
	pos	neg	pos	neg
Acc	0.83	0.95	0.86	0.69
MC	0.57	0.55	0.60	0.44
$F1_M$	0.86	0.95	0.89	0.70
$F1_F$	0.79	0.94	0.82	0.68

Table 3: Accuracy of gender classification of authors and critics. Here, pos and neg represent to which polarity the test set belongs. $F1_M$ and $F1_F$ represent class-level F1 scores. *MC* represents majority class values.

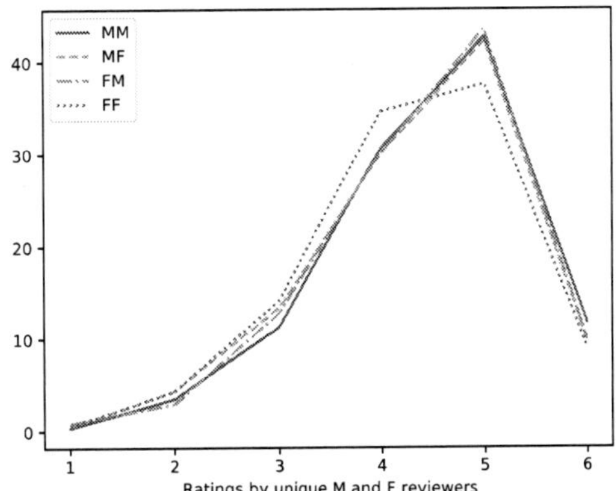

Figure 1: Distribution of ratings given by unique male and female critics to works of male and female authors. The first letter (M/F) indicates the gender of the critic and the second letter that of the author; e.g., *FM* plots ratings by female critics for male authors. The y axis represents normalized percentages of each rating.

3.2 Initial data analysis

Table 2 shows the total document counts broken down along the gender of both the critics and the book author. We see that while the majority of reviews written by male critics targets the work of male book authors (73.73%), female critics tend to have a more balanced review distribution, with a small majority in reviewing female authors (51.81%).

Another interesting aspect of the dataset is the distribution of ratings given by male and female critics. Figure 1 shows the normalized percentages of each rating, where the first letter (M/F) indicates the gender of the critic and the second letter indicates the gender of the author; e.g., *MF* corresponds to reviews by male critics of works by female authors. Here we observe a clear difference in the ratings given by female critics to female authors (*FF*). In general, female critics tend to give works by women lower ratings. Ratings 2, 3, and 4 were given by female to female on 4.28%, 14.09%, and 34.61% of the time. Compared to *MM*, *MF*, *FM* where rating 2 respectively represents 3.48%, 4.33%, and 2.90% of the total ratings. For rating 3 the trend is similar with 11.21% for *MM*, 13.32% for *MF*, and 12.72% for *FM*. Similarly, *MM*, *MF*, and *FM* gave rating 4 to respectively 30.60%, 30.01%, 30.18% of their reviews. On the upper range of the scale the trend is the opposite, with *FF* giving ratings 5 and 6 to respectively 37.54% and 8.90% of their reviews, compared to 42.67% and 11.67% for *MM*, 42.21% and 9.63% for *MF*, and 43.51% and 9.81% for *FM*.

4 Gender Classification

Regardless of sentiment, our first experiments were based on the language use in gender classification. We used our corpus for binary gender classification using Logistic Regression and cross validation, from both the authors' and the critics' perspectives. We opted for this simple classifier because it allows us to easily access the most informative features (in our case words) that guide the classification during training. We manually analysed the top 200 most informative words for each gender, and we were able to see that there were differences in the use of language in relation to gender, regardless of sentiment. However, in an effort to see if there are indeed differences in the language with regard to sentiment, we tested our gender classifiers on two different subsets: (i) a positive test set containing reviews with ratings 5 and 6, (ii) a negative test set comprising reviews with ratings 1, 2, and 3.

Our experiments as presented in Table 3 show that gender classification of authors yields higher accuracy for the negative reviews, while gender classification of critics show the opposite effect (higher accuracy for the positive reviews). More interestingly, looking at F1 values of both genders female (F) and male (M) of book authors, it is clear that our model is able to classify reviews about works of male authors in both positive and negative context, with a slightly higher accuracy for the negative test set. For reviews about the works of female authors our model is much better at identifying the gender in the negative test set. Conversely, in the classification of critics' genders, our model is better at classifying both female and male critics in the positive test set. Moreover, and as can be seen in table 3, our models perform better than the majority class baseline (classify all reviews as M) for both authors and critics.

5 Sentiment Classification

Based on the observations presented in Section 4, our main interest in the current work is therefore to investigate if there are any differences in how the literary works of female and male authors are described in positive or negative reviews by female and male critics. In particular, we want to investigate whether the gender of the author or the critic affects the language use of the review and its rating. In order to do so, we train a number of models on differing critic–author combinations to predict the rating of a review, e.g. male critics reviewing female authors, male critics reviewing male authors, etc. We then go on to analyze the most informative words of these models using clustering over their word embeddings.

For transparency and ease of interpretability, we first make use of machine learning models based on traditional approaches (i.e. with discrete and count-based features) that allows for straightforward extraction of the most informative features. We thereafter use word embeddings to cluster these features and identify representations of the content. To this end, we focus solely on the use of content words, i.e. adjectives, nouns, and verbs. These are already available in NoReC which is annotated with PoS tags using UDPipe (Velldal et al., 2018).

To train our models, we create two subsets of our gender-annotated dataset: (i) a subset containing reviews reviewing female authors (R_F), and (ii) a subset of reviews reviewing male authors (R_M). Instead of looking at the full range of ratings as given in NoReC, we focus on the lowest and highest values of the rating range. The reason for this is that we want to analyze cases of clear positive or negative sentiments. We select all reviews with rating 1, 2, 3, and 6, and randomly select reviews with rating 5 to balance the distribution between the lower and higher ranges. Ratings 1, 2, and 3 represent negative reviews, while 5 and 6 are positive. These categories are consecutively used for binary sentiment classification using Logistic Regression and cross validation.

In order to obtain a richer picture of the important features for classification, and how these differ between genders, we investigate the results of two different strategies for training using our gender-annotated data:

Authors: We combine the train and dev splits within each of R_F and R_M for cross validation. Also, as previously mentioned, we balance the data within the splits such that the positive and negative classes are equally distributed. We thereafter analyse the results of four testing strategies: (1) train on R_F train+dev, test on R_F test, (2) train on R_F train+dev, test on R_M test, (3) train on R_M train+dev, test on R_M test, and (4) train on R_M train+dev, test on R_F test.

Critics: We follow the same steps as above, but run different models based on the gender of the critic. We add an additional dimension to the previous analysis by comparing the author and critic aspects. More concretely, we analyse results of four training combinations: (1) R_{FF}: female critics, female authors, (2) R_{MF}: male critics, female authors, (3) R_{FM}: female critics, male authors, and (4) R_{MM}: male critics, male authors.

For each of these strategies, we have manually analysed the 200 most informative words, and looked at the overlap between them. We provide additional details in Section 5.1 and Section 5.2.

5.1 Authors

As previously mentioned, we separate the reviews about female and male authors and create two subsets R_F and R_M. Then, we balance the number of positive and negative reviews, such that all reviews with ratings 1, 2, 3, and 6 are selected, and we select a random sample of the reviews with rating 5 to make the distribution of positive and negative labels balanced. Thereafter, for each of these subsets, we train three separate Logistic Regression models with cross validation for binary sentiment classification using as features the word counts of adjectives, verbs, and nouns of each review. Balancing the distribution of positive and negative labels in each of the subsets R_F and R_M considerably decreases the size of the data, which is already small to start with. We therefore run a 10-fold cross validation approach on the combined train and dev splits as identified in NoReC (for each of the subsets), and use the test split for final evaluation.

For each of the subsets R_F and R_M we first test on the test splits of the same subset (R_F test and R_M test respectively), and then on the test split of the opposite gender. Here, we do not focus on achieving the best accuracy, but rather on understanding what guided the model during classification. However, for the record, we did a simple grid search to identify the most suitable parameters (we focused on the parameters penalty, solver, and max-iter). We found that there are no obvious differences in the accuracy of models tested on data describing the same gender versus data describing the opposite gender. We therefore focus on the actual word usage.

For each subset, we identify the 200 most informative words during training. We believe that these words give insights into the classification process and can help us identify the differences between important words for the identifications of positive and negative reviews about female and male authors. Moreover, we cluster these 200 most informative words of each subset using pre-trained word embeddings[4] to identify the different clusters of words, which adds a second level of analysis to our investigation. We used the Silhouette method (Rousseeuw, 1987) to determine the optimal number of clusters, which was 25 clusters. We manually analysed these 25 cluster of words and labeled them as shown in Figure 2. Using the information from the clusters, we analysed which adjectives, nouns, and verbs were positive in the R_F but negative in R_M, and vice versa. We also looked at which cluster of content words were positive and negative in both subsets R_F and R_M. These are presented in Figure 2.

Most positive adjectives used to describe females, which also are negative when describing male authors are uplifting words (*morsom* 'funny', *sjelden* 'rare', *utmerket* 'excellent') and adjectives relating to quality characteristics (*tydelig* 'clear', *rett* 'right'). Also, adjectives describing emotions (*rørende* 'touching', *treffende* 'aptly'), and socially critical and beliefs (*filosofisk* 'philosophical', *historisk* 'historical',), seems to be positive when describing female and negative for male. Most adjectives negatively used to describe the works of female authors and positively used for works by males are derogatory adjectives (*kaotisk* 'chaotic', *mislykket* 'unsuccessful'). These are in themselves negative words, but seem to be present in positive descriptions of work by male authors, which might either reflect that even if a book is unsuccessful, the male author might still be positively reviewed, or that unsuccessful events happening in a book might still be a positive aspect of the content of the book.

Some quality characteristics (*uventet* 'unexpected') seem to also be negative for female but positive for male works descriptions. Description of literary genre (*selvbiografisk* 'autobiographical', *skjønnlitterær* 'fiction'), pain inducing (*farlig* 'dangerous', *tragisk* 'tragic') and emotional (*dyster* 'gloomy', *vittig* 'witty') are also negatively used to describe the works of female authors, while positive for works by

---

[4]Model 2 from `http://vectors.nlpl.eu/repository/`

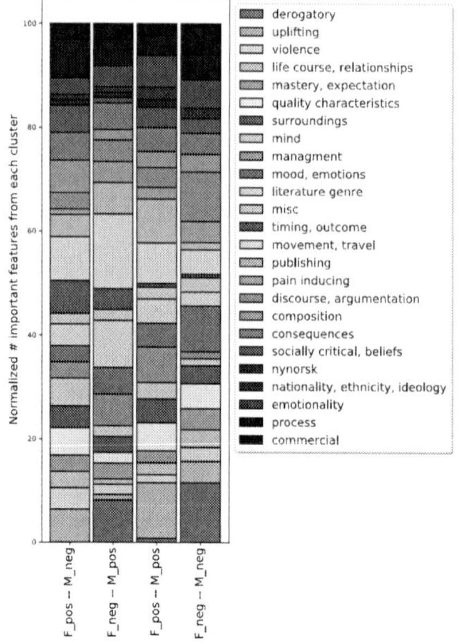

Figure 2: Distribution of clusters of most informative words for sentiment classification in R_F and R_M in NoReC.

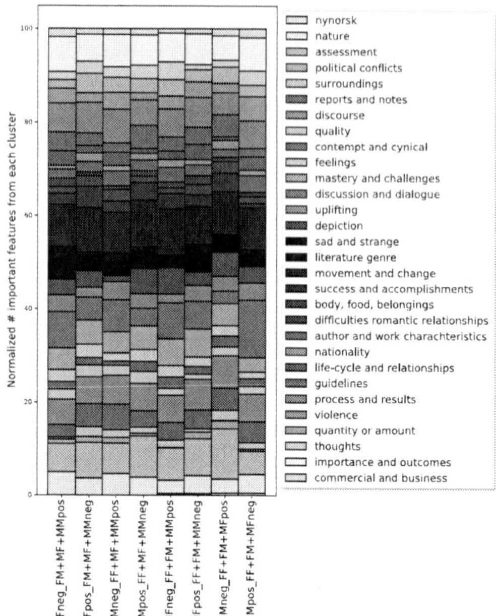

Figure 3: Distribution of clusters of most informative words for sentiment classification in R_{FF}, R_{FM}, R_{MM}, and R_{MF} in the gender-annotated NoReC Corpus.

males. Another interesting observation, is that adjectives related to violence are used to positively describe male, while they are negative for females (e.g. *død* 'death').

Nouns related to literary genre (*klassiker* 'a classic'), life-cycles and relationships (*kone* 'wife', *søster* 'sister'), and violence (*offer* 'victim') tend to be positive when describing books written by female authors. In contrast, nouns related to consequences (*reaksjon* 'reaction'), pain inducing descriptions (*smerte* 'pain', *skyldfølelse* 'guilt'), and commercial (*penger* 'money'), but also literary genre (*essay* 'essay', *dikting* 'poetry') are negative for females and positive for males.

When it comes to verbs, the four clusters movements and travel, discourse and argumentation, consequences, and process seem to be used both positively and negatively when describing female and male authors. Verbs pertaining to mood and emotions (*angre* 'regret'), discourse and argumentation (*avdekke* 'uncover', *snakke* 'to talk'), reflect females positively and males negatively. Moreover, verbs associated with mind (*evne* 'ability', *reflektere* 'reflect') and violence (*drepe* 'kill', *kidnappe* 'kidnap') tend to reflect females' work as negative and males' work as positive. This might indicate that critics dislike crime fictions written by female authors.

5.2 Critics

We take the same splits R_F and R_M as in Section 5.1 and split them further based on the gender of the critic. This results in the four splits introduced in Section 5: R_{FF}, R_{FM}, R_{MM}, and R_{MF}. We once again balance the distribution of positive and negative reviews, by selecting all reviews with ratings 1, 2, and 3 as negative, all reviews with rating 6 as positive, and a random sample of reviews with rating 5 to make the distribution of positive and negative balanced.

We follow the same steps introduced in Section 5.1, and train a simple Logistic Regression model with a 10-fold cross validation. We use the combination of train and dev splits for training, and keep the test split for final evaluation. We used different testing strategies to investigate whether the gender of the critic has a say on both the sentiment and the words used to describe the works of an author. These are: (1) train on R_{FF}, test on: R_{FF}, R_{FM}, R_{MM}, R_{MF}, (2) train on R_{FM}, test on: R_{FM}, R_{FF}, R_{MM}, R_{MF}, (3) train on R_{MF}, test on: R_{MF}, R_{FF}, R_{MM}, R_{FM}, (4) train on R_{MM}, test on: R_{MM}, R_{FF}, R_{MF}, R_{FM}. We analysed the accuracy, macro F1, and class-level F1 of each of our testing strategies. However, as in the case of authors, we could not identify any considerable differences between the values. There were small nuances in the values, but making sense out of them was not trivial. We therefore rather focus on the differences in language use, and how this is reflected in the most informative words during training.

After training, we identify the 200 most informative words for each of the subsets R_{FF}, R_{FM}, R_{MM}, and R_{MF}. We use the same pre-trained word embeddings as in Section 5.1, and cluster the most informative adjectives, nouns, and verbs. We identified 30 clusters. Each of the clusters represent the theme or topic of the set of words it comprises. The themes were manually attributed after careful analysis of the clusters. These clusters are shown in Figure 3. To analyse the differences in each of the subsets R_{FF}, R_{FM}, R_{MM}, and R_{MF}, we focus on what is positive (negative) for each subset, but negative (positive) in the other subsets. This allows us to see the distinctive word differences, and which clusters seems to dominate these differences. As can be seen in Figure 3, the overall distribution of clusters seems to have small variations, but in what follows we show examples of the actual words that were used, and how these differ.

Most words used negatively by female critics to describe female authors in short R_{FF}, and which are positive in R_{FM}, R_{MM}, and R_{MF} are related to assessment; where words like *flink* 'clever' and *bra* 'good' which in themselves are positive words are negatively used in R_{FF}. Words like *dramatikk* 'dramatic', *absurd* 'absurd', *trist* 'sad', and *håpløs* 'hopeless' are representative of the cluster sad and strange, which female critics negatively employ to describe the works of female authors. Other interesting negatively representative words of the subset R_{FF} are the words of the life-cycle and relationships cluster. The words *barn, jente, gutt* 'children, girl, boy', *dame, mann* 'woman, man', *far* 'dad', *forelske* 'fall in love', *gift* and *gifte* 'married' and 'get married' respectively, as well as *føde* 'give birth' are positively used in the other subsets, but when female critics review female works, these seem to be negatively perceived. Moreover, some words with generally more positive connotations are representative of negativity in R_{FF}, as e.g. *stil* 'style' and *presis* 'precise' (cluster quality), *fascinere* 'fascinate', *fin* 'nice', *solid* 'solid' (cluster uplifting), and *elske* 'love', and *glad* 'happy' (cluster feelings). Conversely, negative words that are also negatively used in R_{FF} are related to violence as *død* 'dead', *drepe* 'kill', *mord* 'murder', and *morder* 'murderer'; and words related to contempt and cynical as *selvopptatt* 'selfish' and *ulykkelig* 'unhappy'.

On the other hand, words that are positively used by R_{FF} while negatively used in the remaining subsets are mainly related to the clusters movement and change, and process and results. These exhibit some differences in how simple words can be mostly used to write about a given gender, and not another. The positive words from the life-cycle and relationships cluster are *bror, søster* 'brother, sister', *venn, vennine* 'friend(male and female)', and *forelskelse* 'infatuation'. While this cluster is also negatively used in (R_{FF}), the words are different. The words negatively used seem to be about advanced relationships, either with family members or love relationships (where getting married and having children seem to be negative), while in the positive R_{FF} these words seems to be more about friendships, brothers and sisters, and early or short-term love interests. The same applies to the sad and strange clusters, which in positive (R_{FF}) comprises *dramatisk* 'dramatic', *mystisk* 'mysterious', and *dyster* 'gloomy'. Some of the positive qualities in R_{FF} that are negative in the remaining subsets are *humoristisk* 'humorous', *klasisk* 'classical', *poetisk* 'poetic', and *sentimental* 'sentimental'. On the contrary, Some negative words from the cluster violence are also used positively *blodig* 'bloody', and *dø* 'dead'. Another interesting set of words that are positive in R_{FF} but not elsewhere, are the words *familieliv* 'family life' and *kjærlighet* 'love', which reflect the content of the cluster difficulties in romantic relationships.

In subset R_{FM}, there is an interesting difference in positively and negatively words used from the cluster contempt and cynical. For example, words like *desperat, hevn, løgn* 'desperate, vengeance, lie' are negatively used, while the more feeling oriented words are positive: *ensom, hjertekjærende, ulykkelig* 'lonely, heartbreaking, unhappy'. When it comes to the feeling cluster, female critics use the words *ambisjon, drømme* 'ambition, dream' to negatively describe the work of male authors, while they use *elske, glede* 'love, joy' to positively describe works. As in the previous subset, words from life-cycle and relationships referring to marriage and wives are negatively used, while words referring to love and giving birth are positive. Coming from a female critic, this might be an indication for not adhering to the "traditional" views of relationships. This however, goes in contrast with the words from the political conflicts cluster, where words related to power and Christianity are positively used, while words related to rebellion and religious people are negative.

Some of the same observations can be found in R_{MF}. When it comes to difficulties in romantic relationships, discussing family life, sex, and physical relationships is seen as negative by male critics when discussing the work of females, while using words about love and gender are positive. However, in contrast to the two previous subsets, discussing marriage and fatherhood is positive, while talking about love and giving birth is negative. This difference is particularly interesting, because we can see the effect of having a male or female critic. Another compelling difference, is that male critics perceive female authors who write crime fictions to be negative, while works of female authors are positively described if they are from other genres (e.g. biographies and autobiographical books, novels and novel collections).

When male critics assess the work of male authors, they positively view works that are literary and poetic, but negatively describe biographies and prose. When it comes to difficulties in relationships, erotic works are positively seen, while those triggering anxieties are negative. Moreover, mentions of love, marriage, and children are actually perceived both positively and negatively, which is in contrast to the previous subsets where there was a clear difference in the polarity of early romance and stable relationships. Concerning political conflicts, works about Islam, Christianity, rebellions, and politics are negative, while those covering wars and power are positive. Another fascinating difference in this subset compared to the others, is that male critics who assess the work of male authors seems to be negative to romantic and sentimental books (*romantisk, sentimental*), while classics, witty and entertaining books, or books about music are deemed positive.

6 Non-professional reviews – the Bokelskere corpus

Our gender-annotated literature subset of the NoReC corpus reflects how works by female and male authors are positively and negatively described. However, since these reviews are written by professionals, the language can be expected to be of a more formal and possibly less affective style. In order to investigate to what extent this proves to be correct, we carried out the same analysis done on NoReC on a corpus of non-professional reviews.

We use a corpus comprising user-generated book reviews from `bokelskere.no` compiled by the National Library of Norway (Språkbanken)[5]. We will refer to this corpus as the Bokelskere (*book lovers*) corpus in what follows. The Bokelskere corpus contains the raw texts from discussions and book reviews written by users of the `bokelskere.no` web community. The ratings follow the same scheme as in NoReC, with numerical scores ranging from 1 to 6. The reviews are structured as both reviews and comments on reviews. The corpus is in JSON format and contains a total of 219,000 review comments. For each of these, the corpus provides (amongst others) information about the book being reviewed (title and author), and the rating.

We annotated the Bokelskere corpus with PoS tags using the same version of UDPipe that was used to annotate NoReC (Velldal et al., 2018). Moreover, neither the gender of the users (i.e. critics), nor the gender of the book authors are provided in the Bokelskere corpus. We therefore used our annotations from the NoReC corpus to automatically annotate Bokelskere. We only annotate the authors from our gender-annotated corpus for whom we know the gender. We were able to identify the gender of 9,833 female authors, and 15,544 male authors. However, 1,691 and 2,815 reviews of female and male authors respectively did not contain ratings and were therefore disregarded.

Figure 4 gives an overview of the rating distributions of the remaining 8,142 female and 12,729 male

---

[5]The corpus can be found here: `https://www.nb.no/sprakbanken/en/resource-catalogue/oai-nb-no-sbr-53/`

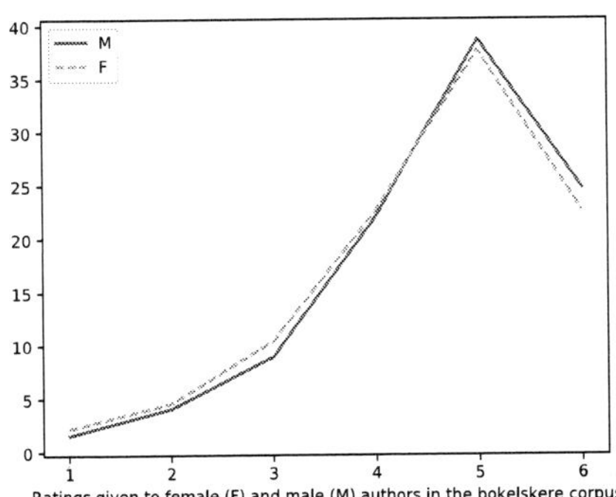

Figure 4: Distribution of ratings given to Female (F) and male (M) authors in the Bokelskere corpus. The y axis represents normalized percentages of each rating.

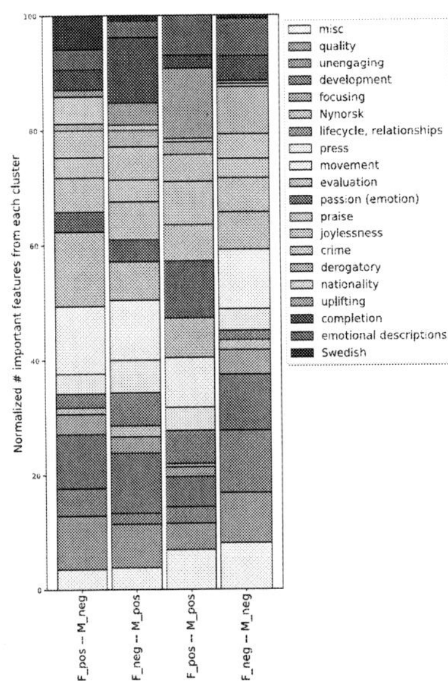

Figure 5: Distribution of clusters of most informative words for sentiment classification in F_{subset} and M_{subset} in Bokelskere Corpus.

reviews. The trend is similar to the distribution of ratings in the gender-annotated NoReC. Female authors tend to get more ratings on the lower range than male authors, while it is the opposite on the higher range. For ratings 1, 2, 3, and 4 female authors are given respectively 2.2%, 4.5%, 10.4% , and 22.6% of the total reviews, and male authors are given 1.5%, 4%, 8.9% , and 22% respectively. On the contrary, for ratings 5 and 6 female authors are respectively given 37.6%, and 22.5% of total ratings, while male are given 38.7%, and 24.7%. Since the gender of the users reviewing books is not available for the Bokelskere corpus, we focus our analysis on the gender of the reviewed authors and follow the same methodology described in Section 5.1.

The Bookelskere corpus do not have predefined train, dev, and test splits. We therefore follow the same strategy as for the splits in NoReC by first sorting the reviews by date and then reserving the first 80% for training, the following 10% for dev split, and the remaining 10% for testing. However, during this work, we combine the train and dev splits, and train a Logistic regression with 10-fold cross validation, and do a final evaluation on the test split. We also balance the distribution of positive and negative reviews for each of the genders.

Clustering the 200 most informative words for binary sentiment classification on Bokelskere, enabled us to identify 20 clusters. These are shown in Figure 5. The distribution of overlap of these clusters based on how often they are used to positively or negatively describe books written by female or male authors also offers an interesting overview (see Figure 5).

When it comes to adjectives, words that are positively used for female authors but negatively used to describe the works of male authors are mostly related to quality and nationality (*mild* 'mild', *solid* 'solid', *engelsk* 'English', *fransk* 'French'). But also words related to the expression of emotions as passion (*inderlig* 'sincerely'), praise (*begeistre* 'exciting'), and general descriptions (*komisk* 'comical'). Adjectives that are negatively used to describe the works of females, but positively used for male, tend also to relate to quality (*åpenbar* 'obvious', *personlig* 'personal', *realistisk* 'realistic'), but also development (*paralell* 'parallel', *tilgjengelig* 'available'), praise (*imponere* 'impress', *positiv* 'positive'), derogatory (*håpløs* 'hopeless', *vond* 'bad') and uplifting words (*gøy* 'fun', *inspirere* 'inspire').

The nouns *venn* 'friend' (related to life-cycle and relationships) is used to positively describe female works and negatively describe male works, while the words *datter* 'daughter' and *søster* 'sister' are negative in female description but positive for male descriptions. Nouns related to crimes seems also to be positive for male, while negative for females (e.g. *gjerningsmann* 'perpetrator'). Most verbs used to positively describe females' while negatively describe males' works are development (*sammenligne* 'compare', *presentere* 'present'), and evaluation (*forestille* 'imagine', *oppfatte* 'perceive'). Conversely, verbs used negatively when describing works of females but positively for males seem to be related to completion (*ende* 'end', *gjennomføre* 'conduct'), development (*lage* 'make'), evaluation (*forstå* 'understand'), life-cycle and relationships (*føde* 'give birth', *gifte* 'marry'), and passion (*forelske* 'fall in love').

7 Conclusion and limitations

We present a gender-annotated dataset of professional book reviews, where both the gender of critics and the book authors are annotated. We also present a corpus of user reviews annotated for the gender of the book authors. We make all annotations and reviews publicly available. We have shown that there are differences in how female and male book authors are positively or negatively described, and that the gender of the critics influences the differences. For example, male critics deem female crime novels and male romantic and sentimental books as negative. This shows that book reviews contain the social hierarchies that tend to focus on emotional traits to describe females as in Menegatti and Rubini (2017).

There are several ways in which the preliminary analysis of the current work can be improved and extended. First, the annotations of the book authors are based on which book is being reviewed, and not if the author is being mentioned in the review. This can lead to issues during classification, since it might be possible that the review in itself contains references to the characters of the book, which might or might not be of the same gender as the author. Therefore, the word usage might not actually reflect the book author, but rather the fictional characters of the book. Secondly, we were able to identify differences in how female and male critics describe the works of female and male authors, but we did not quantify to which degree this is true. The distribution of ratings gives an indication of this, but more extensive analysis is necessary. In future works, we aim to explore how to quantify the amount of bias, but also identify if a review is discussing the quality of the book (as in the work of the author), or if it only focuses on the characters and the storyline.

Acknowledgements

This work has been carried out as part of the SANT project (Sentiment Analysis for Norwegian Text), funded by the Research Council of Norway (grant number 270908).

References

Christine Basta, Marta R Costa-Jussà, and Noe Casas. 2019. Evaluating the underlying gender bias in contextualized word embeddings. In *Proceedings of the 1st Workshop on Gender Bias in Natural Language Processing*, pages 33–39, Florence, Italy, August. Association for Computational Linguistics.

Jayadev Bhaskaran and Isha Bhallamudi. 2019. Good secretaries, bad truck drivers? occupational gender stereotypes in sentiment analysis. In *Proceedings of the First Workshop on Gender Bias in Natural Language Processing*, pages 62–68, Florence, Italy, August. Association for Computational Linguistics.

Su Lin Blodgett, Solon Barocas, Hal Daumé III, and Hanna Wallach. 2020. Language (technology) is power: A critical survey of "bias" in NLP. In *Proceedings of the 58th Annual Meeting of the Association for Computational Linguistics*, pages 5454–5476, Online, July. Association for Computational Linguistics.

Tolga Bolukbasi, Kai-Wei Chang, James Y Zou, Venkatesh Saligrama, and Adam T Kalai. 2016. Man is to computer programmer as woman is to homemaker? debiasing word embeddings. In *Advances in neural information processing systems*, pages 4349–4357.

John D Burger, John Henderson, George Kim, and Guido Zarrella. 2011. Discriminating gender on twitter. In *Proceedings of the 2011 Conference on Empirical Methods in Natural Language Processing*, pages 1301–1309.

Yang Trista Cao and Hal Daumé III. 2020. Toward gender-inclusive coreference resolution. In *Proceedings of the 58th Annual Meeting of the Association for Computational Linguistics*, pages 4568–4595, Online, July. Association for Computational Linguistics.

Marta R. Costa-jussà, Pau Li Lin, and Cristina España-Bonet. 2020. GeBioToolkit: Automatic extraction of gender-balanced multilingual corpus of Wikipedia biographies. In *Proceedings of The 12th Language Resources and Evaluation Conference*, pages 4081–4088, Marseille, France, May. European Language Resources Association.

Jacob Devlin, Ming-Wei Chang, Kenton Lee, and Kristina Toutanova. 2019. Bert: Pre-training of deep bidirectional transformers for language understanding. In *Proceedings of NAACL-HLT 2019*, page 4171–4186, Minneapolis, Minnesota, June. Association for Computational Linguistics.

Joel Escudé Font and Marta R. Costa-jussà. 2019. Equalizing gender bias in neural machine translation with word embeddings techniques. In *Proceedings of the First Workshop on Gender Bias in Natural Language Processing*, pages 147–154, Florence, Italy, August. Association for Computational Linguistics.

Scott Friedman, Sonja Schmer-Galunder, Anthony Chen, and Jeffrey Rye. 2019. Relating word embedding gender biases to gender gaps: A cross-cultural analysis. In *Proceedings of the First Workshop on Gender Bias in Natural Language Processing*, pages 18–24, Florence, Italy, August. Association for Computational Linguistics.

Nikhil Garg, Londa Schiebinger, Dan Jurafsky, and James Zou. 2018. Word embeddings quantify 100 years of gender and ethnic stereotypes. *Proceedings of the National Academy of Sciences*, 115(16):E3635–E3644.

Aparna Garimella and Rada Mihalcea. 2016. Zooming in on gender differences in social media. In *Proceedings of the Workshop on Computational Modeling of People's Opinions, Personality, and Emotions in Social Media (PEOPLES)*, pages 1–10, Osaka, Japan, December. The COLING 2016 Organizing Committee.

Hila Gonen and Yoav Goldberg. 2019. Lipstick on a pig: Debiasing methods cover up systematic gender biases in word embeddings but do not remove them. In *Proceedings of the 2019 Conference of the North American Chapter of the Association for Computational Linguistics: Human Language Technologies, Volume 1 (Long and Short Papers)*, pages 609–614, Minneapolis, Minnesota, June. Association for Computational Linguistics.

Alexander Miserlis Hoyle, Lawrence Wolf-Sonkin, Hanna Wallach, Isabelle Augenstein, and Ryan Cotterell. 2019. Unsupervised discovery of gendered language through latent-variable modeling. In *Proceedings of the 57th Annual Meeting of the Association for Computational Linguistics*, pages 1706–1716, Florence, Italy, July. Association for Computational Linguistics.

Masahiro Kaneko and Danushka Bollegala. 2019. Gender-preserving debiasing for pre-trained word embeddings. In *Proceedings of the 57th Annual Meeting of the Association for Computational Linguistics*, pages 1641–1650, Florence, Italy, July. Association for Computational Linguistics.

Svetlana Kiritchenko and Saif Mohammad. 2018. Examining gender and race bias in two hundred sentiment analysis systems. In *Proceedings of the Seventh Joint Conference on Lexical and Computational Semantics*, pages 43–53, New Orleans, Louisiana, June. Association for Computational Linguistics.

Hugo Liu and Rada Mihalcea. 2007. Of men, women, and computers: Data-driven gender modeling for improved user interfaces. *ICWSM*, 7:26–28.

Juan M Madera, Michelle R Hebl, and Randi C Martin. 2009. Gender and letters of recommendation for academia: agentic and communal differences. *Journal of Applied Psychology*, 94(6):1591.

Rowan Hall Maudslay, Hila Gonen, Ryan Cotterell, and Simone Teufel. 2019. It's all in the name: Mitigating gender bias with name-based counterfactual data substitution. In *Proceedings of the 2019 Conference on Empirical Methods in Natural Language Processing and the 9th International Joint Conference on Natural Language Processing*, pages 5267–5275, Hong Kong, China, November. Association for Computational Linguistics.

Chandler May, Alex Wang, Shikha Bordia, Samuel R. Bowman, and Rachel Rudinger. 2019. On measuring social biases in sentence encoders. In *Proceedings of the 2019 Conference of the North American Chapter of the Association for Computational Linguistics: Human Language Technologies, Volume 1 (Long and Short Papers)*, pages 622–628, Minneapolis, Minnesota, June. Association for Computational Linguistics.

Michela Menegatti and Monica Rubini. 2017. Gender bias and sexism in language. In *Oxford Research Encyclopedia of Communication*.

Arjun Mukherjee and Bing Liu. 2010. Improving gender classification of blog authors. In *Proceedings of the 2010 conference on Empirical Methods in natural Language Processing*, pages 207–217.

Yusu Qian, Urwa Muaz, Ben Zhang, and Jae Won Hyun. 2019. Reducing gender bias in word-level language models with a gender-equalizing loss function. pages 223–228, July.

Francisco Rangel and Paolo Rosso. 2019. Overview of the 7th author profiling task at pan 2019: Bots and gender profiling in twitter. In *Proceedings of the CEUR Workshop, Lugano, Switzerland*, pages 1–36.

Peter J Rousseeuw. 1987. Silhouettes: a graphical aid to the interpretation and validation of cluster analysis. *Journal of computational and applied mathematics*, 20:53–65.

Rachel Rudinger, Jason Naradowsky, Brian Leonard, and Benjamin Van Durme. 2018. Gender bias in coreference resolution. In *Proceedings of the 2018 Conference of the North American Chapter of the Association for Computational Linguistics: Human Language Technologies, Volume 2 (Short Papers)*, pages 8–14, New Orleans, Louisiana, June. Association for Computational Linguistics.

Magnus Sahlgren and Fredrik Olsson. 2019. Gender bias in pretrained Swedish embeddings. In *Proceedings of the 22nd Nordic Conference on Computational Linguistics*, pages 35–43, Turku, Finland, September–October. Linköping University Electronic Press.

Alexandra Schofield and Leo Mehr. 2016. Gender-distinguishing features in film dialogue. In *Proceedings of the Fifth Workshop on Computational Linguistics for Literature*, pages 32–39, San Diego, California, USA, June. Association for Computational Linguistics.

Erik Velldal, Lilja Øvrelid, Cathrine Stadsnes Eivind Alexander Bergem, Samia Touileb, and Fredrik Jørgensen. 2018. NoReC: The Norwegian Review Corpus. In *Proceedings of the 11th edition of the Language Resources and Evaluation Conference*, pages 4186–4191, Miyazaki, Japan.

Rob Voigt, David Jurgens, Vinodkumar Prabhakaran, Dan Jurafsky, and Yulia Tsvetkov. 2018. Rtgender: A corpus for studying differential responses to gender. In *Proceedings of the Eleventh International Conference on Language Resources and Evaluation (LREC 2018)*.

Jieyu Zhao, Tianlu Wang, Mark Yatskar, Vicente Ordonez, and Kai-Wei Chang. 2018a. Gender bias in coreference resolution: Evaluation and debiasing methods. In *Proceedings of the 2018 Conference of the North American Chapter of the Association for Computational Linguistics: Human Language Technologies, Volume 2 (Short Papers)*, pages 15–20, New Orleans, Louisiana, June. Association for Computational Linguistics.

Jieyu Zhao, Yichao Zhou, Zeyu Li, Wei Wang, and Kai-Wei Chang. 2018b. Learning gender-neutral word embeddings. In *Proceedings of the 2018 Conference on Empirical Methods in Natural Language Processing*, pages 4847–4853, Brussels, Belgium, October-November. Association for Computational Linguistics.

Jieyu Zhao, Subhabrata Mukherjee, saghar Hosseini, Kai-Wei Chang, and Ahmed Hassan Awadallah. 2020. Gender bias in multilingual embeddings and cross-lingual transfer. In *Proceedings of the 58th Annual Meeting of the Association for Computational Linguistics*, pages 2896–2907, Online, July. Association for Computational Linguistics.

Ran Zmigrod, Sabrina J. Mielke, Hanna Wallach, and Ryan Cotterell. 2019. Counterfactual data augmentation for mitigating gender stereotypes in languages with rich morphology. In *Proceedings of the 57th Annual Meeting of the Association for Computational Linguistics*, pages 1651–1661, Florence, Italy, July. Association for Computational Linguistics.

Gender-Aware Reinflection
using Linguistically Enhanced Neural Models

Bashar Alhafni, Nizar Habash, Houda Bouamor[†]
Computational Approaches to Modeling Language Lab
New York University Abu Dhabi
[†]Carnegie Mellon University in Qatar
`{alhafni,nizar.habash}@nyu.edu, hbouamor@qatar.cmu.edu`

Abstract

In this paper, we present an approach for sentence-level gender reinflection using linguistically enhanced sequence-to-sequence models. Our system takes an Arabic sentence and a given target gender as input and generates a gender-reinflected sentence based on the target gender. We formulate the problem as a user-aware grammatical error correction task and build an encoder-decoder architecture to jointly model reinflection for both masculine and feminine grammatical genders. We also show that adding linguistic features to our model leads to better reinflection results. The results on a blind test set using our best system show improvements over previous work, with a 3.6% absolute increase in M^2 $F_{0.5}$.

Bias Statement

Most NLP systems are unaware of their users' preferred grammatical gender. Such systems typically generate a single output for a specific input without considering any user information. Beyond being simply incorrect in many cases, such output patterns create representational harm by propagating social biases and inequalities of the world we live in. While such biases can be traced back to the NLP systems' training data, balancing and cleaning the training data will not guarantee the correctness of a single output that is arrived at without accounting for user preferences. Our view is that NLP systems should utilize grammatical gender preference information to provide the correct user-aware output, particularly for gender-marking morphologically rich languages. When the grammatical gender preference information is unavailable to the systems, all gender-specific outputs should be generated and properly marked.

We acknowledge that by limiting the choice of gender expression to the grammatical gender choices in Arabic, we exclude other alternatives such as non-binary gender or no-gender expressions. We are not aware of any sociolinguistics published research that discusses such alternatives for Arabic, although there are growing grassroots efforts, e.g., the Ebdal Project.[1]

1 Introduction

The recent advances in machine learning have propelled the field of Natural Language Processing (NLP) forward at a great pace and raised expectation about the quality of results and especially their impact in a social context, including not only race (Merullo et al., 2019) and politics (Fan et al., 2019), but also gender identities (Font and Costa-jussà, 2019; Dinan et al., 2019; Dinan et al., 2020). Human-generated data, reflective of the gender discrimination and sexist stereotypes perpetrated through language and speaker's lexical choices, is considered the primary source of these biases (Maass and Arcuri, 1996; Menegatti and Rubini, 2017). However, Habash et al. (2019) pointed out that NLP gender biases do not just exist in human-generated training data, and models built from it; but also stem from *gender-blind* (i.e., gender-unaware) systems designed to generate a single text output without considering any target gender information. Such systems propagate the biases of the models they use. One example is the *I-am-a-doctor/I-am-a-nurse* problem in machine translation (MT) systems targeting many morphologically

---

[1]`https://www.facebook.com/EbdalProject/`

Proceedings of the Second Workshop on Gender Bias in Natural Language Processing, pages 139–150
Barcelona, Spain (Online), December 13, 2020.

Input	Gender	Target Masculine	Target Feminine
Âryd HlwlA sryʕħ أريد حلولا سريعة I want quick solutions	B	*Âryd HlwlA sryʕħ* أريد حلولا سريعة I want quick solutions	*Âryd HlwlA sryʕħ* أريد حلولا سريعة I want quick solutions
lÂnny AmrÂħ šqrA' لأنني امرأة شقراء Because I am a blonde woman	F	*lÂnny <u>rjl</u> <u>Âšqr</u>* لأنني رجل أشقر Because I am a blonde man	*lÂnny AmrÂħ šqrA'* لأنني امرأة شقراء Because I am a blonde woman
ÂnA sʕyd blqAŷkm أنا سعيد بلقائكم I am happy [masc.] to meet you	M	*ÂnA sʕyd blqAŷkm* أنا سعيد بلقائكم I am happy [masc.] to meet you	*ÂnA <u>sʕydħ</u> blqAŷkm* أنا سعيدة بلقائكم I am happy [fem.] to meet you

Table 1: Examples covering all possible combinations of input and output grammatical genders. Changed output words are underlined in the transliterations.

rich languages. While English uses gender-neutral terms that hide the ambiguity of the first-person gender reference, morphologically rich languages need to use grammatically different gender-specific terms for these two expressions. In Arabic, as in other languages with grammatical gender, gender-unaware single-output MT from English often results in أنا طبيب *ÂnA Tbyb*[2] 'I am a [male] doctor'/ أنا ممرضة *ÂnA mmrDħ* 'I am a [female] nurse', which is inappropriate for female doctors and male nurses, respectively.

In contrast, gender-aware systems should be designed to produce outputs that are as gender-specific as the input information they have access to. Gender information may be contextualized (e.g., the input 'she is a doctor'), or linguistically provided (e.g., the gender feature provided in the user profile in social media). But, there may be contexts where the gender information is unavailable to the system (e.g., 'the student is a nurse'). In such cases, generating both gender-specific forms is more appropriate.

In this paper, we present an approach for sentence-level gender reinflection using linguistically enhanced sequence-to-sequence models. Our system takes an Arabic sentence and a given target gender as input and generates a gender-reinflected sentence based on the provided target gender. Table 1 shows some input and output examples. Our work is closely related to the one by Habash et al. (2019), as we use the same corpus that is made available and focus on first-person-singular constructions in Arabic. However, the main contributions of this work are the following: (1) we introduce an approach that jointly models the reinflection for both masculine and feminine grammatical genders, unlike Habash et al. (2019)'s segregated systems; (2) we show that adding linguistic features to our encoder-decoder model leads to better reinflection results. Our code, data, and trained models are publicly available.[3]

This paper is organized as follows. In Section 2, we discuss some related work. In Section 3, we present some Arabic linguistic facts related to grammatical gender. Section 4 introduces our model for joint gender reinflection and describes the encoder-decoder architecture. Then, we present the experimental setup in Section 5 and discuss the results in Section 6. An error analysis is given in Section 7. We conclude and present future work in Section 8.

2   Related Work

Many NLP systems have the ability to embed and amplify societal (gender, racial, religious, etc.) biases across a variety of core tasks such as coreference resolution (Rudinger et al., 2018; Zhao et al., 2018a), machine translation (Rabinovich et al., 2017; Vanmassenhove et al., 2018; Font and Costa-jussà, 2019; Moryossef et al., 2019; Stanovsky et al., 2019; Stafanovičs et al., 2020; Gonen and Webster, 2020), named entity recognition (Mehrabi et al., 2019), dialogue systems (Dinan et al., 2019), and language modeling (Lu et al., 2018; Bordia and Bowman, 2019).

For the case of gender bias, various research efforts have shown that this could be caused by either human-generated training datasets (Font and Costa-jussà, 2019; Habash et al., 2019), pre-trained word embeddings (Bolukbasi et al., 2016; Zhao et al., 2017; Caliskan et al., 2017; Manzini et al., 2019), or language models (Kurita et al., 2019; Zhao et al., 2019). To mitigate this problem, several researchers

---

[2] Arabic transliteration is in the HSB scheme (Habash et al., 2007).
[3] https://github.com/CAMeL-Lab/gender-reinflection

proposed approaches in which they focus mainly on debiasing word embeddings (Bolukbasi et al., 2016; Zhao et al., 2018b; Gonen and Goldberg, 2019) or using counterfactual data augmentation techniques (Lu et al., 2018; Zhao et al., 2018a; Zmigrod et al., 2019; Hall Maudslay et al., 2019).

Most of the solutions were mainly proposed to reduce gender bias in English and may not work as well when it comes to morphologically rich languages. Nevertheless, there have been recent studies that explored the gender bias problem in languages other than English. Zhao et al. (2020) studied gender bias which is exhibited by multilingual embeddings in four languages (English, German, French, and Spanish) and demonstrated that such bias can impact cross-lingual transfer learning tasks. Zmigrod et al. (2019) used a counterfactual data augmentation approach and developed a generative model to convert between masculine and feminine sentences in four languages (French, Hebrew, Italian, and Spanish).

For Arabic, Habash et al. (2019) introduced a two-step approach to gender-identify and reinflect first-person-singular constructions. The identification was done through a feature-based classifier, whereas they used a character-level sequence-to-sequence model for the reinflection. They also compared their two-step approach to a single-step joint identification and reinflection model, which under-performed in the case of the Arabic source (not the machine translation source) task. All of their systems modeled grammatical masculine and feminine genders separately. In this paper, we compare to their results using the publicly available Arabic parallel gender corpus they built – a parallel corpus of first-person-singular Arabic sentences that are gender-annotated and reinflected. However, our work is different from theirs in that we jointly learn reinflection for both masculine and feminine genders together. We also model identification implicitly with reinflection in a single architecture. Furthermore, we formulate the problem as a user-aware grammatical error correction task (UGEC). As such, we use as our primary metric the MaxMatch (M^2) scorer (Dahlmeier and Ng, 2012), which is far more meaningful than the BLEU (Papineni et al., 2002) metric used by Habash et al. (2019) for this task.

3 Arabic Linguistic Background

Modern Standard Arabic (MSA) NLP systems and more specifically those using deep learning, face several challenges when it comes to gender expression including morphological richness, orthographic ambiguity and noise.

Morphological Richness and Complexity Arabic has a rich morphological system that inflects for gender, number, person, case, state, aspect, mood and voice, in addition to numerous attachable clitics (prepositions, particles, pronouns) (Habash, 2010). This results in a large number of forms for any particular word, with different morpho-syntactic restrictions. For instance, the adjective مهمٌ *mhmũ* 'important [masculine singular indefinite nominative]', has a related form مهماً *mhmAã* that only differs in being accusative in case. In addition to its richness, Arabic morphology has a lot of idiosyncratic inflectional affixes that are not consistent in indicating specific genders or numbers (Alkuhlani and Habash, 2011). For instance, the *Ta-Marbuta* suffix ة *ħ*, often called the 'feminine singular ending', appears with many words where it does not indicate a feminine-singular feature, and cannot be attached to all masculine singular words to turn them feminine. So, in contrast to the good example of مهمة *mhmħ* 'important [feminine singular]', we find words like خليفة *xlyfħ* 'Caliph [masculine singular]', and سحرة *sHrħ* 'wizards [masculine plural]'. Furthermore, adding the *Ta-Marbuta* to some masculine nouns produces nonsensical forms such as رجلة* **rjlħ* 'man-ess (female man)' from رجل *rjl* 'man'. Similarly, removing the *Ta-Marbuta* is no guarantee that we map from feminine to masculine in every context. For example, the noun word مهمة *mhmħ* 'mission/assignment' is only feminine and has no meaningful masculine form, as opposed to the adjective مهمة *mhmħ* 'important [feminine singular]' discussed above.

These facts pose major challenges to deep learning models attempting to learn from limited supervised or even large unsupervised data. In this work, we make use of morphological analyzers that indicate all the possible gender information of the words in terms of their functional (grammatical) and form-based (affixational) values (Alkuhlani and Habash, 2011).

Orthographic Ambiguity and Noise Arabic uses diacritics to specify short vowels and consonantal doubling. These diacritics are optional and generally unwritten, leaving readers to decipher words using contextual and templatic morphology clues. For example, the verb كنت *knt* can be diacritized as *kuntu* 'I was', *kunta* 'You [masculine] were', or *kunti* 'You [feminine] were'. This is a challenge for identifying the words that need to change for a first-person target gender. In addition to the issue of orthographic ambiguity, *unedited* MSA text is reported to be quite noisy with spelling errors reaching ~23% of all words (Zaghouani et al., 2014). The most important errors involve Alif-Hamza (Glottal Stop) spelling (ﺍ ﺇ ﺃ ﺁ *A, Ā, Ă, Â*), Ya spelling (ﻱ ﻯ *y, ÿ*), and the feminine suffix Ta-Marbuta (ﻩ ﺓ *h, ħ*). In Arabic NLP, Alif/Ya normalization is almost standard preprocessing (Habash, 2010). Generally, the high degree of ambiguity and noise result in a high degree of morphological confusability and model sparsity. For instance, a common spelling error of writing the Ta-Marbuta (ﺓ *ħ*) as Ha (ﻩ *h*) results in interpreting the (ﻩ *h*) as a possessive pronoun clitic attached to a masculine noun: كاتبه *kAtbh* 'his writer [masculine]', vs كاتبة *kAtbħ* 'writer [feminine]'.

Normalizing the text may solve some issues related to noise and ambiguity. In this paper, we follow Habash et al. (2019)'s decision to evaluate within an orthographically normalized space for Alif, Ya, and Ta-Marbuta, since the OpenSubtitles 2018 corpus (Lison and Tiedemann, 2016) they use to build the Arabic parallel gender corpus has many of such spelling confusions.

4 Joint Gender Reinflection Model

In this section, we discuss the motivation behind our model architecture as well as the integration of the linguistic features. We also describe the training settings and the model's hyperparameters for reproducibility.

4.1 Motivation

Sequence-to-sequence models have achieved significant results in grammatical error correction (GEC) (Chollampatt and Ng, 2018; Junczys-Dowmunt et al., 2018; Grundkiewicz et al., 2019) and morphological reinflection tasks (Faruqui et al., 2016; Kann and Schütze, 2016; Aharoni and Goldberg, 2017). Many of these problems are modeled on the word-level, however, such models usually require large amounts of training data to achieve good results. Character-level sequence-to-sequence models can be superior in mitigating the lack of training data and in dealing with subtle morphological reinflection. Further, pre-trained distributed word representations have also shown to be helpful if integrated properly within character-level sequence-to-sequence models (Watson et al., 2018). We formulate the gender reinflection problem as a user-aware grammatical error correction (UGEC) task at the character-level. We also explore leveraging linguistic knowledge on the word-level as well as pre-trained word embeddings to enhance the performance of the model.

4.2 Model Architecture

Given an input sequence $x_{1:n} \in V_x$ containing k words $w_{1:k} \in V_w$, a gender-reinflected output sequence $y_{1:m} \in V_y$, and a target gender $g \in \{F, M\}$, the goal is to model an auto-regressive distribution which is defined over the target vocabulary:[4]

$$P_{V_y}(y_{1:m}|x_{1:n}, g) = \prod_{t=1}^{m} P(y_t|y_{1:t-1}, x_{1:n}, g; \theta);$$

where θ represents the model's parameters.

We implement this model using a character-level encoder-decoder neural network with an attention mechanism.

---

[4]F stands for Feminine and M stands for Masculine.

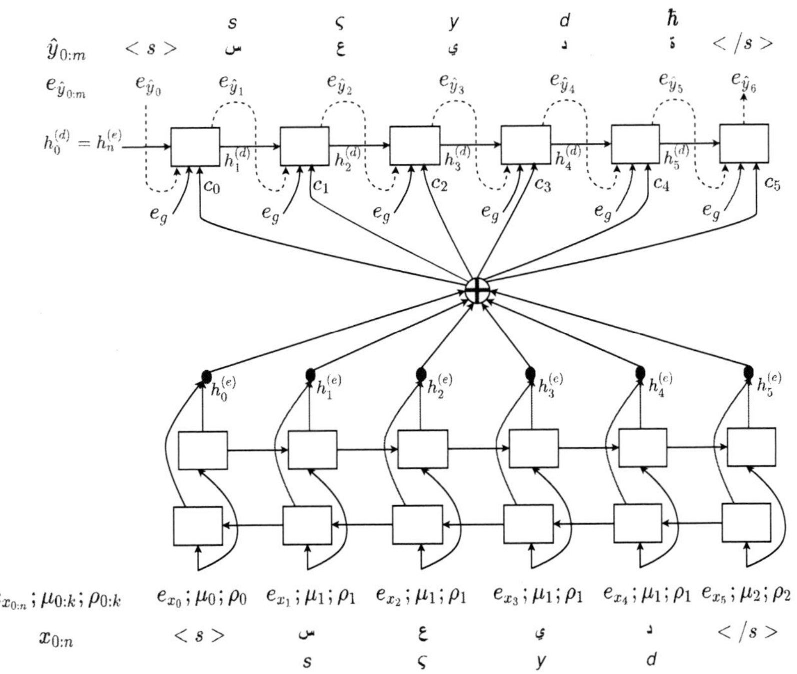

Figure 1: The encoder-decoder architecture for gender reinflection. The input and predicted characters are shown both in Arabic and in the HSB scheme. <s> and </s> indicate the start-of-sequence and end-of-sequence tokens respectively. $\oplus$ refers to the attention mechanism and the filled dot ($\cdot$) indicates a concatenation operation.

Encoder First, each character in the input sequence x_i is mapped to an embedding $\mathbf{e_{x_i}} \in \mathbb{R}^E$. The character embeddings are parameters of the model which are learned during training. We then feed these embeddings to a two-layer bidirectional GRU (Cho et al., 2014) to obtain a sequence of hidden states $\mathbf{h}_{1:n}^{(e)}$. Each hidden state $\mathbf{h}_i^{(e)} \in \mathbb{R}^{2H}$ is the concatenation of the forward and backward GRU outputs when we feed it $\mathbf{e_{x_i}}$.

Decoder For the decoder, we use a two-layer GRU with additive attention (Bahdanau et al., 2015; Luong et al., 2015) over the last layer encoder hidden states $\mathbf{h}_{1:n}^{(e)}$. The initial hidden states of the decoder $\mathbf{h}_0^{(d)} \in \mathbb{R}^H$ are learned by passing the encoder hidden states at the last time step $\mathbf{h}_n^{(e)}$ of the corresponding layers through a fully-connected tanh layer, $\mathbf{h}_0^{(d)} = \tanh(\mathbf{W_a}\mathbf{h}_n^{(e)} + \mathbf{b_a})$. Given the last layer encoder hidden states $\mathbf{h}_{1:n}^{(e)}$ and the last layer decoder hidden state at the tth time step $\mathbf{h}_t^{(d)}$, we learn a context vector $\mathbf{c_t} \in \mathbb{R}^{2H}$ that is used to summarize the source attentional context when we predict target symbol $\hat{y}_t$; we initialize $\mathbf{c_0} = 0$. At each time step, we feed two inputs to the decoder: the context vector $\mathbf{c_{t-1}} \in \mathbb{R}^{2H}$ and the embedding of the predicted decoder output symbol $\mathbf{e_{\hat{y}_{t-1}}} \in \mathbb{R}^E$ from the previous time step. However, it is important to note that we use scheduled sampling (teacher forcing) (Bengio et al., 2015) with a constant sampling probability during training.

The two inputs are then concatenated to create a single vector $\mathbf{v_t} = [\mathbf{e_{\hat{y}_{t-1}}}; \mathbf{c_{t-1}}] \in \mathbb{R}^{E+2H}$, which is then fed to the GRU to obtain a decoder hidden state $\mathbf{h_t^{(d)}} \in \mathbb{R}^H$. The target gender g is mapped to an embedding $\mathbf{e_g} \in \mathbb{R}^J$ which is learned during training and concatenated together with the decoder hidden state $\mathbf{h_t^{(d)}}$, the context vector $\mathbf{c_t}$, and the embedding of the predicted symbol from the previous time step $\mathbf{e_{\hat{y}_{t-1}}}$ to create vector $\mathbf{z_t} = [\mathbf{h_t^{(d)}}; \mathbf{c_t}; \mathbf{e_{\hat{y}_{t-1}}}; \mathbf{e_g}] \in \mathbb{R}^{H+2H+E+J}$. We finally project $\mathbf{z_t}$ to a vector of size $|V_y|$ followed by a softmax layer to model the distribution over the target vocabulary $P_{V_y}(\hat{y}_t) = softmax(\mathbf{W_b}\mathbf{z_t} + \mathbf{b_b})$.

Linguistic Features and Word Embeddings   We explore adding word-level morphological features as well as pre-trained distributed word representations to the character embeddings. We use the CALIMA$_{Star}$ Arabic morphological analyzer (Taji et al., 2018) to obtain word-level functional gender features (Alkuhlani and Habash, 2011).[5] We represent the morphological features for word w_j as a four-dimension one-hot vector $\mu_{\mathbf{w_j}} \in \mathbb{R}^4$. Each element of this one-hot vector represents whether the word w_j is masculine or feminine as well as if the analysis was obtained with or without spelling back-off. We use FastText (Bojanowski et al., 2017) to learn distributed word representations and we denote the FastText word embedding for word w_j as $\rho_{\mathbf{w_j}} \in \mathbb{R}^F$.

Similarly to Watson et al. (2018), we added the word-level features to the character embeddings only on the encoder side. Each character embedding $\mathbf{e_{x_i}}$ is then enriched with $\rho_{\mathbf{w_j}}$ and $\mu_{\mathbf{w_j}}$ to create a single vector $[\mathbf{e_{x_i}}; \mu_{\mathbf{w_j}}; \rho_{\mathbf{w_j}}] \in \mathbb{R}^{E+4+F}$ which we feed to the encoder, where w_j is the word containing character x_i.

Inference   At inference time, we use greedy decoding to find the most likely sequence:[6]

$$\hat{y}_{1:m} = \operatorname*{argmax}_{y \in V_y} P(\hat{y}|x_{1:n}, g) = \operatorname*{argmax}_{y \in V_y} \prod_{\hat{y}_t \in \hat{y}} P(\hat{y}_t|\hat{y}_{1:t-1}, x_{1:n}, g)$$

The architecture of our gender reinflection linguistically enhanced sequence-to-sequence model is shown in Figure 1.

4.3   Training Settings

For all the experiments described in this paper, we use a batch size of 32, a character embedding size of $E = 128$, a gender embedding size of $J = 10$, a hidden size of $H = 256$, a scheduled sampling probability of 0.3, a dropout probability of 0.2, and gradient clipping with a maximum norm of 1. The FastText embeddings have a dimension of $F = 100$ and were trained for 10 epochs using the OpenSubtitles 2018 corpus in a skip-gram manner with context windows of 2 and 3 respectively. We train the model for 50 epochs by minimizing the average cross-entropy loss defined as follows:

$$\mathcal{L}(y_{1:m}, \hat{y}_{1:m}; \theta) = \frac{1}{m} \sum_{t=1}^{m} \mathcal{L}(y_t, \hat{y}_t; \theta); \mathcal{L}(y_t, \hat{y}_t; \theta) = -\log P_{V_y}(\hat{y}_t)$$

We use the Adam optimizer (Kingma and Ba, 2014) with an initial learning rate of 0.0005, decaying by a factor of 0.5 if the loss on the development set does not decrease after 2 epochs.

5   Experiments and Evaluation

In this section, we discuss the data we use to train and evaluate our models. We also discuss the evaluation metrics and the various systems we implemented including the baselines.

5.1   Data

For our experiments, we use the publicly available Arabic parallel gender corpus (Habash et al., 2019), containing 12,238 parallel gender-annotated sentences: F (feminine), M (masculine) or B (gender-ambiguous). The corpus is divided into three parallel balanced corpora: (1) Corpus$_{\text{input}}$ containing F, M and B sentences, (2) Corpus$_{\text{M}}$ containing M and B sentences only, and (3) Corpus$_{\text{F}}$ containing F and B sentences only.[7] Table 1 shows examples of what Corpus$_{\text{input}}$ (Input), Corpus$_{\text{M}}$ (Target Masculine), and Corpus$_{\text{F}}$ (Target Feminine) would look like.

We build our target corpus by concatenating Corpus$_{\text{M}}$ and Corpus$_{\text{F}}$, while our source corpus is a duplication of Corpus$_{\text{input}}$. Since our goal is to build a single user-aware joint gender reinflection model

---

[5]We experimented with both form-based and functional gender features, and found the functional features to be superior in performance; so we only report on them in this paper.

[6]It important to note that we also explored beam search for decoding, however, greedy decoding yield better results.

[7]In this work, we consider the B cases to be masculine in Corpus$_{\text{M}}$ and feminine in Corpus$_{\text{F}}$.

for both grammatical genders, we introduce the notion of target gender g having two possible values: F or M. All of the target sentences from Corpus$_M$ will have an M target gender, whereas all of the target sentences from Corpus$_F$ will have an F target gender. We follow the same data split as Habash et al. (2019). After merging the corpora we ended up with 17,132 sentence pairs for training (TRAIN), 2,448 for development (DEV), and 4,896 for testing (TEST). All of our systems are trained to take a source sentence and a target gender as input to produce a gender-reinflected target sentence as described in section 4.2.

5.2 Metrics

Gender Reinflection We follow Habash et al. (2019) and use BLEU as an evaluation metric (Papineni et al., 2002), however, we believe that BLEU is not a suitable metric for our task due to the high similarity between the input and output sentences. We use SacreBLEU (Post, 2018) to compute the BLEU scores. Additionally, we use the MaxMatch (M^2) scorer (Dahlmeier and Ng, 2012) to compute the word-level edits between the input and reinflected output. We report the precision, recall, and $F_{0.5}$ scores calculated against the gold edits, which were also created by the M^2 scorer. We are aware that there are other tools to consider for word-level edit calculation such as ERRANT (Bryant et al., 2017), but we did not use them as they require additional dependencies to work for Arabic.

Input Gender Identification Our sequence-to-sequence model does not explicitly identify the gender of the input sentence; however, we consider any attempted change (or lack thereof) to the input as a signal for the implicit gender identification: if our model reinflects the source sentence, then we consider the gender of this sentence to be the opposite of the given target gender. But if the model does not reinflect the source sentence, then we consider the gender of this sentence to be the same as the target gender. We report the average F_1 score for M and F gender identification over the source sentences.

We report the results for gender identification and reinflection in a normalized space for Alif, Ya, and Ta-Marbuta as discussed in section 3.

5.3 Baselines

In addition to comparing with the results from Habash et al. (2019), we include two baselines. The first one is a DO NOTHING baseline which simply passes the input to the output as is. This baseline is intended to show how similar the inputs and the outputs are. The second is a baseline in which we define a bigram maximum likelihood estimation (MLE) model: given an input sequence of words $x_{w_{1:n}} \in V_{x_w}$, a target sequence of words $y_{w_{1:n}} \in V_{y_w}$, and a target gender $g \in \{F, M\}$, the MLE model is built as follows:[8]

$$P(y_{w_i}|x_{w_i}, x_{w_{i-1}}, g) = \frac{count(y_{w_i}, x_{w_i}, x_{w_{i-1}}, g)}{count(x_{w_i}, x_{w_{i-1}}, g)}$$

At inference time, we pick the target word $\hat{y}_{w_i}$ which maximizes the probability defined above. If $\hat{y}_{w_i}$ was not observed in the training data along with x_{w_i} and $x_{w_{i-1}}$, we back-off to a lower-order distribution (unigram) $P(\hat{y}_{w_i}|x_{w_i}, g)$. In the worst case scenario, where $\hat{y}_{w_i}$ was not observed in the training data along with x_{w_i}, we pass x_{w_i} to the output.

The MLE baseline is suitable for our case because the input and output sentences are perfectly aligned on the word-level.

5.4 Systems

We explore four variants of the model described in section 4.2. In the first, we provide the encoder with the character embeddings without any morphological features or FastText embeddings and we refer to it as JOINT. The second variant is where we add the morphological features to the character embeddings but without the FastText embeddings and we refer to it as JOINT+MORPH. For the third variant, we explore adding both the morphological features and the FastText embeddings to the character embeddings, we refer to it as JOINT+MORPH+FT. To build the fourth one, we selected the best variant and trained it in a similar fashion to Habash et al. (2019). We trained two systems disjointly; one using Corpus$_M$ and the

---

[8]We experimented with different n-gram sizes for the MLE model, the bigram yielded the best results.

	Reinflection				Identification
	Precision	**Recall**	**$F_{0.5}$**	**BLEU**	**F_1**
Do Nothing	100.0	0.0	0.0	97.1	91.8
MLE (bigram)	65.5	41.5	58.7	97.8	95.0
Habash et al. (2019)	74.0	48.2	66.8	98.0	96.3
Joint	70.6	51.3	65.6	98.2	96.2
Joint+Morph	**75.3**	**58.5**	**71.2**	**98.4**	**96.8**
Joint+Morph+FT	64.8	50.9	61.4	97.9	95.9
DisJoint+Morph	63.6	49.1	60.0	98.0	96.0

Table 2: Results of a number of systems on the Dev set.

	Reinflection				Identification
	Precision	**Recall**	**$F_{0.5}$**	**BLEU**	**F_1**
Do Nothing	100.0	0.0	0.0	97.1	91.8
MLE (bigram)	70.8	48.9	64.9	98.0	95.6
Habash et al. (2019)	77.7	52.0	70.8	98.3	96.6
Joint+Morph	**79.0**	**60.3**	**74.4**	**98.5**	**97.0**

Table 3: Results of baseline systems and the best system on the Test set.

other using Corpus$_F$ and reported the average performance of both systems. We refer to this last variant as DisJoint+Morph.

6 Results

The results of our evaluation on the Dev set are presented in Table 2. The best performing system is Joint+Morph. It improves over the previous SOTA on this task, Habash et al. (2019), in every compared metric, including a 4.4% absolute increase in M^2 $F_{0.5}$. The biggest contribution to the performance increase is from recall (10.3% absolute). In fact, all of the neural models we introduced in this paper improve over the Habash et al. (2019) results in terms of recall (at varying degrees); however, only Joint+Morph improves in terms of recall and precision. The MLE results are surprisingly competitive in terms of precision, scoring higher than some of the weaker neural models; while being the worst (barring Do Nothing) across all other metrics.

The two aspects of our best system (being joint and using morphological features) are important to its performance. When we compare Joint+Morph to its Joint counterpart, we observe an 5.6% absolute increase in the M^2 $F_{0.5}$ score and a corresponding 0.6% increase in identification F_1 score. This confirms that morphological features are helpful for both gender identification and reinflection.

An ablation experiment comparing the best system Joint+Morph to the disjoint variant of it (DisJoint+Morph) demonstrates the large added value of using a joint model: an 11.2% absolute increase in M^2 $F_{0.5}$ score, 0.45 BLEU points , and 0.8% absolute improvement in identification F_1 score. The use of word embeddings was not helpful to our best system. One possible explanation is that the use of semantically oriented embeddings may not be optimal for fine-targeted rewriting tasks.

The results on the Test set using the baselines and the best system from the Dev experiments are given in Table 3. These results show consistent conclusions with the Dev results. Our best system improves over the previous SOTA in every compared metric, including a 3.6% absolute increase in terms of M^2 $F_{0.5}$.

	M Target		F Target		M+F Target	
No Change	35	64%	52	71%	87	68%
Wrong Change	17	31%	14	19%	31	24%
Case form	9	16%	0	0%	9	7%
Uninflectable word	4	7%	5	7%	9	7%
Odd characters	2	4%	6	8%	8	6%
Other	2	4%	3	4%	5	4%
Gold Error	3	5%	7	10%	10	8%
Total	55	100%	73	100%	128	100%

Table 4: Summary of the errors found in the Dev set organized by target gender (M or F) and in combination (M+F).

7   Error Analysis

We conducted a manual error analysis examining all of the errors in the output of our best system on the DEV set. In total, there were 106 sentences with errors (or 4.3% out of 2,448). In those erroneous sentences, there were 128 words with problems. Table 4 presents the detailed scores, which we discuss next.

Around two thirds of the word errors were false negatives, i.e., where a change should have happened but did not (Table 4 No Change). In a quarter of the No Change cases, a clear copular construction context for first person gendered expression is seen. For example, the word فنان *fnAn* 'artist [masc]' in

أنا فنان يا سيدي *ÂnA fnAn yA sydy* 'I'm an artist, sir' is not correctly reinflected to its F target form فنانة *fnAnħ* 'artist [fem]'. The No Change errors with target gender F are 50% higher than the target gender M; this suggests that the system is more adept at identifying feminine source text than the other way around. This is plausible given that the Arabic feminine form is the marked variety.

Returning to the rest of the errors, an additional quarter of them involved a false positive (Table 4 Wrong Change). Three types of incorrect changes are noteworthy. First is imperfectly reinflecting the masculine form by failing to indicate case (Table 4 *Case form*), e.g., generating كنت مشغول *knt mšγl* instead of كنت مشغولا *knt mšγlA* 'I was busy [masc]'. It should be noted that such cases are commonly used and are 'accepted' since most modern dialects of Arabic lost the productive generation of case. Second is reinflecting words that are not inflectable for gender (Table 4 *Uninflectable word*). One example is adding the feminine nominal suffix ة *ħ* to the first person imperfective verb أمثل *Âmθl*

in إنني أمثل جشع الشركات *Ânny Âmθl jšς AlšrkAt* 'I represent corporate greed'. This results in creating a nonsensical verbal form أمثلة *Âmθlħ* which is a homograph with the word 'examples'. The third type of change errors involves random generation of odd repetitive character sequences (Table 4 *Odd characters*), a side effect of using character sequence-to-sequence models. One example in our data is the generation of the nonsensical form ققق *qqq* from the word قلق *qlq* 'worried [masc]' instead of قلقة *qlqħ* 'worried [fem]'. Finally, about $1/12^{th}$ of all counted errors are miscounts due to Gold annotation fails, where our system actually generated the correct output (Table 4 Gold Error).

Considering the detailed scores for the whole DEV set and for M target and F target cases, we note the following. As expected, the F target setting has more errors than the M target setting. No Change errors and Gold errors are more common for the F target setting. The Case form errors are only seen in the M target setting. Errors with uninflectable words are almost equally present. These errors suggest that more work needs to be done on identifying when a reinflection should take place. Furthermore, to address the errors of uninflectable forms and case-marked forms, we may have to incorporate more linguistic knowledge or more powerful language models.

8 Conclusion and Future Work

In this paper, we proposed a solution to single-output NLP systems that allows users to specify their grammatical gender preference in Arabic. Our intention is to enable users to reduce the harm that may be produced by NLP systems propagation of biased representations. Our joint approach for sentence-level gender reinflection uses linguistically enhanced sequence-to-sequence models and frames the problem as a user-aware grammatical error correction task. Our system takes an Arabic sentence and a given target gender as input and generates a gender-reinflected sentence based on the provided target gender. We showed that linguistic knowledge helps in learning gender identification implicitly which improves reinflection results. In future work, we would like to explore different architectures such as Transformer-based models (Vaswani et al., 2017). Furthermore, we are interested in exploring the added value of combining syntactic and morphological features. We would also like to apply our approach to different languages and dialectal varieties. Lastly, we plan to extend the Arabic parallel gender corpus beyond first-person-singular constructions and adapt our models accordingly.

Acknowledgements

This research was carried out on the High Performance Computing resources at New York University Abu Dhabi (NYUAD). We would like to thank the Computational Approaches to Modeling Language Lab at NYUAD for their help and invaluable suggestions throughout this project. We also would like to thank Professor Dima Ayoub for helpful conversations.

References

Roee Aharoni and Yoav Goldberg. 2017. Morphological inflection generation with hard monotonic attention. In *Proceedings of the 55th Annual Meeting of the Association for Computational Linguistics (Volume 1: Long Papers)*, pages 2004–2015, Vancouver, Canada, July.

Sarah Alkuhlani and Nizar Habash. 2011. A corpus for modeling morpho-syntactic agreement in Arabic: Gender, number and rationality. In *Proceedings of the 49th Annual Meeting of the Association for Computational Linguistics: Human Language Technologies*, pages 357–362, Portland, Oregon, USA, June.

Dzmitry Bahdanau, Kyunghyun Cho, and Yoshua Bengio. 2015. Neural machine translation by jointly learning to align and translate. In *Proceedings of the International Conference on Learning Representations (ICLR)*.

Samy Bengio, Oriol Vinyals, Navdeep Jaitly, and Noam Shazeer. 2015. Scheduled sampling for sequence prediction with recurrent neural networks. *CoRR*, abs/1506.03099.

Piotr Bojanowski, Edouard Grave, Armand Joulin, and Tomas Mikolov. 2017. Enriching word vectors with subword information. *Transactions of the Association for Computational Linguistics*, 5:135–146.

Tolga Bolukbasi, Kai-Wei Chang, James Zou, Venkatesh Saligrama, and Adam Kalai. 2016. Man is to computer programmer as woman is to homemaker? debiasing word embeddings.

Shikha Bordia and Samuel R. Bowman. 2019. Identifying and reducing gender bias in word-level language models. In *Proceedings of the 2019 Conference of the North American Chapter of the Association for Computational Linguistics: Student Research Workshop*, pages 7–15, Minneapolis, Minnesota, June.

Christopher Bryant, Mariano Felice, and Ted Briscoe. 2017. Automatic annotation and evaluation of error types for grammatical error correction. In *Proceedings of the 55th Annual Meeting of the Association for Computational Linguistics (Volume 1: Long Papers)*, pages 793–805, Vancouver, Canada, July.

Aylin Caliskan, Joanna J. Bryson, and Arvind Narayanan. 2017. Semantics derived automatically from language corpora contain human-like biases. *Science*, 356(6334):183–186.

Kyunghyun Cho, Bart van Merriënboer, Caglar Gulcehre, Dzmitry Bahdanau, Fethi Bougares, Holger Schwenk, and Yoshua Bengio. 2014. Learning phrase representations using RNN encoder–decoder for statistical machine translation. In *Proceedings of the 2014 Conference on Empirical Methods in Natural Language Processing (EMNLP)*, pages 1724–1734, Doha, Qatar, October.

Shamil Chollampatt and Hwee Tou Ng. 2018. A multilayer convolutional encoder-decoder neural network for grammatical error correction. In *Proceedings of the AAAI Conference on Artificial Intelligence*.

Daniel Dahlmeier and Hwee Tou Ng. 2012. Better evaluation for grammatical error correction. In *Proceedings of the 2012 Conference of the North American Chapter of the Association for Computational Linguistics: Human Language Technologies*, pages 568–572, Montréal, Canada, June.

Emily Dinan, Angela Fan, Adina Williams, Jack Urbanek, Douwe Kiela, and Jason Weston. 2019. Queens are powerful too: Mitigating gender bias in dialogue generation. *ArXiv*, abs/1911.03842.

Emily Dinan, Angela Fan, Ledell Wu, Jason Weston, Douwe Kiela, and Adina Williams. 2020. Multi-dimensional gender bias classification. *arXiv preprint arXiv:2005.00614*.

Lisa Fan, Marshall White, Eva Sharma, Ruisi Su, Prafulla Kumar Choubey, Ruihong Huang, and Lu Wang. 2019. In plain sight: Media bias through the lens of factual reporting. *arXiv preprint arXiv:1909.02670*.

Manaal Faruqui, Yulia Tsvetkov, Graham Neubig, and Chris Dyer. 2016. Morphological inflection generation using character sequence to sequence learning. In *Proceedings of the 2016 Conference of the North American Chapter of the Association for Computational Linguistics: Human Language Technologies*, pages 634–643, San Diego, California, June.

Joel Escudé Font and Marta R. Costa-jussà. 2019. Equalizing gender biases in neural machine translation with word embeddings techniques.

Hila Gonen and Yoav Goldberg. 2019. Lipstick on a pig: Debiasing methods cover up systematic gender biases in word embeddings but do not remove them.

Hila Gonen and Kellie Webster. 2020. Automatically identifying gender issues in machine translation using perturbations.

Roman Grundkiewicz, Marcin Junczys-Dowmunt, and Kenneth Heafield. 2019. Neural grammatical error correction systems with unsupervised pre-training on synthetic data. In *Proceedings of the Fourteenth Workshop on Innovative Use of NLP for Building Educational Applications*, pages 252–263, Florence, Italy, August.

Nizar Habash, Abdelhadi Soudi, and Tim Buckwalter. 2007. On Arabic Transliteration. In A. van den Bosch and A. Soudi, editors, *Arabic Computational Morphology: Knowledge-based and Empirical Methods*, pages 15–22. Springer, Netherlands.

Nizar Habash, Houda Bouamor, and Christine Chung. 2019. Automatic gender identification and reinflection in Arabic. In *Proceedings of the First Workshop on Gender Bias in Natural Language Processing*, pages 155–165, Florence, Italy, August.

Nizar Y Habash. 2010. *Introduction to Arabic natural language processing*, volume 3. Morgan & Claypool Publishers.

Rowan Hall Maudslay, Hila Gonen, Ryan Cotterell, and Simone Teufel. 2019. It's all in the name: Mitigating gender bias with name-based counterfactual data substitution. In *Proceedings of the 2019 Conference on Empirical Methods in Natural Language Processing and the 9th International Joint Conference on Natural Language Processing (EMNLP-IJCNLP)*, pages 5267–5275, Hong Kong, China, November.

Marcin Junczys-Dowmunt, Roman Grundkiewicz, Shubha Guha, and Kenneth Heafield. 2018. Approaching neural grammatical error correction as a low-resource machine translation task. In *Proceedings of the 2018 Conference of the North American Chapter of the Association for Computational Linguistics: Human Language Technologies, Volume 1 (Long Papers)*, pages 595–606, New Orleans, Louisiana, June.

Katharina Kann and Hinrich Schütze. 2016. Single-model encoder-decoder with explicit morphological representation for reinflection. In *Proceedings of the 54th Annual Meeting of the Association for Computational Linguistics (Volume 2: Short Papers)*, pages 555–560, Berlin, Germany, August.

Diederik P Kingma and Jimmy Ba. 2014. Adam: A method for stochastic optimization. *arXiv preprint arXiv:1412.6980*.

Keita Kurita, Nidhi Vyas, Ayush Pareek, Alan W Black, and Yulia Tsvetkov. 2019. Measuring bias in contextualized word representations. In *Proceedings of the First Workshop on Gender Bias in Natural Language Processing*, pages 166–172, Florence, Italy, August.

Pierre Lison and Jörg Tiedemann. 2016. OpenSubtitles2016: Extracting large parallel corpora from movie and TV subtitles. In *Proceedings of the Tenth International Conference on Language Resources and Evaluation (LREC'16)*, pages 923–929, Portorož, Slovenia, May. European Language Resources Association (ELRA).

Kaiji Lu, Piotr Mardziel, Fangjing Wu, Preetam Amancharla, and Anupam Datta. 2018. Gender bias in neural natural language processing.

Thang Luong, Hieu Pham, and Christopher Manning. 2015. Effective approaches to attention-based neural machine translation. In *Proceedings of the Conference on Empirical Methods in Natural Language Processing (EMNLP)*, pages 1412–1421, Lisbon, Portugal.

Anne Maass and Luciano Arcuri. 1996. Language and stereotyping. *Stereotypes and stereotyping*, pages 193–226.

Thomas Manzini, Yao Chong Lim, Yulia Tsvetkov, and Alan W Black. 2019. Black is to criminal as caucasian is to police: Detecting and removing multiclass bias in word embeddings.

Ninareh Mehrabi, Thamme Gowda, Fred Morstatter, Nanyun Peng, and Aram Galstyan. 2019. Man is to person as woman is to location: Measuring gender bias in named entity recognition.

Michela Menegatti and Monica Rubini. 2017. Gender bias and sexism in language. In *Oxford Research Encyclopedia of Communication*. Oxford University Press.

Jack Merullo, Luke Yeh, Abram Handler, Alvin Grissom II, Brendan O'Connor, and Mohit Iyyer. 2019. Investigating sports commentator bias within a large corpus of american football broadcasts. *arXiv preprint arXiv:1909.03343*.

Amit Moryossef, Roee Aharoni, and Yoav Goldberg. 2019. Filling gender & number gaps in neural machine translation with black-box context injection. In *Proceedings of the First Workshop on Gender Bias in Natural Language Processing*, pages 49–54, Florence, Italy, August.

Kishore Papineni, Salim Roukos, Todd Ward, and Wei-Jing Zhu. 2002. BLEU: a Method for Automatic Evaluation of Machine Translation. In *Proceedings of the Conference of the Association for Computational Linguistics (ACL)*, pages 311–318, Philadelphia, Pennsylvania, USA.

Matt Post. 2018. A call for clarity in reporting BLEU scores. In *Proceedings of the Third Conference on Machine Translation: Research Papers*, pages 186–191, Brussels, Belgium, October.

Ella Rabinovich, Raj Nath Patel, Shachar Mirkin, Lucia Specia, and Shuly Wintner. 2017. Personalized machine translation: Preserving original author traits. In *Proceedings of the 15th Conference of the European Chapter of the Association for Computational Linguistics: Volume 1, Long Papers*, pages 1074–1084, Valencia, Spain, April.

Rachel Rudinger, Jason Naradowsky, Brian Leonard, and Benjamin Van Durme. 2018. Gender bias in coreference resolution. In *Proceedings of the 2018 Conference of the North American Chapter of the Association for Computational Linguistics: Human Language Technologies, Volume 2 (Short Papers)*, pages 8–14, New Orleans, Louisiana, June.

Artūrs Stafanovičs, Toms Bergmanis, and Mārcis Pinnis. 2020. Mitigating gender bias in machine translation with target gender annotations.

Gabriel Stanovsky, Noah A. Smith, and Luke Zettlemoyer. 2019. Evaluating gender bias in machine translation. In *Proceedings of the 57th Annual Meeting of the Association for Computational Linguistics*, pages 1679–1684, Florence, Italy, July.

Dima Taji, Salam Khalifa, Ossama Obeid, Fadhl Eryani, and Nizar Habash. 2018. An Arabic Morphological Analyzer and Generator with Copious Features. In *Proceedings of the Fifteenth Workshop on Computational Research in Phonetics, Phonology, and Morphology (SIGMORPHON)*, pages 140–150.

Eva Vanmassenhove, Christian Hardmeier, and Andy Way. 2018. Getting gender right in neural machine translation. In *Proceedings of the 2018 Conference on Empirical Methods in Natural Language Processing*, pages 3003–3008, Brussels, Belgium, October-November.

Ashish Vaswani, Noam Shazeer, Niki Parmar, Jakob Uszkoreit, Llion Jones, Aidan N. Gomez, Lukasz Kaiser, and Illia Polosukhin. 2017. Attention is all you need. *CoRR*, abs/1706.03762.

Daniel Watson, Nasser Zalmout, and Nizar Habash. 2018. Utilizing character and word embeddings for text normalization with sequence-to-sequence models. In *Proceedings of the 2018 Conference on Empirical Methods in Natural Language Processing*, pages 837–843, Brussels, Belgium, October-November.

Wajdi Zaghouani, Behrang Mohit, Nizar Habash, Ossama Obeid, Nadi Tomeh, Alla Rozovskaya, Noura Farra, Sarah Alkuhlani, and Kemal Oflazer. 2014. Large Scale Arabic Error Annotation: Guidelines and Framework. In *Proceedings of the Language Resources and Evaluation Conference (LREC)*, Reykjavik, Iceland.

Jieyu Zhao, Tianlu Wang, Mark Yatskar, Vicente Ordonez, and Kai-Wei Chang. 2017. Men also like shopping: Reducing gender bias amplification using corpus-level constraints.

Jieyu Zhao, Tianlu Wang, Mark Yatskar, Vicente Ordonez, and Kai-Wei Chang. 2018a. Gender bias in coreference resolution: Evaluation and debiasing methods. In *Proceedings of the 2018 Conference of the North American Chapter of the Association for Computational Linguistics: Human Language Technologies, Volume 2 (Short Papers)*, pages 15–20, New Orleans, Louisiana, June.

Jieyu Zhao, Yichao Zhou, Zeyu Li, Wei Wang, and Kai-Wei Chang. 2018b. Learning gender-neutral word embeddings. In *Proceedings of the 2018 Conference on Empirical Methods in Natural Language Processing*, pages 4847–4853, Brussels, Belgium, October-November.

Jieyu Zhao, Tianlu Wang, Mark Yatskar, Ryan Cotterell, Vicente Ordonez, and Kai-Wei Chang. 2019. Gender bias in contextualized word embeddings. In *Proceedings of the 2019 Conference of the North American Chapter of the Association for Computational Linguistics: Human Language Technologies, Volume 1 (Long and Short Papers)*, pages 629–634, Minneapolis, Minnesota, June.

Jieyu Zhao, Subhabrata Mukherjee, Saghar Hosseini, Kai-Wei Chang, and Ahmed Hassan Awadallah. 2020. Gender bias in multilingual embeddings and cross-lingual transfer.

Ran Zmigrod, Sabrina J. Mielke, Hanna Wallach, and Ryan Cotterell. 2019. Counterfactual data augmentation for mitigating gender stereotypes in languages with rich morphology. In *Proceedings of the 57th Annual Meeting of the Association for Computational Linguistics*, pages 1651–1661, Florence, Italy, July.